SPIRITUAL SUBJECTS

FIGURE 1. Sultantepe Özbekler Tekkesi, interior courtyard, 2018. Photograph by author.

SPIRITUAL SUBJECTS

*Central Asian Pilgrims and
the Ottoman Hajj
at the End of Empire*

LÂLE CAN

STANFORD UNIVERSITY PRESS
Stanford, California

STANFORD UNIVERSITY PRESS
Stanford, California

© 2020 by the Board of Trustees of the Leland Stanford Junior University. All rights reserved.

No part of this book may be reproduced or transmitted in any form or by any means, electronic or mechanical, including photocopying and recording, or in any information storage or retrieval system without the prior written permission of Stanford University Press.

Printed in the United States of America on acid-free, archival-quality paper

Library of Congress Cataloging-in-Publication Data

Names: Can, Lâle, author.
Title: Spiritual subjects : Central Asian pilgrims and the Ottoman hajj at the end of empire / Lâle Can.
Description: Stanford, California : Stanford University Press, 2020. | Includes bibliographical references and index.
Identifiers: LCCN 2019017972 | ISBN 9781503610170 (cloth : alk. paper) | ISBN 9781503611160 (pbk.) | ISBN 9781503611177 (epub)
Subjects: LCSH: Muslim pilgrims and pilgrimages—Saudi Arabia—Mecca—History. | Muslim pilgrims and pilgrimages—Asia, Central—History. | Central Asians—Legal status, laws, etc.—Turkey—History. | Panislamism—Political aspects—History. | Turkey—History—Ottoman Empire, 1288–1918.
Classification: LCC BP187.3 .C36 2020 | DDC 297.3/52409034—dc23
LC record available at https://lccn.loc.gov/2019017972

Cover photo: Sultantepe Özbekler Tekkesi, entrance. Undated, but believed to be late 1970s. Courtesy of the author.

Typeset by Kevin Barrett Kane in 10.25/15 Adobe Caslon

For my mother, Saliha,
and in memory of my father, Mehmet (1925–2014),
two people who taught me what is at stake in remembering those
whose names would otherwise be forgotten.

And, for Kuzum (2006–18),
my companion and guide through much of the journey.

CONTENTS

List of Maps and Illustrations	ix
Note on Translation and Transliteration	xi
PREFACE: On Twists and Turns	1
INTRODUCTION: The Terrain of Transimperial Pilgrimage	5
1 Rewriting the Road to Mecca	34
2 Sufi Lodges as Sites of Transimperial Connection	65
3 Extraterritoriality and the Question of Protection	94
4 Petitioning the Sultan	125
5 From Pilgrims to Migrants and De Facto Ottomans	149
CONCLUSION: A Return to Sultantepe	175
Acknowledgments	185
Notes	191
Bibliography	225
Index	245

MAPS AND ILLUSTRATIONS

Maps

1	Central Asia and the Ottoman Empire	xii
2	Central Asia political map	xiv
3	Mirim Khan's journey through Istanbul, c. 1902	44
4	Central Asian Sufi lodges of Istanbul	72
5	Major cities of origin of guests at Sultantepe	79

Illustrations

1	Courtyard of Sultantepe Özbekler Tekkesi	ii
2	Interior of Hagia Sophia	42
3	Galata Bridge, Istanbul	45
4	The Sultan's procession to the Hamidiye Mosque	46
5	Central Asian hajj travelers in an Eyüp cemetery	50
6	Sample page from Sultantepe Özbekler Tekkesi guest register	70
7	Ottoman-Bukharan statesmen, shaykh Süleyman Efendi	118
8	Ottoman petitioners and petition-writer	128
9	Quarantine station at Anadolukavağı, Istanbul	137
10	Central Asian pilgrims in Eminönü, Istanbul	150
11	A street in Mecca	162
12	Medina "the Illuminated"	163
13	Sultantepe Özbekler Tekkesi guest register	183

NOTE ON TRANSLATION AND TRANSLITERATION

Writing about people who traveled through the vast multilingual Ottoman Empire and who originated from a wide range of Turkic polities calls attention to both major similarities and differences in how they communicated, wrote, and recorded history. These complexities are embedded in archival sources in Ottoman Turkish and Chaghatay/Turki. A note here is in order to clarify that Chaghatay was a lingua franca of Central Asia (alongside Persian) that was used from the 1400s through the 1950s and written in Arabo-Persian script. It is distinct from Ottoman and Tatar. In the interest of consistency, I have chosen to transliterate all Central Asian personal names and place names recorded in Ottoman sources according to the modified *International Journal of Middle East Studies* method. Ottoman Turkish is rendered in modern Turkish with minor exceptions. For transliterating Chaghatay, I use the system for modern Uzbek. In translating passages from Mirim Khan's hajj account, I have stayed true to the original text and have taken only minor liberties with syntax. All manuscript and document translations are my own unless otherwise specified.

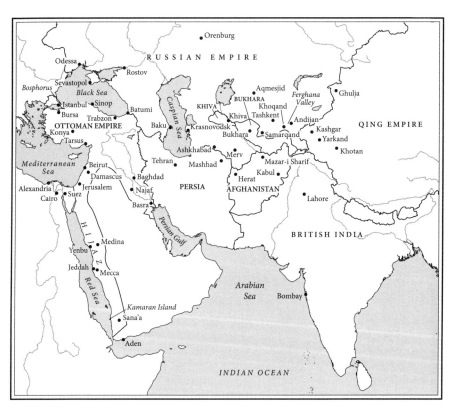

MAP 1. Central Asia and the Ottoman Empire in inter-Asian perspective, c. 1900.

SPIRITUAL SUBJECTS

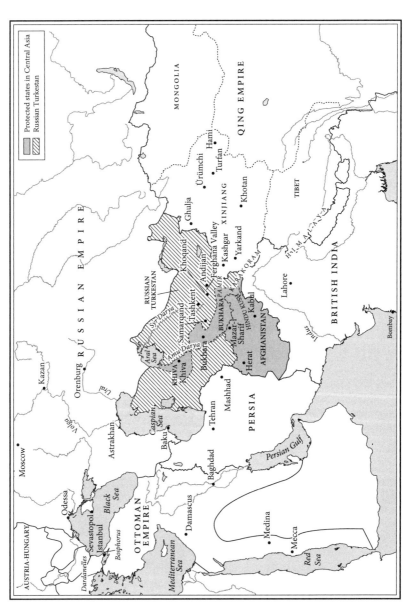

MAP 2. Central Asia political map, early twentieth century.

{ PREFACE }

ON TWISTS AND TURNS

AFTER LIVING THE FIRST THREE DECADES of his life in the Soviet Union, China, and Saudi Arabia, the peripatetic Uzbek merchant Hajji Muhammed Jon became a Turkish citizen in 1956. He had first emigrated from the Soviet Union in 1932 and settled in Kashgar as a young child. In 1949, Muhammed fled China for an uncertain future in Saudi Arabia, this time on his own. Traveling via Lahore and Bombay, he took old roads that merchants and pilgrims had used for centuries, with only the last leg of his journey, from India to Arabia, replaced by air carrier rather than ship. After about five years of residence in Mecca, where there was a sizable Uzbek and Uyghur diaspora but little prospect of naturalization, he applied for Turkish citizenship. He hoped to continue studies in Turkey that had been upended in China. But rather than a student, he found himself a soldier. And in lieu of the Muslim army he imagined joining, the hajji was conscripted into a joint Turkish-Greek NATO force in Izmir (Smyrna), his name registered in the Turkified form of Mehmet Can. When he completed his service in late 1957, his plans to return to Mecca were interrupted by countrymen (*hemşeri*) from back home—"home" itself now an ever-changing geography—who introduced him to a seamstress named Saliha. The two were married shortly thereafter in an old Istanbul mosque where her father was the prayer reciter (*müezzin*). To make a living, the hajji opened a small restaurant in the Grand Bazaar, but he found that he did not have the temperament for this type of work. Within a few years he returned to Mecca, a wife and two young daughters in tow, and worked as a pilgrimage guide. Uzbek acquaintances with a home close to the Noble Sanctuary hosted them. Although the family did not remain long, the Holy Cities occupied a special place in their memory. The children would remember joining the crowds of pilgrims and melodically chanting *labbayka allahumma labbayk* as they arrived in Mecca and declared their intention to perform the hajj. Saliha, a child of the young Turkish Republic, would for decades describe arriving in Medina and finding a city illuminated by prophetic light.

The two hajjis were my parents, the two girls my sisters, and I grew up listening to their stories—tuning them out mostly. Or so I thought. It was very late in the writing of this book that I saw the parallels between their lives and those of people I studied at the end of empire, and I realized that I was, in part, writing a history of how the hajj shaped my father's path to Mecca and then Istanbul. Perhaps willfully, perhaps by chance, this seemingly obvious fact had escaped me. In part, it was because I began this project with a different research question: how travel on the hajj had shaped the political imaginaries of participants in a failed anticolonial revolt in Russian Turkestan. This was the 1898 Andijan Uprising, a rebellion led by a Sufi shaykh in the Ferghana Valley who claimed to have Ottoman support in a holy war against the Russian tsar. Although the likelihood of Ottoman involvement was negligible, the question of why the leader invoked Sultan Abdülhamid II's (r. 1876–1909) backing in his battle against Russian colonialism served as the point of departure for studying social and political connections between Central Asia and the Ottoman Empire. As the project evolved, small detours into the study of hajj networks took on a life of their own, and I began to focus on the links between sacred travel, migration, and imperial belonging. Rather than religio-political or ethnic ideology—the pan-Islamism and pan-Turkism of intellectuals and statesmen that constituted the topic of hundreds of books—all signs in the archive pointed to pilgrimage as *the* major force connecting people across a vast expanse of what would later be called the Turkic world.

To a large extent, these connections were obscured by the world that took shape after the First World War and the Turkish Republic's rejection of much of its Ottoman legacy. But while the republic established by Mustafa Kemal (later Atatürk) in 1923 was avowedly secular (adapting the French model of laïcité), religion continued to inform the basis for determining who was or could become a "real" Turk. Whereas Armenians, Greeks, and Jews became what one historian has likened to the nation's step-citizens,[1] many Central Asians and other Turkic Sunni peoples were welcomed as blood relations. Turkish nationalist narratives of a glorious, shared past in lands stretching from Kashgar to Ankara had great force among disenfranchised Turkic migrants. For people like my father, it provided a focus for their nationalist yearnings and something to hold on to in a world where communism had forced them into exile, sometimes more than once.

But, like most nationalist myths, this narrative stood in for a much more complex history characterized by simultaneous processes of inclusion and exclusion that dated to the late Ottoman period. For Central Asians, the paths to becoming subjects of the sultan and, later, citizens of the Turkish Republic were built on old hajj routes and networks—not primarily ethnic brotherhood or kinship—and included major obstacles and moments of dissonance. Like the young man who left Mecca to study in Turkey and found himself in a NATO force rather than a Muslim army, Central Asians from all over Russian- and Chinese-ruled lands found an empire that both welcomed them as pilgrims and simultaneously began to define them as foreigners, restrict their rights in the Holy Cities, and view them as potential threats to Ottoman political sovereignty. With the expansion of Russian and British colonial rule and extraterritorial legal jurisdiction—a system in which European powers insisted on their right to adjudicate the legal affairs of their citizens, as well as their colonial subjects—the Ottoman central government became increasingly apprehensive about foreign nationals on its soil. This included Muslim colonial subjects, Turkic and otherwise.

Yet Central Asians' routes through and roots in the empire allowed them to carve out spaces and new types of relationships that I reconstruct in the pages that follow. Like Hacı Muhammed Can's journey to Istanbul (where he would become Mehmet) and my own road to writing this book, their paths were full of twists and turns that pivoted on the hajj. These paths opened up into multiple directions that guide us toward a new understanding of pilgrimage in Ottoman history and an alternative genealogy of imperial subjecthood and citizenship in global history.

{ INTRODUCTION }

THE TERRAIN OF TRANSIMPERIAL PILGRIMAGE

IF YOU WALK UP one of the steep paths leading from the waterfront through the hills of Üsküdar, you will soon approach a restored Sufi lodge—referred to in Turkish as a *tekke* or *dergah*—that was historically a destination for Central Asians traveling to Istanbul. Known as the Sultantepe Özbekler Tekkesi, the lodge is perched high above the Bosphorus on the Asian side of the city. Its wood and stone architecture are now something of an anomaly amid the concrete and steel that dominate the urban landscape. A little more than a hundred years ago, it was surrounded on all sides by verdant neighborhoods named after streams and nightingales and was in close proximity to the many mosques and tekkes that informed the rhythms of religious and social life.[1] This was a time when Sultantepe overlooked quays where imperial ships still departed for Mecca, transporting the faithful on the annual pilgrimage established by the Prophet Muhammad before his death in 632 CE. By the turn of the twentieth century, the lodge had become a major node in the city's Central Asian pilgrimage networks, which grew alongside the rise of hajj traffic through imperial Russia. Men and women from Bukhara, the Ferghana Valley, and East Turkestan in China took Russian rail and steam lines to Istanbul, where they might—the men at least—see the sultan-caliph at Friday prayers. After receiving his ceremonial blessing, they would continue their journey to visit the House of God in Mecca. In doing so, they followed customs established in the early modern period by the expansionist Naqshbandi order, the dominant mystical brotherhood of Central Asia.²

Marked by a sign that only hints at its storied past, the lodge has big wooden doors that open onto a welcoming courtyard surrounded by small-scale buildings that were home to Sufi shaykhs of Central Asian extraction, their families, and the pilgrims they served. A veranda to the left of the main entrance connects the family quarters to a room where shaykhs presided over visitors and recorded their names and details in ledgers kept for the central government. Just beyond is a small mosque and a room for weekly religious gatherings. Across these spaces of devotion and prayer, a separate structure houses a kitchen where resident cooks prepared meals, using grains and meat provided by the Ottoman government and various sources that funded the lodge's Islamic endowment. Adjacent to the lodge is a cemetery, with the graves of luminaries from Ottoman and Turkish history sharing space with pilgrims and migrants.

If, like me, you have spent years poring over the lodge's archives, it is not difficult to imagine scenes of everyday life in the times when Istanbul was a crossroads of transimperial pilgrimage. There, just over by the small mosque, is the Bukharan dervish Hacı Baba, recently arrived from a Sufi lodge associated with Kashgaris, because he needed a "change of air."³ He is getting ready for the weekly congregational *dhikr*, the remembrance of God. By the fountain are Ahmed Efendi and members of his family. In a few days, they will leave for Bursa, only to return to Sultantepe a month later.⁴ Men are sitting in the back, drinking tea and exchanging pleasantries. They have just returned from long days of work, doing odd jobs here and there to earn money before going to Mecca or departing for home. In the women's section of the kitchen, the wives, mothers, and daughters of male pilgrims—whom the shaykh described in only this way in his records—are busy preparing for the evening gathering. After a day spent going through accounting ledgers and writing petitions on behalf of guests for travel arrangements, the shaykh is chatting with the latest group of arrivals about when they can expect to depart. Men of all ages are gathered underneath trees that still grace the courtyard. One of these trees is an old magnolia. If it could speak, it might share the stories this book seeks to tell: how the hajj connected Central Asians to the Ottoman

Empire, what forms these connections took, and how the roads to Mecca paved paths to becoming Ottoman.

Rooted in Asia and overlooking the straits that connected pilgrims from Russia's Black Sea ports to Ottoman Istanbul, the magnolia might begin its story in 1869. This was the year that marked the opening of the Suez Canal, an event that symbolized an age of expanded Muslim mobility and European power in the Middle East and Indian Ocean world. It was also the year that the Ottoman government, in its ongoing battle against European legal imperialism, promulgated the Law on Ottoman Nationality (*Tabiiyet-i Osmaniye Kanunnamesi*), which defined who was an Ottoman and who was a foreigner (*ecnebi*; plural, *ecanib*) and effectively included all non-Ottoman Muslims in the latter category. Or maybe it would begin in the 1880s, when the lodge began to host increasing numbers of guests who had recently become subjects of Tsarist Russia, Qing China, and, to a lesser extent, the British Empire. Spurred by major advances in technology and colonial infrastructure that made long-distance travel more accessible, thousands of Central Asians combined pilgrimage with labor migration, trade, and religious study. Russian investment in railroad and steamship lines, in particular, enabled unprecedented mobility, and by the beginning of the twentieth century, as many as twenty-five thousand pilgrims traveled via Black Sea ports to Istanbul each pilgrimage season.[5] They set out from the oasis cities of Xinjiang, the Ferghana Valley, Bukhara, and Afghanistan, and included single male artisans, merchants, farmers, laborers, and scholars, as well as families who would settle in the empire after completing the hajj, and people headed to Mecca and Medina to devote themselves to lives of piety and prayer. While some pilgrims fulfilled their religious duties and quickly departed, for others the hajj became a conduit to various forms of short- and long-term migration.[6]

Long before its time, the magnolia would tell you, the Ottomans had assumed custodianship of the Holy Cities of Mecca and Medina (the *Haremeyn*, or two sacred precincts) and become patrons of the hajj. When Sultan Selim (r. 1512–20) conquered Mamluk Egypt and extended his sovereignty into the region of Arabia known as the Hijaz, he had added "Caliph" and "Servitor of the Holy Cities" (*hadimü'l-Haremeyn*) to a long list of titles acquired by his predecessors. Assuming the title of caliph—the religious and political leader of the worldwide Muslim community (*umma*)—brought the

Ottomans religious legitimacy and prestige. It also brought new responsibilities, as sultans became charged with provisioning the Haremeyn and ensuring the safe passage of pilgrims traveling across dangerous terrain. Although the caliphate was integrated into the structure of Ottoman power in the sixteenth and seventeenth centuries, it was only in the eighteenth that sultans actively began to use it to assert authority over people beyond their domains. The first iteration of this was with the signing of the 1774 Treaty of Küçük Kaynarca, concluded with Russia after the loss of the Crimean Khanate. According to the treaty, the Ottomans recognized Catherine II ("the Great"; r. 1762–96) as the protector of Orthodox Christians in Ottoman lands and established the sultan as the religious authority of Muslims in the former khanate.[7] Such claims would expand under Sultan Abdülhamid II, even as they remained nebulous. By 1903, an Ottoman statesman contemplating the rights of foreign Muslims in the Hijaz province would invoke the sultan's religious leadership as a matter of course, writing that Abdülhamid II "possesses spiritual leadership (*riyaset-i ruhaniye*) over all of Islam owing to the Caliphate" and that "according to the requirements of this illustrious title, he is the great leader and esteemed sovereign of all of the people of Islam, regardless of which nation they are subjects of, not only Muslims found in his own country."[8]

Yet as the "people of Islam" came into closer contact with the sultan, they did so as subjects of colonial powers, many of whom actively challenged the sultan's sovereignty through their engagements with a changing legal order. Throughout the 1860s and 1870s, formerly independent Muslim states were conquered and annexed to major world empires: the Khiva Khanate and Bukhara Emirate became Russian protectorates; the Khoqand Khanate became a Russian colony ruled by a military governor-general; and, after the rise and fall of the short-lived Emirate of Kashgar during the so-called Muslim uprisings (1864–77), the Qing reconquered the region and created the province of Xinjiang.[9] This "new frontier" province (later part of Republican China) would become an Anglo-British "buffer zone of ambiguous sovereignty."[10] Just to the south, the British took control of Kabul's foreign affairs after the Second Anglo-Afghan War (1878–80) and established a protectorate where the emir retained nominal independence but the British controlled foreign policy.[11] As Ottoman Foreign Ministry officials monitored developments in this growing arena of imperial competition, they started using calques derived from Russian and English, such as "Asya-yı Vustâ" (Middle Asia) and "Türkistan-ı Çini" (Chinese Turkestan, also referred to widely as East Turkestan). The Foreign Ministry also began to address issues relating to the legal status and rights of Bukharans, Afghans, and Kashgaris (sometimes referred to as Chinese Muslims) together, grouping them as people from informally colonized lands. At times, they used *Bukhara* to refer to Russian Central Asia more generally, hinting at their unfamiliarity with "distant lands" (*mahall-i baide*) that were historically outside the Ottoman sphere of interest.[12] As with the contemporary usage of *Central Asia* and *Central Asians*, there was no term that fully captured where these Muslim migrants were from or how they identified. Only later would they refer to themselves and identify as "Türkistanlı" (from Turkestan), Uzbek, Tajik, and Uyghur. At the fin de siècle, they were usually defined in official correspondence by the states from which they originated: Bukhara, Russian Turkestan, Chinese Turkestan, and Afghanistan. The tekke shaykh often referred to them collectively as *hemşeri* (countrymen, compatriots), invoking alternative understandings of belonging that persisted alongside imperial legal categories.

After long stories about the years when pilgrims flowed into the tekke like a stream and sometimes a tide, the magnolia's tale would continue into the First World War, when the Ottoman dynasty lost control of Islam's holiest cities and the routes to Mecca ceased to wind through Istanbul. These were difficult days, and the Mudros Armistice that ended the war for the Ottomans was followed by an Allied occupation of Istanbul that shook the community at Sultantepe. The shaykh in those years, Atâ Efendi (1883–1936), helped the resistance by smuggling weapons to fighters in Anatolia—an act that would link Sultantepe to the national struggle and inadvertently overshadow a long history of service to pious pilgrims. After the dislocations of the war and the collapse of empires, pilgrims were replaced in the 1930s through 1950s by émigrés fleeing communism in the Soviet Union and then China. Many of them settled in and around Central Asian lodges in Istanbul and other cities on the old overland hajj routes to Mecca. When Atatürk closed the nation's Sufi lodges in his aggressive secularization campaigns in the 1920s and 1930s, many of the Central Asian tekkes continued to operate informally. Thus, even though Sultantepe's days as a way station between Istanbul and Mecca had come to a close, it continued to connect people from

East Turkestan, the Ferghana Valley, Bukhara, and Samarqand as they started new lives in the old Ottoman capital.[13]

What the magnolia would likely not tell you is how the intersection of mass pilgrimage and European pressures informed Ottoman relations with these "foreign Muslims." At the end of the Crimean War (1853–56)—a conflict spurred by European competition in Ottoman lands, particularly Russian demands to exercise protection over the sultan's Orthodox Christian subjects in Palestine—the Great Powers welcomed the empire to the Concert of Europe. The Paris Peace Treaty of 1856 gave the Ottoman Empire the same legitimacy and rights to territorial integrity and sovereignty as other member nations.[14] But in the context of the "Eastern Question"—the issue of how European empires could pursue their ambitions in Ottoman domains without upsetting the balance of power between them (and inaugurating another war like the one fought in the Crimean Peninsula)—these guarantees did not materialize. Specifically, the treaty formalized and further entrenched capitulatory agreements granting European nationals and protégés extraterritorial rights and privileges (*imtiyazat*), such as immunities from Ottoman law, that undermined jurisdictional sovereignty.[15] These treaties—collectively referred to as the Capitulations—led to a system of extraterritoriality where European powers were able to extend their legal authority into the sultan's domains and exert their jurisdiction in a range of matters that affected the legal and financial interests of their subjects and protégés.

As the British and Russians became active in the politics and regulation of the hajj, they quickly availed themselves of opportunities to project their power into the Hijaz, Greater Syria, and Iraq via Muslim subjects. By the late nineteenth century, foreign Muslims could count on their consular representatives for various forms of financial, logistical, and legal support. Hajjis, like non-Muslim European protégés, nationals, and citizens, were becoming a population covered by the capitulatory regime that had plagued the Ottomans. When foreign Muslims sought to benefit from imtiyazat that were originally meant to "protect" Christians from the perceived injustices of Islamic law, the Sublime Porte (the central government in Istanbul) responded with legislation that curtailed their rights to landholding and property. It also sought to more consistently classify Muslims from abroad as foreigners. In the case of Central Asians, this designation proved difficult to enforce, since they had deep roots in communities that did not view them as foreigners or outsiders. Nevertheless, by the 1880s, the rising incidence of Bukharans seeking to circumvent Ottoman jurisdiction led the Porte to adopt a radically new position. Drawing on contemporary norms in international law, the Foreign Ministry claimed that subjects of informally colonized lands such as the emirates of Afghanistan and Bukhara were not "real" (*asıl, sahih*) European subjects and that they were therefore ineligible for capitulatory privileges.[16] While they were in Ottoman lands, these "protected persons" (*mahmi*) were under the exclusive protection of their spiritual sovereign, the caliph.

For the Central Asian pilgrims resting in the shade beneath the magnolia's branches, these legal distinctions would change their experience of being hajjis in Ottoman lands. What would it mean to be a foreign Muslim who was protected by the caliph? And, if being a foreigner meant having one set of rights and privileges—and restrictions—and being an Ottoman promised another, where did Central Asians fit in?

Many Ottoman statesmen would grapple with these questions between 1869 and the First World War, as they tried to situate Central Asian pilgrims and migrants in the categories of "Ottoman" (*Osmanlı*) and "foreigner" (*ecnebi*) and to determine how to accord or deny them rights and privileges based on nationality. Likewise, Central Asians charting a course through empires where obtaining some form of imperial protection had become crucial would pose these questions to different branches of the Ottoman government. This book reconstructs their efforts—and the points where Ottoman statesmen and hajjis overlapped and conflicted—and argues that Central Asians effectively transcended the Porte's legal categories of subjecthood, as well as those that historians have used to analyze membership in the late Ottoman Empire. As the empire sought to simultaneously promote a universal Islamic caliphate and to narrowly define Ottoman subjecthood, Central Asians tested both imperial projects and became what I term the sultan's "spiritual subjects."[17] These subjects were Muslim migrants who asserted a type of membership in the empire that derived from Islamic networks like the one that took shape at Sultantepe, as well as the state's pronouncement of spiritual authority over the umma by dint of the caliphate—specifically, its claim of being the exclusive protector of Bukharans, Afghans, and Kashgaris in its domains. Spiritual subjects were not legal nationals but subjects of the caliph, pulled into the Ottoman orbit through pilgrimage and the politics of protection. In this book's telling, they were also subjects of history, whose interactions with Ottoman state and society prompted continual engagement with the questions of what it meant to be an Ottoman or a foreigner. Their experiences shed new light on Ottoman nationality reform and reveal a fuller picture of the hajj in Ottoman and global Islamic history during the age of high imperialism.

The Sufi lodge at Sultantepe offers an ideal starting point for an investigation into the ways that hajj created enduring transregional connections and allows us to see how Islamic spaces shaped Central Asians' experiences and trajectories in Ottoman lands—despite sometimes contentious interactions with the state stemming from disputes over nationality and capitulatory privileges, and the manifold hardships that characterized the journey. Like similar nodes in vast Sufi networks that extended from Istanbul to Medina, the lodge was crucial to integrating Muslims from abroad and facilitating their travels. It was the community within its walls—presided over by a shaykh who vouched for those who needed guarantors, found jobs for those who needed employment, arranged for medical care for those who needed treatment, and buried those who died thousands of miles from their native lands—that helps us to grasp the elusive idea of transimperial connection. In an empire in the midst of large-scale transitions, Sultantepe provides a unique perspective for understanding how Central Asians' experiences in spiritual communities—many of which preceded and, in some cases, survived the Ottomans—opened up paths to integration and naturalization.

In the chapters that follow, we meet a range of Central Asian "hajjis"—not just pilgrims on a journey with a beginning and end but also people who traveled back and forth, migrated, studied, and worked before, during, and after the hajj. From literate men of religion urging others to see Istanbul, to savvy merchants trying to obtain foreign nationality for material benefit, down-on-their-luck artisans and farmers petitioning the sultan while stuck in transit, and deceased migrants whose legal nationality was contested only in death, these individuals demonstrate that hajj connections were wide-ranging—and, often, tense. They also show how these foreign Muslims both challenged the Ottoman subjecthood and nationality boundary and reified the spiritual power of the caliph.[18] If these seem like somewhat dissonant developments, that is because they were. In investigating the transimperial hajj in Ottoman history, I have chosen to dwell on seeming paradoxes to reveal a fuller picture of tensions of empire and to elucidate how this rite intersected with legal and political developments occurring throughout the Eurasian, Mediterranean, and Indian Ocean worlds. While "spiritual subjecthood" is arguably an elusive concept, the juxtaposition of religious and political belonging is meant to conjure broader questions about the centrality of Islam and the caliphate in the late Ottoman Empire. Rather than focusing on pan-Islam—the politics of Muslim political and religious unity—or the instrumentalization of religion, this book investigates the burdens and limits of the Ottoman caliphate, as well as its integration into the structure of power in the late nineteenth century.

By connecting the fragmented histories of Islamic patronage, imperial reform, and international law, I seek to answer the following questions: How did the hajj as a form of migration converge with extraterritoriality? How did ordinary people understand the sultan's "spiritual" (*ruhani, manevi*) authority? What kinds of new connections and tensions did the hajj produce within the umma? And, ultimately, what lessons can be drawn from engaging with the idea of spiritual subjecthood? What does it tell us about imperial subjecthood and nationality? A rich body of published and unpublished, official and private archival sources from Uzbekistan and Turkey help us answer these questions. In mapping the changing religious, social, and legal terrain of the hajj, our guides are none other than Central Asian hajjis. Before we join them, however, the remainder of this introduction takes us through a number of questions in Ottoman, transimperial, and global history that help us understand the roads ahead.

When Hajjis Became Protégés

When Ottoman sultans of the early modern period first issued charters and formal pledges (*ahdname*) to European states granting their subjects extraterritorial privileges—including immunities from Ottoman law, tax exemptions and low customs duties, and guarantees of safe residence and passage—they likely never imagined a world in which Muslims, let alone hajjis, would benefit from these agreements. Yet this is exactly what began to happen in the nineteenth century, as mass pilgrimage brought more Muslim colonial subjects and European protégés (protected persons who were not necessarily subjects or citizens) into contact with the Ottoman state and society. What were meant in the early modern era to be revocable grants to foster political and commercial links with Europeans had morphed into a wide-ranging system of extraterritorial concessions. In the nineteenth century, ahdname were enshrined in bi- and multilateral treaties and granted to an ever-growing class of protected persons who were able to register with foreign consuls and obtain certificates of protection (*berat*). A system to "protect" Christian merchants from Islamic law had become a widely (ab)used mechanism that undermined the sultan's sovereignty, since berat holders—even those who maintained their Ottoman nationality—were not subject to the sultan's justice.[19]

As the Porte became quickly aware, Russian and British conquests and rivalry in Asia facilitated the emergence of protégés among Central Asians, including people from lands in East Turkestan that were ruled by the Qing and then Republican China, neither of which had diplomatic relations with the Ottoman Empire. Like the boundary-crossers and "legal chameleons" of Alexandria, Shanghai, or Tunis who "used the capitulatory system to manipulate their official identities, juggling at times two or three 'nationalities,'"[20] Central Asians began to assert rights to European nationality, with the goal of obtaining the most advantageous legal affiliation in a particular setting. In practice, this meant that Bukharans and others began to claim European nationality to benefit from preferential tariffs and customs duties or to evade Ottoman taxation, conscription, and prosecution. In other instances, foreign Muslims would become naturalized as Ottomans in order to purchase land, without formally renouncing their foreign nationality (leading to problems when they died and foreign consuls did not recognize their Ottoman nationality, or when they tried to revert to their previous nationality to avoid Ottoman jurisdiction). These developments were spurred in part by a growing network of European consuls in the bustling Red Sea port of Jeddah, which offered pilgrims services that included everything from storing valuables and buying steamer tickets, to helping people escape Ottoman prosecution. For hajjis whose journeys extended beyond the rites at Mecca and involved longer residence in cities like Basra, Damascus, and Istanbul, European consuls were likewise willing to provide protection to cultivate protégés among Muslims who would expand their economic interests in the empire.[21] For the Porte, the most pressing problems were driven not by pilgrims but by hajjis who settled in the empire.

Ottoman statesmen struggled to understand why subjects of the Bukharan emir or people subject to sharia law in Russian Turkestan should be "protected" from Islamic law by colonial European powers. This not only subverted the logic of the Capitulations but also threatened to open the empire—particularly the Hijaz—to foreign intervention.[22] Yet, in reality, Central Asians' engagements with the law were not exceptional. Throughout the Mediterranean world, Moroccans and Tunisians tried to pass as Algerians to benefit from French nationality, and Maltese protégés in Alexandria insisted that they were British subjects in order to benefit from the attendant rights. In the treaty ports of China, Andijani and Bukharan émigrés to Xinjiang sought Russian identity papers to profit from the advantageous terms of economic treaties, while Baghdadi Jews in Shanghai frequently registered with British consuls to obtain the status of protected persons. From Kashgar to Casablanca, the world in the long nineteenth century was shaped by forms of imperialism that went beyond direct conquest and relied on legal and "diplomatic" instruments of power legitimized by the "international" state system.[23] Both protector and protected benefited in different ways: the former by establishing jurisdiction through consular courts and the presence of particular groups in strategic economic and political arenas, the latter by obtaining preferential status.

Whereas citizenship represented the fullest form of state membership and was accompanied by political enfranchisement, nationality was primarily a form of legal affiliation and a tool of international law that defined rights and protections of subjects. For individuals in settings of overlapping, divided, and contested sovereignty, it was not a tool of identity but of advantage. As Will Hanley convincingly argues, it was "first and foremost to assume civil rights and legal advantages, rather than as an expression of an upsurge of political, cultural, or national identity."[24] Native Bukharans who claimed to be Ottomans in Medina, but Russians when arrested in Istanbul, or British when they wanted to avoid taxes in Baghdad—and who may have petitioned the tsar *and* the sultan for financial aid or support—did not evince loyalty or allegiance to any particular state through their actions. Conquered peoples actively participated in colonial legal orders regardless of whether they viewed their rulers as just or legitimate—even when they were engaged in revolts against the imperial order. Rather than signs of allegiance or legitimacy, the use of law to personal advantage through a variety of strategies was indicative of "sophisticated understandings of the jurisdictional complexity [legal pluralism] and politics."[25]

For the Porte, the problem was that these sophisticated engagements with the law were occurring on its terrain and at its expense: hajjis were becoming unlikely agents of expanding European jurisdiction. The Porte's responses were consistent with strategies employed by authorities in polities as varied as China, Japan, Tunisia, and Morocco, who worked within the parameters of the international legal order to limit the power of foreign consular courts and to rein in the privileges of European protégés.[26] That said, the Ottoman Foreign Ministry's utilization of the caliphate—a vaunted Muslim institution representing leadership of the worldwide Islamic community—to deprive rights to Muslims seeking European nationality (many of them on a journey symbolizing the unity of the umma) adds a unique spin to a global story of legal pluralism and imperialism. These dynamics also challenge long-held assumptions about the role of religio-political ideology and ethnic identity that impede our understandings of Central Asian connections to the empire.

Confronting the Specter of Pan-Islamism and Pan-Turkism

Throughout the period of Ottoman political reforms during the Tanzimat era (1839–76), and the tumultuous years of the Hamidian and Young Turk periods (1876–1909 and 1909–18, respectively), the regulation of mass pilgrimage developed in step with efforts to maintain Ottoman legitimacy at home and among the powers in the Concert of Europe. A major component of this was the promotion of the sultan's power as caliph and renewed emphasis on his position as defender of the Holy Cities of Mecca and Medina and leader of the umma. Through Islamic motifs and a reinvigoration of the language of the caliphate, the Ottoman state sought to symbolically legitimate power in response to the challenges of nationalism and European political and economic encroachments. As Muslims across the world faced the expansion of Western colonial rule, disparate groups from Central Asia to Indonesia pledged their devotion to the caliph and sought military and political support from the sultan, coalescing in what has been defined as a broad-based religio-political movement that was essentially anticolonial in nature. In this rendering, pan-Islamism—often defined as the ideology of Muslim religious and political unity—has been understood from one of two perspectives: first, as an undefined radical and anticolonial movement that people were exposed to, influenced by, and provoked by; second, as something that could be harnessed by the sultan to buttress his authority. More recent scholarship has sought to "demilitarize" the ideals of Islamic unity and to shift our thinking from pan-Islamic to inter-Islamic connections, as well as to historicize the very idea of the "Muslim world." Yet the paradigm for thinking of pan-Islamism as a cohesive ideology remains in place to explain seemingly all matters involving Muslims in the realm of politics. Few scholars have considered how it was exercised or what kinds of expectations and challenges it brought to bear on the Ottoman state. By shifting focus from the orchestration and imagination of authority to the way it was understood by a specific group within the umma, we see concepts of pan-Islamic loyalty, allegiance, and brotherhood in a new light.[27]

Rather than a powerful weapon that could be deployed to win Muslims' hearts and minds, or to threaten European powers, the pages that follow show the range of concerns driving Ottoman hajj patronage. A case from the Interior Ministry archives, in the later part of the period examined in this book, provides a concrete example of the struggles inherent in managing pilgrimage and pilgrims' expectations and the reasons why pan-Islamism is not a useful analytical framework in this study. This case begins in the spring of 1910, when several groups of Central Asian hajjis stranded in Istanbul petitioned the Ottoman state, asking to be repatriated to Russian and Chinese Turkestan. After completing the pilgrimage to Mecca, these men and women had run out of money and found themselves "sleeping and waking on the stones, and in the mud" on the streets and corners of Istanbul, desperate to go home. As they described their plight, they drew on various discursive models and asked for patronage from "their Islamic government" and "the Muslim treasury," and they presented themselves as subjects (*kul*) of the sultan.

Although they were subjects of Tsarist Russia, the Bukhara Emirate, and the Qing and Republican China, the petitioners invoked the caliph's obligations, not only as the custodian of hajj but as their self-designated protector (*hami*) in Ottoman lands.

The supplications ultimately landed on the desk of an official in the Interior Ministry. That spring, the official—whose early eagerness (and perhaps naiveté) suggest he was new on the job—worked alongside many others to make arrangements to send them home. In a memorandum to the Istanbul municipality, he advised that "if the current Islamic government (*hükumet-i hazira-yı islamiye*) wants to secure its power through [Islamic] union, it ought to treat these pilgrims with affection and to ardently protect (*himaye*) them." The pilgrims, he added, "should be regarded as a delegation of envoys, and their hearts should be satisfied toward the abode of the caliphate." But as he would realize over the course of the next year, satisfying hearts was not so easy. The cash-strapped government of the Committee of Union and Progress (CUP) could not afford to continually pay for the pilgrims' passage as far as Odessa, let alone to distant cities in Russian and Chinese Turkestan. The problems of governance posed by hajj were daunting and, at times, exasperating. The extensive file of related inter- and intraministerial correspondence revealed that these guests of the caliph were not universally welcomed by municipal authorities, who were concerned about the dangers itinerant populations posed to public health and safety, as well as the openings they presented for foreign consuls to become involved in their affairs. By the beginning of the next pilgrimage season, the same official—now seemingly beleaguered by his duties—proposed working with the police to prevent Central Asians who were traveling to Mecca from disembarking in Istanbul. If this was done, he reasoned, "in the following years, we'll see an end to their numbers. And the government will be relieved of its spiritual responsibility (*mesuliyet-i maneviye*) toward them."[28]

The official's change of heart—captured in this succinct turn of phrase—revealed the burdens of "spiritual" (*manevi*) responsibility. His use of *spiritual* did not signify something symbolic or in contradistinction to the temporal or political realms. As with the dual nature of Ottoman legitimacy, which was derived from the sultanate and caliphate and then invested in one sovereign who presided over both, it was complementary to and enmeshed in the material (*maddi*) world of governance. The terms *maddi manevi*—commonly paired in Ottoman Turkish—were complementary and interconnected rather than dichotomous. Although the caliphate is often imagined as a symbolic institution, a locus of emotional attachment, or a tool of empire, it was much more than that: it was part and parcel of the Ottoman government, including the Interior Ministry (as well as the Foreign Ministry and the Istanbul Municipality).[29] This is not to say that religion and politics were one in Islam, or in the Ottoman Empire, but to recognize that the Ottoman caliphate was built on a vision of the caliph as a universal Islamic leader who could bridge "Islamic and non-Islamic notions of rulership" and hence intertwined temporal and spiritual realms.[30] As the hajj became subject to the same processes of globalization as the Middle East at large, the Ottoman obligations toward the umma grew and changed in step with the central government's domestic and international priorities. It was not possible to promote the caliphate as only a spiritual figure, distinct from or outside of politics and governance of the empire.

The Porte's position on Central Asians was somewhat paradoxical: on the one hand, its claim of being their "hami" (protector) put forward a connection to the caliphate that could be read regardless of intent as constituting a special bond. On the other hand, the 1869 Ottoman Nationality Law and related legislation excluded Central Asians from Ottomanness and rights they had traditionally enjoyed. At the same time, their position as liminal subjects was taking shape alongside uneven changes in how people experienced mobility during the "Age of Steam and Print"—the period from roughly 1850 to 1930, defined by heightened circulations of people (pilgrims, merchants, intellectuals), commodities, texts, and ideas. This age also lent its name to the "steamship-era hajj," which was distinguished by the introduction of railroads and steamships. After the construction of the Suez Canal—one of the most potent symbols of the age of high imperialism and increasingly networked connections across the Mediterranean and Indian Ocean—European investment in rail and steam lines cut travel times and lowered the costs, so people who would not have previously been able to afford to leave work, home, and harvests for multiple seasons could now travel to Mecca and back in a matter of months.[31] Yet, as Valeska Huber compellingly articulates in her study of mobility in the Suez Canal Zone, the revolutions of this period were marked as much by the deceleration of certain types of movement as they were by the acceleration of others. Biopolitical controls such as quarantine and passports, and the hardening of political boundaries and identities, created chokepoints that slowed down many migrants and travelers, even as they sped up the mobility of others.[32]

Huber's analysis of the tensions inherent in this period of globalization is instructive for thinking about the relationship between mass pilgrimage and colonialism in new ways. Despite the rhetoric of pan-Islamic unity in this period, the reality was that as Muslims entered Ottoman realms, they were concurrently becoming legal outsiders—primarily because they had been colonized. If 1869 represented a watershed for transregional mobility and connections, it also marked a major legal shift in the relationship between the sultan-caliph and Muslims from abroad. The Ottoman central government took a category (ecnebi) previously associated with Christians and applied it to hajjis. It was one thing to list Bukharans and Kashgaris in a guest register (like the ones the state required at Sultantepe) and to annotate their legal nationality, but it was another to classify them as legal outsiders and limit their rights. Not surprisingly, these legal distinctions were difficult to enforce, particularly in the Hijaz, where Bukharans and Kashgaris were part of mercantile, scholarly, and religious communities with their own visions of what it meant to be a local or an outsider (not necessarily an Ottoman and a foreigner). Resistance from these communities raised continual questions about how to balance the prestige and honor of the caliphate against the interests of the empire at large, and it struck at the core of tensions in trying to create a subjecthood boundary in an empire that claimed a form of power over Muslims who were not Ottoman subjects. These tensions, I argue, were indicative of the limited power of pan-Islamism in shaping policies vis-à-vis the umma within the empire's domains. Despite the grip it maintains on approaches to religious politics in late Ottoman history, ideology, I contend, does not explain the kinds of dynamics we see in what we might imagine as the archetype of a pan-Islamic ritual—the hajj. Even as intellectuals and ideologues discussed pan-Islamic ideals, the Ottoman Foreign Ministry enunciated policies that gave rise to differentiated relationships within the umma based on the types of European colonies and protectorates Muslim migrants originated from.

Recognizing the empire's approach to Muslims based on nationality opens up fruitful paths for revisiting assumptions not only about pan-Islamism but also about pan-Turkism. Driven in large part by attention to intellectuals and ideologues, Ottoman rhetoric about the caliphate, Russian and British fears of religiously inspired colonial uprisings, and post-Ottoman assertions about the role of Turkic identity in politics, these twin theses stubbornly persist.[33] Particularly after the collapse of the Soviet Union in 1991 and the emergence of independent new nation-states in Central Asia, Turkish politicians, scholars, and journalists breathed new life into an idea that first gained traction in the early twentieth century. The end of the Soviet era prompted renewed interest in Central Asia, and Turkey positioned itself as a regional political and economic leader for people imagined as kin in countries cut off from one another by communism. Publishers and governmental ministries responded to this new climate by producing glossy coffee table books and archival editions that celebrated and sought to document a multitude of political, religious, and cultural connections dating to the early Ottoman era. In doing so, they presented a curated vision of the past that ignored the problematic reality that the Ottoman dynasty and elite had no abiding interest in Central Asia throughout its history and that the major vector of connection was religion rather than ethnicity.[34] They also revived ideas that originated in the late Ottoman and early Republican eras, when the interests of pan-Turkists, nationalists, and Turkic émigrés and irredentists began to coincide. While the founders of the Republic sought to distance themselves from their Ottoman forebears and find alternate sources for the construction of a new national identity, Turkic émigrés like Yusuf Akçura, Ismail Gasprinskii, and Ahmet Ağaoğlu created narratives that helped make sense of their displacements from imperial Russia and connect them to their new homelands. Their "marketing" of identity[35] was not only a Turkic identity but a Muslim one that played an important role in determining the basis for full membership in the Turkish Republic, as well as the imagined collective of the Turkic world. This laid the foundation for ideas that still maintain currency in Turkey and that create the conditions for studies that posit Central Asian lodges as "spiritual bridges between fatherland [*ata yurt*] and motherland [*ana yurt*]," or the notion that modern Turkey and Central Asia share an "ancient" and "familial" geography.[36]

The discourses of pan-Turkish ideology created a myth about a special Ottoman–Central Asian relationship that does not hold up to historical scrutiny. Julia Phillips Cohen's study of imperial citizenship and the Ottoman-Sephardi "romance" in this era offers valuable insight into what is at stake in deconstructing such ahistorical visions of the past. "Through their frequent repetition," Cohen writes, tropes and narratives about such purportedly special relationships take on "the aura of unquestionable truth" and obscure "other stories that have not served the agendas of different authors throughout the ages."[37] In the Ottoman–Central Asian context, rather than an exceptional relationship predicated on ethnicity, we see a history shaped by ambivalence and contestation. Attention to records from the Interior and Foreign Ministries, for example, makes clear that there were no Turkist policies guiding the Porte's dealings with Central Asians—and nothing to suggest a cohesive or guiding commitment to pan-Islamist or pan-Turkist foreign policies. Many Ottoman statesmen were untutored in the finer points of the dynastic states' postconquest status, unclear as to what differentiated entities like Bukhara and Turkestan in legal terms, and unsure as to whether there was indeed a basis for Russian—or Ottoman—protection of Muslims from any part of the region. A closer look at the conferral of patronage reveals that it was informed by both the expanded duties of the caliphate and concerns about order. There were no strings attached to these funds, pan-Islamic treatises provided with steamship tickets, or attempts by Ottoman officials and bureaucrats to instill a sense of Turkic brotherhood among those who benefited from imperial patronage and philanthropy. As the case involving the state's "spiritual responsibilities" referenced above suggests, even as Ottomans took the caliph's obligations seriously, these were not the main priorities of people within the government.

While I am not suggesting that pan-Islamism played no role in shaping Central Asians' views of the sultan, or that Turkic identities did not facilitate integration in certain contexts, I am arguing that both have limited power to explain how people—statesmen and hajjis—made decisions. Despite its hold on the imagination, the ideal of geopolitical unity was not consistent with the range of political behaviors and decisions taken by ordinary Muslims or government officials, including interactions that centered on the hajj. This was not a failing of Muslims or a sign that religion was not consequential to their worldviews. Rather, it is an indication that pan-Islamic unity was an aspiration, not a model or paradigm for historical analysis of how states or people behaved. In an era when Muslims worldwide began to imagine the Ottoman sultan-caliph as the leader of "the Muslim world" (*alem-i İslam*),[38] the empire was in fact working to minimize the threats that foreign Muslims could pose to Ottoman sovereignty through their engagement with the Capitulations. Drawing on a growing body of scholarship on the transforming Ottoman legal landscape, this study suggests a new way to think about imperial subjecthood and spiritual and political belonging: through attention to Islamic networks and the use of law.[39] By disaggregating pan-Islamism from Islam, and pan-Turkism from historical connections forged by ordinary Central Asians to Ottoman communities, we can reconstruct, first, how migrants and hajjis responded to simultaneous processes of inclusion and exclusion and understood their legal place in empire; and second, how pilgrims and statesmen struggled with changing parameters of legal and political nationality and, ultimately, created a hybrid form of membership defined by both law and the idea of spiritual connection.

The Ottoman Empire and the Hajj

By tracing pilgrims' trajectories in Ottoman lands and their attempts to engage with different regimes of protection, *Spiritual Subjects* sets out to present a new history of the hajj in the late Ottoman era. Specifically, it reconstructs unstudied imperial dilemmas that stemmed from being a Muslim power charged with custodianship of a phenomenon that impinged on many facets of its domestic and international policy, but that it was not able to freely regulate. These dilemmas were set in motion by the expansion of European colonial power in Asia and Africa and the unprecedented circulations of people, goods, and ideas—many of which flowed through Ottoman lands. Indeed, by the second half of the nineteenth century, European powers had become actively engaged in hajj politics and administration, ushering in an influx of foreign Muslims. Although European, particularly British, involvement was first prompted by regulatory measures to address sanitation and security concerns—what William Roff described as "a kind of twin infection [of cholera and pan-Islamism] . . . against which defenses had to be devised"[40]—by the late nineteenth century, there was a major shift toward accommodation of this annual rite. For example, Great Britain and Russia—the two powers whose involvement arguably had the greatest impact on Central Asians and our story—actively invested in hajj infrastructure and offered support to pilgrims abroad. In part, they were motivated to buttress their authority among their growing Muslim colonial subjects. This support also promised dividends in extending British and Russian commercial and political interests further into the Ottoman Empire, particularly in regions throughout Arabia, Greater Syria, and Iraq. Thus, where there were pilgrims, there were soon British and Russian consuls, who worked through Muslim intermediaries to provide their subjects and protégés with logistical, legal, and financial assistance. Pilgrims actively drew on this support, which helped to facilitate what was indeed a journey marked by hardship. And while both empires would continue to grapple with fears of the potentially destabilizing effects of pan-Islamism, as well as ambivalence about appearing to endorse this ritual, historians have argued in recent works that they ultimately became "Muslim powers" and "hajj sponsors" and "patrons."[41]

The robust scholarship on European empires and hajj has opened up fruitful paths to comparative research.[42] But it tells us very little about the impact of the steamship-era hajj on Ottoman state and society or about the ways that it reconfigured relationships between the sultan-caliph and Muslim subjects of colonial empires. In fact, new approaches to empires and hajj often assume that late Ottoman patronage was driven by the same dynamics that characterized the early modern period. *Spiritual Subjects* offers the first in-depth examination of the hajj in the last decades of empire and makes a number of interventions that have implications beyond the field of Ottoman studies. First, it significantly revises conventional understandings of the relationship between imperial support and legitimacy or loyalty. Historians interested in questions of Ottoman hajj patronage have thus far relied heavily on Suraiya Faroqhi's seminal study of the early modern era, *Pilgrims and Sultans*, which traces how the Ottoman dynasty drew on sponsorship of this ritual to buttress its legitimacy in the central Islamic lands conquered by Sultan Selim (r. 1512–20). Over the next two centuries, the empire integrated custodianship of the Holy Cities into a broader repertoire of Islamic patronage that included the construction of Sufi lodges, caravanserais, mosques, madrasas, and public works, as well as philanthropic activities that supported the activities of pious Muslims from within and without Ottoman domains. Needless to say, the industrialized hajj was a very different political and social phenomenon. Historical comparisons to the early modern Ottoman state—particularly in nineteenth-century European empires that approached Islamicate lands as part of quasi-civilized and barbaric civilizations—are not especially fruitful. The notion that European empires could become Muslim powers or be perceived as sponsors of hajj (rather than rulers of Muslims or sponsors of hajjis) dehistoricizes hajj patronage: first, by taking it out of a particular historical context informed by discursive conditions, structures, practices, negotiations, and traditions among a broad range of actors; and second, by schematizing what makes something "Islamic" or "Muslim" and mapping it onto empires characterized by vastly different sets of relations with their Muslim subjects.[43]

By shifting our focus to pilgrims and the spaces and networks that enabled Central Asians' integration into the Ottoman Empire, this study questions the utility of thinking about Islam, hajj, and Islamic networks as things or objects that empires (Ottoman and European) could co-opt, harness, or instrumentalize. Through attention to both law and communities, and the ways that Central Asians engaged with petitioning, nationality, and protection, I suggest that we need to disentangle the use of colonial legal structures and discourses of loyalty with the conferral of Islamic legitimacy. Although writing global history invites comparison across empires, one of its pitfalls is that it produces a kind of conceptual flattening, where the specificity of certain relationships and dynamics gets lost, or, as in the Ottoman case, remains to be fully excavated. This problem is evident not only in the use of phrases such as "Muslim power" and "hajj patron" but in the emphasis on mapping hajj routes. Doing so highlights the impressive scope of interimperial connectivity, but insufficient attention to the scale and the depth of connections along various points in these maps runs the risk of distorting—flattening—the pilgrimage experience. As Anna Tsing provocatively argues, the allure or "charisma" of globalization as a concept "draws our enthusiasm because it helps us imagine interconnection, travel, and sudden transformation."[44] But whereas shifting to a wider global or cross-regional frame of analysis promises an antidote to the confines of area studies, jumping scales and registers is not always illuminating.[45] What does it mean, for example, when we say that hajj was itself a global network? What does this tell us about the parameters, actors, and mechanics involved or why diverse groups of Muslims (e.g., Tunisians, Indians, Javanese) had different experiences in Ottoman lands? How do we compare Christian empires, which could not officially sponsor the hajj, with a Muslim empire that had to support it as part of its custodianship of the Haremeyn—a form of power established long before the hajj became subject to these new global forces?

By treating the hajj as a form of open-ended migration, this book recenters this annual ritual as a central force in Ottoman history. Rather than an event taking place in a distant province that is at once treated as central to Islamic legitimacy and somehow exceptionally exceptional (largely because the Hijaz was exempt from many of the Tanzimat reforms), much of the story I tell takes place between the Hijaz and Istanbul and unfolds within the context of Ottoman political and legal reforms. Through attention to the experiences of a particular group within the umma, specifically Central Asians' engagements with competing regimes of protection, we see that there was no one-size-fits-all approach to ruling foreign Muslims in the empire or to the experiences of foreign Muslims.[46] As M. Christopher Low's innovative study of the materiality of hajj shows, for example, concerns about British intrigues to install a rival caliphate, as well as the threat of extraterritoriality gaining ground in the Holy Cities (which were exempt from the Capitulations),[47] led the Porte to view Indians and Jawis with extreme suspicion—particularly since they were "real" subjects of Indian Ocean powers who were recognized as having extraterritorial rights.[48] While Low highlights the deep colonial anxieties about the power of these foreign Muslims—reflecting the Porte's fears that they might constitute a fifth column[49]—his findings support one of this book's central claims: that the Porte managed foreign Muslims using the same tools of empire as their subjects: through the rule of difference.[50]

What was unique in the Ottoman context was the fact that although the sultan-caliph was recognized as the leader of the umma, he was not the legal ruler of migrants moving through his domains. Pilgrims and migrants—as subjects of history—pushed questions about hajj patronage, extraterritoriality, and imperial subjecthood to the fore and set in motion new relationships to the sultan as caliph that extended beyond "the spiritual." In the context of British and Russian imperial rivalries and the proliferation of the

Capitulations, anxieties surrounding foreign Muslims turned on questions of territorial and jurisdictional sovereignty. As the Ottomans continually adapted to new political realities and configurations—now in the form of Muslim extraterritoriality—the Foreign Ministry had asserted a form of caliphal protection that forged a new relationship (*rabıta*) to "mahmi": the sultan was not their political leader, but in Ottoman lands he was their exclusive protector. As the sultan tried to defend the sovereignty of his empire, he became the spiritual sovereign of those who might undermine his authority through their engagement with the international legal order.[51]

A Story of Pilgrims

At the turn of the twentieth century, the routes from Central Asia to Mecca were riddled with disorienting encounters: pilgrims came into contact with unfamiliar languages, geographies, modes of transportation, and onerous regulations of their bodies and movement. The phenomenon of what social scientists call space-time compression, "the reordering of distance, the overcoming of spatial barriers, the shortening of time-horizons, and the ability to link distant populations in a more immediate and intense manner," was remarkably uneven.[52] Even as spatial barriers between cities like Tashkent and Odessa were shrinking, social and political barriers between Russians and colonial Muslim peoples remained largely intact. Yet other places were closer in ways that could not be measured, such as in travelers' hearts. Mecca, for example, had always occupied a key place in the Muslim religious imaginary as a shared holy landscape, and going there was a symbolic act of return. But getting to Mecca involved traveling through multiple empires, and the journey was rife with problems that I have alluded to above. Nevertheless, throughout the late nineteenth century, more and more pilgrims embarked on the pilgrimage, and roughly half of them chose the route through Istanbul. How can we understand their choices?

The first two chapters of this book show how texts, Sufi lodges, and pilgrimage networks connected Central Asians to Istanbul and transformed it into a gateway to Mecca. Both chapters are microhistorical in their approach, and each examines intimate encounters, specific texts and sites, and the process of meaning-making that accompanied such large-scale revolutions and transformations. They focus on how belonging to the empire was wrapped up in both deeply symbolic instantiations of religion and prosaic acts and experiences that paved the way to integration into Ottoman communities. Visiting the tomb of a companion of the Prophet Muhammad, finding work in a coffeehouse, or being treated for illness at an Ottoman hospital for the Muslim poor were just as much a part of the experience of modern hajj as was quarantine or obtaining mobility documents.

In Chapter 1, we meet Mirim Khan, the author of an early twentieth-century hajj account that described in great detail the hardships pilgrims encountered on the roads to Mecca. During his trip, the bane of his existence was other travelers—particularly Kashgari pilgrims whom he uncharitably described as disorderly, loud, and stupid. This was the irascible pre-hajj pilgrim talking, who had much to complain about as he waited in crowded train stations, rode in crowded train cars, and sailed on crowded ships on a journey that frequently took him to the precipice of death. Although he was ostensibly writing to convince other pilgrims to follow in his footsteps, he was disarmingly honest—and human—about what they could expect in terms of challenges. But Mirim Khan had more interesting things to tell us than *how* he traveled to Mecca or what empires did (or did not do) to expedite his journey. This chapter captures what he wanted to communicate to his audience of listeners and readers and how he described the *feeling* of travel across this complex and shifting terrain. Specifically, it highlights how one pilgrim made sense of and responded to hardship through spiritual experiences. Engaging with these facets of the hajj, I argue, is integral to understanding where it diverged from other forms of migration. Like many of his fellow travelers, Mirim Khan was influenced by Sufism (*tasavvuf*), the mystical and esoteric approach to Islam.[53] While not every pilgrim might describe him- or herself as an adept of a particular order—and was certainly not a dervish or an ascetic—the majority of Central Asians in this period engaged in practices associated with Sufism. They would be at home in places like Sultantepe, the subject of Chapter 2.

The culture of Sufism was supported by the Ottoman state and a vast network of lodges that stretched from Istanbul to Jeddah and were referred to in Ottoman, Arabic, and Persian as *tekke*, *dergah*, *zawiya*, and *hankah*. As pilgrimage practices grew and changed, so did the functions these lodges performed, which included registering and keeping tabs on foreign Muslims for the central government. They also provided various forms of social welfare to those in need—Ottomans and non-Ottomans alike—and were entrenched in and constitutive of tightly knit communities. In every neighborhood of Istanbul and every quarter of Medina or Jerusalem, one could find a lodge that fed the poor, provided them with a place to pass the night, and helped people find health care and employment. The state-appointed shaykhs helped people write petitions to the state, acted as guarantors, helped arrange marriages, and assisted in burying the dead. When someone took their last journey—an aphorism for death—it was the shaykh who tried to find kin and countrymen and who sent news to their families. And when no one was found, they noted this in the registers of their lodges, both for future travelers and as a testament to the loss of someone from their community. Although they were often underfunded and dilapidated, these structures played a major role in shaping a transregional religious and social world. Through a bottom-up history of the Sultantepe Özbekler Tekkesi, Chapter 2 traces concrete movements and trajectories that uncover the specific "social mobilizations in which new identities and interests are formed and travels from one place to another through which place-transcending interactions occur."[54]

As the book investigates Central Asians' trajectories in the empire, it provides a thread connecting the hajj to major developments in Ottoman and global history, particularly in the realm of imperial sovereignty and extraterritoriality. Chapter 3 offers a window into these issues through an investigation of complex cases involving the legal claims of contested subjects who were living for all intents and purposes as Ottomans. While the majority of Central Asians never advanced extraterritorial claims, the exceptions to the rule were cause for worry—particularly since European consuls frequently insisted on jurisdiction over their affairs and, in death, their estates. This threatened to open up the Hijaz to foreign penetration and, more important, threw into question the fundamental stability of the caliph's power and claims to pan-Islamic power. When Central Asian migrants began to assert rights to British and Russian nationality—often after decades of living as de facto Ottomans—or were claimed as such in death, the Foreign Ministry Office of Legal Counsel drew on international law to articulate a new position on "protected persons." As nationality and hajj converged, the Porte tweaked its repertoire, borrowing from its own tool kit of ruling subjects through difference, to simultaneously deny Central Asians access to the Capitulations and claim to be their protector. But failure to enunciate what caliphal protection meant in practice, and to effectively challenge European extraterritoriality, meant that many Central Asians remained in a sort of limbo. Through attention to the many dead ends in archival records, the study counters the view that competing jurisdictional sovereignty increased legal opportunities for people via practices such as "shopping" in multiple legal forums. Imperial competition, I argue, often led to a narrowing of legal horizons and possibilities.

If Ottoman rulers and statesmen viewed the caliphate as a means to counter extraterritoriality or assert power over Muslims from beyond their domains, Chapter 4 suggests that they did not anticipate the ways they would be called to account. The chapter follows the path of numerous petitions asking for logistical, material, and legal support—often couched in the language of "spiritual assistance." I read them alongside extensive Ottoman inter- and intraministerial correspondence, which details how and why the Porte sponsored foreign Muslims in the empire and contributed to their repatriation. These records illustrate that while the Porte took its obligations toward pilgrims seriously, it struggled with their potentially destabilizing presence: pilgrims taxed the government's resources, threatened imperial order, and needed to be moved quickly through Ottoman space. The chapter also calls into question conventional wisdom about petitioning and imperial patronage and helps us to see how the caliph's claims of protection shaped a rights discourse among people who were effectively excluded from a nascent citizenry and rights to a viable legal nationality.

Through an exploration of long-term migrants in Istanbul and the Hijaz, Chapter 5 investigates why many of the tensions between hajj patronage and nationality reform could not be eradicated. Specifically, it shows how Ottomans treated Central Asians as locals and examines the role of communities in determining belonging. Working back from the First World War, it shows how people who finally gave up their foreign nationality were accepted into the Ottoman fold, without incident. By telling this story from the perspective of Medina and Istanbul, I explore the deep roots Central Asians planted in the empire and why they defied the categorization as ecnebi. In concert with

Chapter 2, the chapter demonstrates that the connections foreign Muslims forged to the empire depended heavily on local networks rooted in specific sites but with broad regional connections.

My conclusion reflects on the intractability of the protection question and what the experiences of Central Asians tell us about nationality and becoming Ottoman. The study ends where it began, in the courtyard of Sultantepe, and offers a window into the legacy of the lodge in the Turkish Republic.

A final word here on the book's approach to its subjects. As hajjis guide us through the vast and shifting terrain of the pilgrimage in the late Ottoman Empire, they remind us that they did not represent some ideal Muslim type that acted according to pan-Islamic ideals or mores that scholars sometimes ascribe to their subjects. As the chapter on Sultantepe demonstrates, they drank, smoked, had affairs, and tried to take advantage of Ottoman philanthropy. They were a motley assortment of multifaceted people with their own struggles and dreams. They were not zealots, nor were they irrationally drawn to Mecca because trains and steamships could take them there. "Ordinary people" are at the center of this study. I call them this because of the clumsiness of terms like *nonelites* and the disparate contexts for *subaltern*.[55] Throughout, I have tried to accord them the ability to defy our preconceptions about how they should behave. Even in the most formulaic sources, individual voices shine through. They include Bukharans who wrote Persian poems to the sultan as requests for assistance on the way to Mecca and a woman who asked the government for a stipend because her (good-for-nothing) husband said he was going to help some pilgrims in Eyüp in Istanbul but, instead, boarded a train for Russia and never came back. These are the kinds of people—alongside Ottoman legal advisers, foreign consuls, and statesmen—who animate this book.

Uneasily situated between emerging legal categories of Ottoman and foreigner and colonial subject and protected person, these migrants were liminal persons traveling on a journey that we can imagine as a threshold between the structure of home and Mecca.[56] In the Holy Cities, pilgrims achieved a temporary state of relations characterized by the leveling of difference and a transcendental sense of religious brotherhood. This is the *communitas*—the relationship or feeling of great social equality, solidarity, and togetherness characteristic of people experiencing liminality together—explored most famously by Victor Turner,[57] that we see described again and again by pilgrims in varied contexts and eras: it is what Mirim Khan's travelogue recounts when he says that at Mecca and Medina, beggars and kings became one; and it is what, decades later, the African American civil rights activist Malcolm X communicated in his letters from Mecca, when he wrote that participating in the circumambulation of the Kaaba led him to rethink everything he knew about race. As he wrote in a much-quoted passage:

> On this pilgrimage, what I have seen and experienced has forced me to rearrange much of my thought-patterns previously held and *to toss aside* some of my previous conclusions.... During the past eleven days here in the Muslim world, I have eaten from the same plate, drunk from the same glass, and slept in the same bed (or on the same rug)—while praying *to the same God*—with fellow Muslims, whose eyes were the bluest of blue, whose hair was the blondest of blond, and whose skin was the whitest of white.... We were *truly* all the same (brothers)—because their belief in one God had removed the "white" from their minds, the "white" from their behavior, and the "white" from their attitude.[58]

Malcolm X's idealization of his journey, which we know was not characterized by the equality he describes (for one thing, he was originally treated poorly and then as a guest of the king when he was able to mobilize connections that garnered him royal favor), is important because it is a classic example—perhaps a textbook case—for how communitas shaped the recounting of the experience by the faithful. As he "rearranged" his thoughts and "toss[ed] aside" his previous views, he rewrote his experience to fit a certain paradigm. The pilgrim, to paraphrase Michael Wolfe, brought to Mecca what she or he hoped to find there.[59] If for Malcolm X, this was an idealized vision of Islam that offered a path to transcending the structural constraints of racism in America, for some Central Asian pilgrims in the age of high imperialism, it was the possibility for strong Muslim leadership and community in a world dominated by Christian powers. Even as the hajj connected people in a multitude of ways, its ritual—and spiritual—dimensions reinforced ideals of unity that were not always in step with how pilgrims or sultans pursued their interests.

Here, one may ask, if colonial subjects in Mecca and other Ottoman cities actively sought consular support and capitulatory privileges, why would they view the world in these terms? I would answer by saying that religion mattered, and we need to bring it back into our analysis of hajj. This does not mean that it dictated how Central Asians understood political belonging or religious legitimacy or that they viewed their attempts to benefit from either Ottoman or European nationality as an espousal of allegiance. Religion influenced their subjectivity but not necessarily their understanding of subjecthood or legal nationality. As in other legally plural orders, people operated within the extant system to maximize the benefits available to them because that was how things were done. Reconstructing the experiences of pilgrims—and not only those of Muslim elites and intermediaries—helps us see them as more than bodies to be influenced, regulated, policed, and monitored by empires. Instead, these individuals—their desires, beliefs, and experiences—become productive of the very categories (subjecthood and nationality above all) that the state used to constitute itself.

(CHAPTER 1)

REWRITING THE ROAD TO MECCA

Bismillāhirraḥmānirraḥīm. After reciting the name of God and declaring his intention to perform the hajj, Mirim Khan "pulled his heart" from his family and boarded the first of many trains on the long journey from Russian Turkestan to Ottoman Mecca.[1] When he left Tashkent, it was just around six o'clock and the beginning of Hayit (Ramadan) in the year 1902. He would arrive in Samarqand around daybreak and continue his travels with a group of fellow aspirants on a series of "fire wagons" and "fire ships" through Bukhara, Ashkhabad, Krasnovodosk, Rostov, Akmasjid, Sevastopol, Istanbul, Alexandria, Suez, and Jeddah. It was by turns an exhausting and exhilarating journey, marked by numerous near-catastrophes. One of the more devastating ones occurred as the travelers were on the cusp of arriving in Mecca and experienced a harrowing Bedouin attack that killed members of the caravan and left many destitute and "laid bare . . . with thirst and hunger." In Mirim Khan's telling, however, the experience only increased the spiritual rewards for those who had survived. When they reached Mecca, he declared, "Sorry and worry left [our hearts] and we were freed." He continued:

> Can one reach their goal without hardship?
> Without hardship there is no gain
> The one who took on hardship was now *majnun* [mad with love]

> Without diving, one cannot find *durr-i maknun* [the hidden pearl, i.e., the concealed truth].²

Hardship, love, and the Sufi way were essential elements of Mirim Khan's account, a turn-of-the-twentieth-century hajj narrative written in vernacular Turki (Chaghatay) and rooted in the idiom of Central Asian Islam: Sufism. The text, catalogued as *Hajjnoma-i Turkiy*, chronicled the journey of a middling religious scholar who was by turns irascible and amusing and was consistently strident in his admonitions to embark on the hajj. While the author referred to himself after a short prayer in Istanbul as Mirim Khan (the name I use here), archivists attribute the manuscript to a certain Muhammad Oxund Toshkandi.³ Despite questions about its authorship, the hajjnoma's publication in three lithograph editions between 1907 and 1915 suggests that it had become a popular title in Russian Turkestan. Mirim Khan's frequent habit of using the imperative to tell his audience of pious friends and brothers to listen (*quloq soling!*) indicated an awareness that it would be read aloud—a common practice in the manuscript cultures of Central Asia.⁴ Men who gathered in teahouses and tekkes would likely be eager to learn about the distant lands to which their friends and family were traveling. In Mirim Khan's stories, they may have envisioned people like themselves: aspirants navigating new routes and foreign cities, trying to catch a glimpse of the Ottoman sultan-caliph at Friday prayers, and ascending to the Mount of Mercy, where the Prophet Muhammad delivered his Farewell Sermon in 632 CE.

Like other works in this burgeoning genre, *Hajjnoma-i Turkiy* described various facets of the industrialized hajj: trains and steamships, routes through Russia, mobility controls and regulations, and the jarring experiences of quarantine. It was clearly not lost on the author that in a paradox of globalization, "the industrialized Hajj [had become] at once easier and more difficult than before."⁵ He not so subtly hinted at how the ruptures of modernity provoked anxiety among believers and created oppressive conditions with which pilgrims would have to contend. He described both the wonders of technology and the darker sides of global capital, writing about how passengers on ships were packed like cargo and stacked one on top of the other, like melons or jugs, and how boarding a cramped vessel could feel like entering a tomb or coffin.⁶ He and his travel companions faced hostile administrators, outbreaks of cholera, and other harsh conditions that could be incredibly dehumanizing. The text prepared people for what they could expect and did the work of convincing them to go, despite the hardships they would encounter.

But this was not a book about death, nor was it another guide describing the rituals that pilgrims would perform once they reached Mecca. Mirim Khan situated the challenges of steamship-era hajj within a mystical framework where worldly suffering was presented as an intrinsic part of the Sufi path to spiritual transformation. In long poems interspersed with prose descriptions of the mundane dimensions of travel, he recounted experiences that would lighten the believer's heart and invoked mystical goals such as the annihilation of the ego (*fana'*) through union with God. *Meshaqqatsiz hajj bo'lmas*. "There is no hajj without hardship," he admonished. "Go, if you are able," and, "Go, if God allows," he wrote. He claimed that his reed pen could not do justice to Istanbul or Alexandria, let alone to Mecca, where the Kaaba cleansed away one's sins, redeemed the ignorant, and transformed "kings and beggars" into equals.⁷ The text's dialogic nature thus yields insight not only into the journey of this one person but also the concerns of a much wider audience in early twentieth-century Turkestan. His repeated exhortations suggested that readers and listeners were not—as colonial officials feared and present-day historians often assume—religious fanatics drawn to Mecca like so many moths to a flame. Rather, they resembled the birds in Farid ud-Din Attar's *Conference of the Birds*, a mystical allegory of a pilgrimage to find spiritual truth. In this twelfth-century tale, the hoopoe tries to convince his fellow birds to travel to China in search of a mythical bird called the Simorgh, who would be their king. The hoopoe is met with resistance from those who have heard of the travails that lie ahead. The text reminds us that, like the nightingale that could not bear to leave the rose, or the partridge that chose wealth over spiritual fulfillment, pilgrims had worldly attachments and legitimate fears about leaving their loved ones and embarking on the arduous journey.⁸ At the same time, it helps us keep sight of a seemingly banal fact: the hajj was at heart a religious journey.

In the first part of this chapter, Mirim Khan guides us from Russian Turkestan to Istanbul and introduces us to *his vision* of the Ottoman capital. Next, given the frequency with which he admonishes readers to retrace his steps and go on hajj, the chapter pauses to consider the broader context of Mirim Khan's exhortations. It examines an 1890s Russian hajj account published in Turkestan, which reflected colonial anxieties about Muslim travel to Mecca. While the attempts of the series to desacralize Arabia likely gained little traction among local Muslims, it highlights the influence of the hajjnoma genre as a perceived space for shaping public views and reflects the abiding tsarist hostility toward hajj that would have informed the lives of people like Mirim Khan and his readers. In the last section, the chapter considers how Mirim Khan's experience of communitas—what anthropologists describe as a spontaneous sense of brotherhood and equality experienced by people undergoing a liminal journey together—can help us to understand how religious experience informed Central Asian migrations and travels in Ottoman lands.

This chapter follows Mirim Khan through segments of his hajj from Russian Turkestan to Mecca (a discussion of the entire text would merit an entire monograph), with the purpose of beginning our journey with a pilgrim whose name we know (sort of), who was neither ordinary nor extraordinary, and who helps us to see hajj as more than a rite to be regulated by empires. Rather than wade into historiographical debates about ordinary people, subalterns, and elites, my goal is to introduce a figure that subverts these categories and compels us to think about how often people crossed these boundaries. While literate and educated, Mirim Khan was one among thousands of people traveling in third-class railcars and on steamships, in a sea of people often referred to disparagingly as "pauper pilgrims." All too often, the literature on hajj treats them as stock characters in a story animated by elites and empires; as bodies to be counted, quarantined, and disinfected; or as subjects whose loyalties were sought by competing imperial powers.[9] Heeding Shahzad Bashir's caution against "mining" sources (in his case, hagiographies) for useful facts and verifiable information and treating the remainder as "historiographic waste matter," I reconstruct a worldview and voices that are conspicuously absent in much extant literature.[10] As we will see, the Istanbul that Mirim Khan describes was one that many contemporary travelers and flaneurs of the upper classes would not recognize; instead of a cosmopolitan city of Christians, Jews, and Muslims, in his telling it was a fundamentally Sunni Muslim space. Thus, while the hajjnoma helps us excavate the experiences and concerns of travelers during this period, it is not simply a window on pilgrims' already shaped subjectivities. Rather, I argue that Mirim Khan was an active mediator of a journey altered by colonial infrastructure and intervention. The process of making Istanbul into more than just another transit point on the industrialized hajj involved eliding its cosmopolitan character; focusing on sites that connected the city to a more expansive, pre-Ottoman, Sunni Muslim past; and emphasizing its location as the seat of a modern Islamic caliphate.

Finding Islam in the Ottoman Capital

Historically, travel to Istanbul was not an easily realized goal: the vast overland distance between Central Asia and the lands of "Rum" (a reference to Byzantium) was prohibitive, and throughout much of the early modern period, those who set out for Mecca did so by taking routes through India, the Caucasus, and then Anatolia to Damascus, or through Persia.[11] Russian investment in an extensive network of rail and steamer lines made it possible for Mirim Khan to travel from Russian Turkestan to Ottoman Istanbul and from there to Arabia in a matter of weeks rather than the months it would have taken in the past. By the early twentieth century, as many as twenty-five thousand pilgrims traveled through Odessa alone and had to move quickly through Istanbul. Additional waves of pilgrims traveled via Sevastopol.[12] With the opening of the Suez Canal in 1869, the two most popular routes were through Bombay and Istanbul. Those who went via Afghanistan and India could travel from Peshawar to Bombay by rail and then take any number of established steamship services to Jeddah. This option was popular among subjects of Russia's colony and protectorates in Central Asia but also among Afghans who had no direct links to rail lines in tsarist territory, merchants with trade connections to the Indian subcontinent, and Russian and Chinese subjects who were unwilling or unable to obtain visas from the tsarist government.[13] With the opening of the Trans-Caspian and Tashkent-Orenburg rail lines in 1899 and 1906, and investment in steamship lines that crossed the Black Sea, travel through Russia became, for many, a faster and cheaper option. This was the route Mirim Khan chose, and it took him through Istanbul, then on to Egypt, and from there to Jeddah. In 1904, Russia's introduction of regular direct service from Odessa to Jeddah sped up the trip but was not ideal for those who wanted to spend time in the Ottoman capital.[14]

While it was comparatively easier than traveling entirely overland (which people continued to do), the Black Sea route was in no sense easy. Shortly after leaving Sevastopol, Mirim Khan described how the ship hit rough waters, leading him to think that he might not live to see dry land again. In scenes that evoked the end of days, he recounted how panicked passengers cried and embraced one another and begged God to pardon their sins.[15] Then, just as quickly as the storm had come, it cleared away, and their awkward embraces hung in the thick air of the ship's cramped quarters. The pilgrims continued to sail for another thirty hours, the sun rising and setting on the same monotonous horizon over the Black Sea until the ship approached Istanbul and the banks of the Bosphorus came into view. After what seemed like an eternity at sea, the vista of Istanbul's imperial mosques would greet them.

As they arrived in the strong currents of the straits, the weary travelers disembarked onto a small rowboat that bobbed in the sea like an unbalanced scale. These were waters that imperial Russia had long sought to control, leading to centuries of intermittent warfare and rivalry with the Ottomans. Mirim Khan, however, was not thinking about history; he was eager to figure out his next steps. His brief moment of disorientation quickly subsided when he met a porter from Turkestan who helped the travelers get their bearings and manage their many bags. It was an encounter that immediately rendered the city somewhat familiar and that contrasted starkly with Sevastopol, which remained foreign to him throughout his time there. Within hours, a group of travelers had checked into Davud Han in Tahtakale (a neighborhood near the Golden Horn), an inn that catered to Central Asian migrants and pilgrims. After breaking their fast in the small and cramped inn, the author and his companions set about seeing the city. Their first destination was the Hagia Sophia, the famous Byzantine cathedral built by Emperor Justinian I (r. 527–65) and that Sultan Mehmed II converted to a mosque when he conquered Constantinople in 1453. Mehmed's military victory over Byzantium was the realization of a dream shared by his father and grandfather before him, as well as the Prophet Muhammad, who believed that Muslims would one day capture the city and the cathedral.[16] Although Arab armies first laid siege to the city in 674 CE, it took nearly eight centuries for this shared dream to be realized. After fifty-three days of continuous shelling of the city walls, Ottoman armies hoisted ships onto dry land to circumvent the blockade of the Bosphorus. Finally, they triumphed, and the seventh Ottoman sultan—henceforth "Mehmed the Conqueror"—entered the city on 29 May 1453. One of his first acts was to visit the cathedral, where he is said to have "dismounted at the door . . . and bent down to take a handful of earth, which he then sprinkled over his turban as an act of humility before God."[17] Constantinople had never fully recovered from the Crusader sack of 1204, and Mehmed II set about returning it to its former glory through a program to rebuild and repopulate the city.

The Ottoman conquest marked the beginning of a new epoch in which Arabo-Islamic traditions were integrated into the dynasty's Turco-Mongol and Byzantine heritage. In the sixteenth century, when Selim "the Grim" defeated the Mamluks and extended the empire's domains into the central Islamic lands, the need to establish an Islamic basis for authority took on added significance. With the conquest of Islam's three holiest cities—Mecca, Medina, and Jerusalem—the sultan added the title of Custodian of the Two Holy Cities to a long list that had started with "Beg" and grown to include khan, gazi, sultan, padishah, and Caesar. Custodianship of Mecca and Medina inaugurated new imperial projects, with court historians weaving legend and myth into official histories of the House of Osman and connecting distant Mecca and Medina and early Islamic history to the Ottoman capital. As the work of Gülru Necipoğlu details, Ottoman chroniclers began to circulate legends that the Prophet had sanctioned the cathedral's reconstruction during his lifetime and that water from a holy spring in Mecca (Zamzam) and the Prophet's saliva had gone into its mortar. Ostensibly, the goal was to connect the Ottoman conquest of the church and Byzantium to the Prophet and Muslim holy spaces. Zamzam was the well that miraculously sprang up as Abraham's handmaiden, Hagar, desperately searched in the desert for water for her infant son, Ishmael. It was this search that pilgrims reenacted as they ran back and forth between the hills of Safa and Marwa seven times during the hajj ritual known as *sa'y*. According to Necipoğlu, the court historian İdris-i Bidlisi also compared the Hagia Sophia to both al-Aqsa in Jerusalem—where the Prophet ascended to heaven on a night journey—and to the Kaaba itself. Over time, others would compare it to "a second Ka'ba for the poor who could not afford the pilgrimage to Mecca."[18]

Sultan Abdülhamid II's promotion of the mosque as the seat of the caliphate and the site where the last Abbasid caliph had allegedly transferred power to Sultan Selim in 1519 added to the Hagia Sophia's prestige.[19] Central Asians, who are said to have held the mosque in particularly high esteem, propagated its significance as an integral part of the pilgrimage to Mecca. Soon after Mirim Khan visited, the ulema of the cities of Hami and Turfan wrote to Sultan Abdülhamid II in 1906, saying that the people of Chinese Turkestan "believe a visit to your lofty residence prior to making the hajj is as much a religious obligation as the trip to the Hijaz itself, and consider a pilgrimage to the caliphal seat as the fulfillment of the hajj."[20] Thus, even as Mirim Khan referred to the Hagia Sophia as "Ayaz Sufi"—in what seems to have been a common corruption of the Greek name and perhaps a claiming of the mosque for Sufism—he was clearly aware that it was a destination that merited visiting.[21] By making it the first stop on his visit to Istanbul, he sought to affirm its position in the geography of hajj.

As he set out that first night, Mirim Khan likely followed a route through the old city that would impress on him the festive nature of Istanbul during the holy month of Ramadan. Everywhere, the streets would be full of people headed to perform the supererogatory prayers, and the tall spindly minarets of the imperial mosques would be festooned with strings of lights (*mahya*) that lit up the night sky and spelled out messages to welcome what was popularly referred to as "the sultan of the eleven months." As he described the mosque, the author contributed to the rich layers of meaning the Hagia Sophia had acquired over time and immersed his readers in the visual, aural, and spiritual experience of visitation. Although he began by claiming he would not be able to depict its beauty, he immediately began to do just that: there was no counting, he said, the domes upon domes, porticos, and arches or the lights and lanterns illuminating the vast space (fig. 2). The floors were adorned with rich and colorful carpets in lieu of worn prayer mats, and the sounds of Quranic recitation reverberated across its walls to produce a uniquely Ottoman soundscape.[22] He noted the rhythmic chanting of the *tekbir* ("God is great")—*Allahu ekber allahu ekber, la ilahe illallahu vallahu ekber, allahu ekber ve lillahil hamd*—after each recitation of a Quranic chapter and its effect: it lightened his grief, reduced his woes, and cleansed his heart of the dust that had gathered there.

In invoking the heart, the author was influenced by a literary tradition Shahab Ahmed terms "the *madhhab* [way] of Love." This was an extensive textual corpus passed down through the generations, in which human love for God and divine beauty was considered the "paramount human sensation, sensibility, action and condition," essential for being able to experience knowledge of God, or Truth.[23] As Ahmed explains, the concepts and images of this way were so widespread that they constituted a lingua franca of sorts across the Islamicate world. In writing about his experiences, Mirim Khan invoked Sufi ideals such as diving into a metaphorical sea, uncovering that which was concealed, or going "mad" (*majnun*), signaling that he was versed in this language. He and his writing were products of Persianate societies, where the heart was considered one of the most important organs and believed to have its own senses, which mirrored those of the body and ensured its correct functioning. Mirim Khan invoked it often, beginning on the very first page of his account when he described how he "pulled" it from his family during his departure. The heart helped to make sense of the

FIGURE 2. Interior of Hagia Sophia, 1860s–1910, undated. Digital image courtesy of the Getty's Open Content Program.

material world, and its internal senses brought "sensations of the interior world into the heart's purview: its eyes see the sights of the unseen, its ears hear God's speech, its nose smells the perfumes of the heavenly realm, its tongue tastes divine love and interior knowledge, and the sense of touch, which is spread all over its exterior, gives a comprehensive experience of the unseen world." The heart's senses allowed the believer to experience a type of spiritual intelligence and to travel into the metaphysical realm.[24] While one only needed a sound body to travel to Mecca, it was the heart that allowed the Sufi to experience the city's grace. Tending to this organ in the steamship era, when the hajj threatened "to become its own undoing," was more important than ever.[25]

By signaling the moments and places along the way where one could unburden and enrich the heart, Mirim Khan was mapping an itinerary rooted in a particularly mystical view of the hajj—and that was a response to its reconfiguration through new cities and experiences (map 3). After visiting a mosque that "the sultan's mother built" (Valide Camii), and then the Süleymaniye, the second major stop on his tour of what we might imagine as "Islamic Istanbul" was the Yıldız Hamidiye Mosque. Mirim Khan refers to crossing an impressively large bridge, likely the Galata Bridge (fig. 3), indicating that he walked across the thoroughfare connecting the old city to the district of Karaköy—with Pera just up any number of the hills that connected the waterfront to the European quarters. From this crossing, he would have an unparalleled view of Yeni Camii, Sultanahmet, Hagia Sophia, Süleymaniye, and the Golden Horn. Once he reached the other side, he could see the tramway that made its way up and down Meclis-i Mebusan Caddesi (Chamber of Deputies Avenue) and could follow its path from the shoreline toward the Dolmabahçe Palace, and then continue his walk to Hamidiye Mosque.

With its single minaret and relatively small scale, Hamidiye did not rival the Hagia Sophia or Süleymaniye Mosque. Yet through association with the caliph, it had a profound effect on Mirim Khan, who followed a brief prayer invoking the umma with a description of a sublime structure reaching to the heavens. The Friday prayers were where the performance of Ottoman power and Islamic tradition converged along pan-Islamic lines, and Mirim Khan was clearly influenced by the pageantry that visitors to Friday prayers commented on in written accounts from this period. In a faithfully rendered

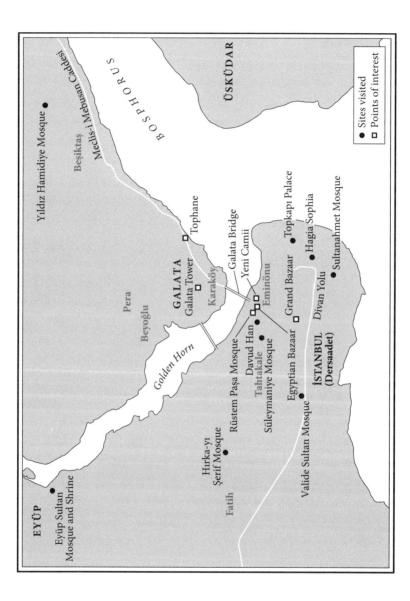

MAP 3. Mirim Khan's travels through Greater Istanbul, c. 1902.

scene that corresponds to many foreigners' descriptions, he explained how the "Master of Victorious Islam"—whom he wanted to see with his heart and soul (*bajon u dil*)—displayed himself to the public. Like the choreographed projections of the tsar's power in Russia, or the Habsburg emperor's authority in Austro-Hungary, the Ottoman sovereign had invested a long-standing sultanic tradition of appearing at the Friday prayers with new ceremonial elements that emphasized his power and patrimony.[26] Mirim Khan commented on the soldiers surrounding Sultan Abdülhamid II, whose imposing appearance contributed to the great pomp of the imperial procession from the palace to the mosque. Although it was a short distance from Abdülhamid's palace at Yıldız to the Hamidiye, "the sultan would be driven to the mosque in his landau, but on the return journey he would mount a simpler caleche, and take the reins himself. Male members of the dynasty, his palace retinue, leading bureaucrats, and high ranking military, in that order, would

FIGURE 3. Pedestrians on the Kara-Keui (Galata) Bridge, Constantinople, Turkey, c. 1890–1900. The bridge spans the Golden Horn at Eminönü, Istanbul (note minarets and mosques in the background). Library of Congress, Prints and Photographs Division.

then line up behind him."²⁷ According to Selim Deringil, this was a symbolic representation of the ruler taking in hand the reins of the state. After the prayers, special officials would collect petitions from the people, Ottoman and non-Ottoman Muslims alike, signaling the paternalism and care of the sultan for his subjects. Mirim Khan insisted that his readers witness it all and see the Caliph—his face, "the station of heaven."²⁸

The spectacle was meant to create "vibrations of power" in a state that had seen its authority steadily decline over the nineteenth century.²⁹ Although the Hamidian regime poured extensive financial resources into Istanbul and maintained the appearance of a well-ordered modern city, the empire at the turn of the century had seen much better days: the numerous wars and territorial losses of the long nineteenth century, combined with extensive—and expensive—modernization programs dating to the late 1700s, eventually led to massive indebtedness to European creditors and, ultimately, Ottoman bankruptcy. The government had taken out its first foreign loans during the Crimean

FIGURE 4. The Selamlık (Sultan's procession to the mosque) at the Hamidiye Camii (mosque) on Friday, created between 1880 and 1893. Library of Congress, Prints and Photographs Division.

War (1853–56), and by the mid-1870s it was unable to service the growing debt. Defeat in the 1877–78 Russo-Ottoman War only compounded the problem, and by 1879, the Porte had defaulted on its loans. Within two years, Sultan Abdülhamid II was forced by foreign powers to sign the 1881 Muharrem Decree, which created the Ottoman Public Debt Administration (OPDA), a vast, essentially independent bureaucracy within the Ottoman administration that was run by a council comprising members from creditor countries.[30]

The creation of the OPDA was emblematic of the loss of fiscal sovereignty, which was only one dimension of the impact of continuous European intervention in Ottoman affairs. Faced with two types of legitimation crises—an internal one stemming from the Tanzimat "reordering" of 1839 to 1876 and the increasing demands made by the state on its subjects, and an external one that derived from the loss of real power in the Concert of Europe and European manipulation of the Capitulations—the Hamidian government responded with new survival strategies. These included engagement with a developing international legal order (the focus of Chapter 3) and efforts to legitimize the sultan's power and authority through the institution of the caliphate. The procession at the Hamidiye Mosque was part of the latter—the promotion of the institution through public displays and pageantry designed to leave viewers with an impression of a strong, modernizing, and Islamic empire.[31] In addition to Ottoman subjects, the sultan's intended audience included European foreign observers and Muslims from abroad. Mirim Khan had faithfully reproduced the procession and the message for an audience thousands of miles away. His depiction of the Friday prayer procession adhered closely to a script that informed other travel accounts and gave away the hajjnoma's carefully curated message to Central Asians. Had there been a Hamidian public relations office, it could not have asked for better publicity.

A Culture of Visitation

Although we tend to think of a pilgrimage as a journey to a specific location, before the advent of air travel, the hajj signified a journey that did not generally go from point A to point B and back. Instead, it was marked as much by detours and digressions as it was the circumambulation of the Kaaba. But as the routes to Mecca shifted during the second half of the nineteenth century, they bypassed many of the shrines that shaped greater pilgrimage journeys that had taken pilgrims in earlier eras from Bukhara to Bombay, Mazar-i Sharif, Najaf, and Jerusalem. The "quicker and cheaper alternative offered by train and steamship ... came at a symbolic price: the old shrines of the saints had to be sacrificed for a speedier and timelier arrival in Mecca."[32] Yet pilgrims did not remain passive observers to these changes; they responded by making alternative calculations: they not only found new shrines but also ascribed greater meaning to those that may not have earlier merited the costs of veering from the overland routes. For Central Asians traveling via the Black Sea and then through Istanbul, this could be a challenging feat: cities like Odessa, Sevastopol, and Batumi could not easily be coaxed to yield graves of old Sufi "saints" and other Muslim holy persons; and Istanbul and its environs were not rich in the shrines of major figures in Islamic history—even those whose bones seemed to have traveled quite extensively or those who had shrines honoring them in multiple places.

Nonetheless, the sheer volume of people traveling through Istanbul meant that by the early twentieth century, it had established its spot in this changing religious geography. Mirim Khan was likely one of many hajjnoma authors who worked to make the case for Istanbul's credentials as a major Muslim city and, in a sense, to promote its attractions. Of all the places he visited after leaving Russian Central Asia, Istanbul was where he performed his first veritable shrine visit. This was at the tomb complex at Eyüp Sultan, built in honor of Halid bin Zeyd Ebu Eyüp el-Ensari (Arabic: Khalid bin Zeyd Abu Ayyub al-Ansari), the standard-bearer and companion of the Prophet Muhammad who was believed to have been killed on the European shores of the Bosphorus during the first Muslim siege of Constantinople in 674–78 CE.[33] In the Sunni Hanafi tradition, Eyüp el-Ensari was considered one of those charismatic figures who had enjoyed God's divine favor and who, in turn, could bestow blessings on those who visited his shrine. Mirim Khan summarized this by explaining that Eyüp el-Ensari was a helper and friend of the Prophet, known for hadiths that his audience could learn more about "by reading books." It was true that he was believed to be a companion (*sahaba*), as well as a helper, of the Prophet (*ansar*) who had aided God's messenger as he migrated from Mecca to Medina in 622 CE. This migration marked the formation of the first Muslim community and the beginning of the Islamic calendar. After Mehmed II's conquest of the city in 1453, he ordered the construction of a shrine in honor of this companion. Somewhat improbably, the construction of this tomb forged a direct link between the Ottomans, the Prophet, and the first Muslims in Islamic history. Mehmed also designated the complex as the location where Ottoman sultans would ascend to the throne. Until the end of empire, new sovereigns were invested with power in a sword-girding ceremony (*kılıç kuşanma*) that involved being given the sword of the state, which was named after Osman, the founder of the dynasty. The ritual embedded the shrine complex in Ottoman political history and the city's sacred geography. As one scholar writes, "If the Ottoman Fatih Sultan Mehmet is known as the conqueror of Constantinople, Halid bin Zeyd is often described as the city's spiritual conqueror; where the Ottoman conquest of 1453 marked a political triumph, it was Halid bin Zeyd's death—and the miraculous rediscovery of his body—that marked the religious conquest of the city."[34]

Mirim Khan's journey to Eyüp moved the reader from the first descriptions of religious grace at Hagia Sophia, and a subsequent rendering of Ottoman political and religious authority at the Hamidiye Mosque, to the site where one of the most powerful of sultans—whom he referred to as a *gazi* (holy warrior)—had forged deep connections between the dynasty and early Islamic history. Mirim Khan described Eyüp foremost as a place that was full of blessings and miracles that could dispel a visitor's pain and grief[35]—concepts that would be familiar to readers who were part of a culture of shrine visitation, or *ziyara*, and likely receptive to learning about sacred spaces they could visit on the way to Mecca. From Kashgar to Bukhara, there was a widespread practice of visiting the graves and shrines of venerated Sufi shaykhs and pirs and other holy personages regarded as "friends of God" (*veli*, pl., *evliya*). These individuals were believed to have special spiritual and healing powers and blessings (*karama*), and men and women sought their intercession for relief from physical, mental, and spiritual ailments and saw them as intermediates for prayers for themselves and their ancestors. The shrines ranged in size and ornamentation and included structures such as the mausoleum commissioned in 1389 by Amir Timur (Tamerlane) in commemoration of the great mystic Khoja Ahmed Yesevi (1093–1166) in Turkestan (formerly Yasi, in today's Kazakhstan), to makeshift shrines in remote spots in the desert outside Kashgar, where pilgrims left small devotional offerings or tied ribbons to trees to mark their wishes. In his study of religious practice and identity formation in Xinjiang, Rian Thum shows the extent to which these practices were interwoven with the transmission of oral and written hagiographies of so-called saints—what he calls the "tazkirah-shrine system" that shaped not only local praxis but also a collective identity among inhabitants of the oasis cities of East Turkestan known as Altishahr.[36]

Local and regional differences notwithstanding, this culture of shrine visitation was widespread across the Islamic world, connecting people to sacred space and genealogies across oceans and centuries. In the Eurasian or Silk Road context, entire cities such as Mazar-i Sharif (in today's Afghanistan) and regions in Iraq developed around mausoleums and cemeteries devoted to figures from the Prophet's family, particularly through the lineage of Ali, and were visited by Sunni and Shi'a Muslims alike. Prior to the shift from overland to sea routes in the nineteenth century and, later, the intensifying Wahhabi opposition to these practices (and the subsequent destruction of sites where people engaged in practices deemed un-Islamic innovations), pilgrims to Mecca would plan their journeys to include trips to shrines in Afghanistan, India, Iraq, and Anatolia. They would also allot time for Medina, where prior to the Saudi destruction of the tombs at Jannat al-Baqi and Jannat al-Mu'alla in the 1920s, many members of the Prophet's family and his companions were buried. Pilgrims also often

FIGURE 5. Central Asian hajj travelers in an Eyüp cemetery, Istanbul. Undated, likely early 1900s. *Hac, Kutsal Yolculuk* (İstanbul: Denizler Kitabevi, 2014).

visited Jerusalem to see al-Aqsa (the Dome of the Rock). This was the location where in 621 CE the Prophet Muhammad ascended to heaven and led the other prophets in prayer. His miraculous night journey and ascension was a prominent feature of Islamic world histories, miniatures, and hagiographies and were echoed in Sufi saints' biographies, where mystics traveled in space and time to perform miracles or receive certificates of transmission (*ijaza*) from great masters who had long since departed.[37]

The diachronic linking of Ottoman space to early Islamic history continued in Istanbul proper, as Mirim Khan recounted visiting Topkapı. This was the fifteenth-century palace where the Ottoman dynasty preserved and displayed holy relics such as the Prophet's mantle (*hırka-i şerif*) and hairs from his beard (*mu-yı mübarek*) during Ramadan. After rubbing the relics on his face and saying a prayer of thankfulness, Mirim Khan journeyed to see another cloak of the Prophet, likely at the Mosque of the Blessed Mantle (Hırka-i Şerif Camii) in Fatih. This one was said to be given by him to Uwais al-Qarani, a seventh-century Muslim from Yemen who was acquainted both with the Prophet and with Ali, the fourth caliph for Sunni Muslims and the imam in Shi'i Islam.[38] Mirim Khan twice mentioned rubbing the relics on his "blackened face"—in yet another allusion to his sinfulness and the redemptive power of the sacred objects and places.

Some of the work Mirim Khan did to Islamicize Istanbul was achieved via silences. With the exception of a disparaging passage describing Armenian merchants and comments on the markets of the city, Mirim Khan largely ignored non-Muslim life. Instead of the busy streets of Pera, the Armenian and Greek neighborhoods along the Bosphorus, and the many gardens and coffeehouses populated by people of various ethnicities and confessions, he focused on sites and experiences that portrayed Istanbul as fundamentally Sunni. This was in stark contrast to Alexandria—his favorite of all the cities he visited, and which he discussed in extended detail as a tourist taking in the sights (and the smells of flowers and the tastes of fruits). There, he held out the steamship-era hajj as adventure, not only spiritual endeavor.[39] The juxtaposition in his approach suggested that he sought to fix Istanbul's position in the industrialized hajj—much of which involved a journey outside "Muslim memory space" and "into a world governed by ideas, people, and technologies of non-Muslim provenance"[40]—as a point of reentry into a shared world of mosques, pan-Islamic power, shrine visitation, and relics from the Prophet Muhammad. In a recurring refrain, he told his audience that they needed to go see the city with their own eyes:

> If I try to describe Istanbul and Rum
> I won't be able, my faculties not sufficient
> Go and see it, if God facilitates [your travel]
> What I say will never approximate its praise
> If I took up the pen for life
> If I took a step toward this path
> Not one in a thousand would be expressed
> Like trying to sing the praises of a youthful lad.[41]

His description again rested on the embodiment of experience and stressed the importance of being, seeing, and feeling Istanbul and its effects on the senses, eyes, and—most important—the heart. This was a deeply subjective and strategic portrayal of the Ottomans, which contrasted greatly with other cities along the way, particularly in the Russian Empire.

Hardship and the Colonial Hajj

In 1910, the former Russian consul to Jeddah, M. E. Nikol'skii, voiced concerns about the bad impression that Muslim pilgrims might form of Tsarist Russia. Exposed only to the empire's lesser cities and "drab train stations, where they encountered thieves and bandits," he worried that they would imagine the "hajj journey through Russia as one of hardship and abuse" and that this would "reinforce their positive impressions of Constantinople when they arrived in the Ottoman capital."[42] Nikol'skii's concerns were valid, particularly about the abuses and hardships that informed the journey. Throughout the *Hajjnoma*, Mirim Khan made clear that even as the pilgrimage had become faster and cheaper, it was still marked by great difficulty and sacrifice. Despite "promises of superior safety, comfort, and speed,"[43] he recounted traveling in uncomfortable, unsafe, and unhygienic conditions. During the trip from Tashkent to Istanbul, for example, he described an encounter with Russian officials who taunted the pilgrims and alternated between referring to them as infidels (*ahl-i kuffor*), dishonorable men, and men of oppression who did not recognize that they were "hajjis heading to sacred territory." In his telling, this was not an isolated incident and continued at another station, where the group was locked up in a room "like prisoners" and forced to wait for more than eight hours. During this time, more "infidels" gathered around the travelers and mocked their clothing and turbans, even as they prayed. As Mirim Khan endured this ridicule, women cried and wailed, and people were trampled as they tried to get out of the station. The policemen guarding the door, meanwhile, were taking plentiful bribes. As he recounted the chaos, Mirim Khan said it felt like nothing less than the end of the world.[44] The pilgrims were subject to the whims of tsarist officials and, like in the tight quarters of the trains and ships, oppressed spiritually and physically by the journey.

Mirim Khan's depictions of his trip from Russian Turkestan to Istanbul highlighted the deep-rooted ambivalence that informed Russia's approach to the hajj in the late nineteenth and early twentieth century. While some statesmen saw potential avenues for expanding influence and lucrative opportunities to employ the empire's underutilized passenger fleet and extensive railroad lines in the service of growing Muslim populations, others continued to harbor paranoia about pan-Islamism. Like their British and Dutch counterparts, Russian officials in St. Petersburg were concerned about the potentially destabilizing effects of travel to Ottoman lands—particularly their subjects' "exposure" to pan-Islamism and pan-Turkism. Even as they began to accommodate the hajj, many within the government continued to view it as "a clandestine, conspiratorial activity, and a symbol of Muslims' 'fanaticism.'"[45] After intermittent attempts to cease issuing passports in the 1880s and 1890s—efforts that were largely unsuccessful, since pilgrims could easily bypass these restrictions by taking routes through porous borders, such as the southern route through India[46]—the empire sought to create an official, state-sanctioned route that would facilitate surveillance and control of pilgrims, while also directing income into imperial coffers.

Despite efforts to streamline the journey and the protection of subjects abroad by Nikol'skii and his colleagues, the Russian government's relationships with Central Asian Muslims remained fraught. As in the Ottoman Empire, religious tolerance was a prerequisite for ruling diverse, multiethnic and multiconfessional populations. But tolerance did not correspond to equal treatment of people of different faiths.[47] For example, while the tsar officially sponsored Christian Orthodox pilgrimages to the Holy Land in Palestine, the same was not true for the Muslim pilgrimage to Mecca. The empire was an Orthodox Christian polity, and despite policies of accommodating and "ignoring" Islam (*ignorirovanie*), Muslim subjects complained of hostility toward them and their faith. The frequent bans in the 1880s and 1890s, for example, generated discontent at the local level and were likely remembered well into the early 1900s as part of the expansion of colonial rule. The leader of an important 1898 anticolonial uprising in the Ferghana Valley, for example, stridently complained about repeated attempts to prohibit hajj pilgrimage and cited this as one of the reasons why the Russians needed to be driven out of the lands that previously constituted the Khoqand Khanate.[48] The failed uprising had stoked concerns that provincial authorities had been naive and dismissive about the threat of pan-Islamism. In the aftermath of the revolt, the local population saw its village burned and the leaders of the uprising publicly hanged, and Muslims faced a renewed level of scrutiny of religious practices in the Ferghana Valley into the early twentieth century.[49]

Muslims in the governor-generalship of Turkestan could feel the tensions of empire in various ways—not only during their travels through Russian imperial space but also in the regimes of power that shaped daily life.[50] One organ of the state that reflected the local government's attitudes was the semiofficial colonial newspaper of Russian Turkestan, *Turkiston Viloyatining Gazeti* (*TVG*). The paper was first established as a weekly supplement to the *Turkestanskie Vedomosti* in 1870 by the influential governor-general of Russian Turkestan,[51] K. P. Kaufman, who envisioned it as a vehicle of tsarist administration that would "inform the populace of all manner of decrees issued by the governor-general."[52] Nikolai Petrovich Ostroumov, a Russian Orthodox missionary and Orientalist, became its editor in 1883. Although Ostroumov's formal missionary activity was circumscribed by tsarist policies that prohibited proselytizing in Russian Turkestan, he served as an inspector of schools and in various capacities as the director of a teacher's college and a Russian school for boys after arriving in Tashkent in 1877. Ostroumov was considered a resident expert on the local population and was an influential figure who advised tsarist administrators, including Kaufman and later governors-general. Under his tenure, the paper evolved from a weekly designed to publicize imperial decrees (in Russian and Turki) to a paper that eventually included the work of local poets and writers, entertaining installments of well-known stories such as *The Thousand and One Nights*, and useful information on agriculture and the economy. It became an instrument of the Russian civilizing mission and the "policy of cautious enlightenment," as well as a space where "enlighten[ed] orientals" could debate the issues of the day—so long as "their interests coincided with those of the autocracy."[53]

Just a few years prior to Mirim Khan's journey, the gazette began to publish a series of articles that depicted all of Arabia as Turkestan's unwelcoming, inhospitable other. As late as 1897, almost every issue of *TVG* published official decrees, issued by the Ministry of the Interior, that prohibited all Muslims—Sunni and Shi'i—from visiting Mecca and Medina and holy sites in India. The prohibitions were not limited to Russian Turkestan: in February, the paper noted, "Their Royal Excellencies the Khans of Bukhara [*sic*] and Khiva" had also stopped issuing passports for travel to Mecca.[54] Although the ban had gone into effect on 24 January 1897, announcements continued throughout the year. The paper ran numerous articles on epidemics in India and the Hijaz. For example, the first issue of 1897 featured "a story on an epidemic in India," followed in February by news on the appearance of a plague (*toun*) in India, referred to as "Chuma kasali." The article stated that the government had banned travel "so that the aforementioned epidemic does not spread to and appear in Russia." It was followed by short pieces on various diseases and then a letter of advice or admonition (*nasihatnoma*) about personal hygiene, which was clearly related to public health concerns.[55]

Authorities were certainly aware that with limited men on the ground and porous borders, imperial bans were an ineffective means of preventing pilgrimage. In this context, the series might be understood as a novel way of dissuading travel to Mecca. In early March of 1897, a local *alim* (Muslim scholar) by the name of Sayyid Muhammad Amin Khudayor Marhumoghli wrote a long letter in defense of the bans, which he said were passed by the merciful and compassionate "padishah-emperor" to protect the people of Turkestan from diseases ravaging foreign (*ajnabi*) lands. As M. Christopher Low details, on "at least twenty-two, but possibly as many as forty, occasions between 1831 and 1914 cholera spread from India to the Hijaz and was then dispersed far and wide by returning pilgrims." In particular, a global pandemic between 1881 and 1895–96 killed tens of thousands of people during each outbreak and inflicted as many as thirty to fifty thousand casualties in the hajj of 1893.⁵⁶ But rather than focus on the toll of these cholera outbreaks—which would have driven home the point of the severity of the pandemic—Marhumoghli put forth arguments that drew on the Quran, recorded traditions of the customs of the Prophet (*hadith*), and nonbinding legal opinions (*fatwa*). He argued that it was permissible to delay the hajj under present conditions (without explicating their actual severity) and warned that those who chose to ignore the law risked being stranded abroad, far from their homes, wives, and children, and praying for assistance from the tsar.

Sandwiched between these announcements and warnings was a series that ran from March through August of 1897. The first installment coincided with the beginning of pilgrimage season in Shawwal, when thousands of pilgrims would be preparing to board the new train line that had reached Tashkent that year. Almost two and a half pages in length (in a paper totaling, on average, eight pages), the first story ran with the title "Description of the Pilgrimage to Mecca-Jeddah: One Hajji's Account of Going to Mecca the Honored to Perform the Hajj" (*Opisanie palomnichestvo v Mekku-Dzheddah: Makka-i mukarrama'ga hajj qilmoq uchun bormoq xususida bir hajjining bayon qilgan so'zidur*). Although the title began in Russian, the account was written in a Turkic language—signaling to Russian settlers that the story was only of interest to Muslim readership. But this was an odd and sterile Turki, peppered with Russian words for common things like candy and soldiers. Along with frequent admonitions to readers to learn Russian and to return quickly after completing the hajj, the prose suggested that the author was not a native speaker and likely a colonial official. Here was a completely different kind of hajj account that readers familiar with the Islamo-Persian texts and discursive traditions would find jarring. In the first story, for example, we find the following description of Jeddah:

> Due to the presence of large numbers of subjects and merchants and all sorts of travelers from surrounding areas, the city's customs, traditions, and people are not of a high level. In the aforementioned city there is boy and child prostitution (*javon va bachchabozliq*), and it is not very clear if the people of Turkestan have taken this wicked custom from Arabia, or if the people of

Arabia imitate the customs of Turkestan in this matter. And, in the environs of the city there are all sorts of places where wicked people congregate, and which government officials and the lawful do not attend to.[57]

This followed a description of Jeddah's barren terrain, the ominous numbers of wealthy merchants and Turkish soldiers, and unusual local customs such as eating locusts. The story's goal of forging an association between Arabia and pederasty, a practice that both tsarist officials and Muslim reformers from the Jadidist movement associated with "backwardness," broke with genre conventions. As it moved to Mecca, titillating allusions to illicit behavior gave way to dry description and preoccupations with cost, order, and disease. The author described how people were forced to patronize expensive coffeehouses and eateries, intimating that only the wealthy could perform the hajj in peace, while poor pilgrims were left to sleep in the streets and subsist on tiny pieces of bread, at best, and die amid wretched conditions, at worst.[58] While the series described many harsh realities, it stripped the landscape of Quranic revelation of any spiritual power. In a genre that typically included practical advice and spiritual guidance, only one installment mentioned the meaning and rituals of hajj. In the same story, the author cast aspersion on these, too, and warned readers to avoid practices proscribed by the shari'a and to not get carried away with the symbolic stoning of Satan at Muzdalifa. Even Arafat—the plain where the Prophet delivered his farewell sermon, and where pilgrims spent the night supplicating for forgiveness of their sins—was portrayed as a site of death and of rushed burial.[59] The focus on death was continuous. In a section on the city of the Prophet, the author explained that "among those who travel to Medina, many pass away. There are many reasons, such as those who die from hardship in the desert. Others die from epidemics and disease along the way, while most die at the hands of bandits and thieves."[60]

By associating Arabia exclusively with danger, the newspaper serial sought to counter the rise of an imagined community of Muslims that transcended Russian imperial space—the very type of community that Mirim Khan and other writers of hajj accounts were trying to forge. The world was divided into binaries of rich and poor; familiar (*bizning Turkiston viloyati*) and foreign (the Hijaz, Arabs, Turks); and the lush and civilized (Russian Turkestan) and the barren and uncivilized (Arabia). Nothing could compare to Turkestan: not the mountains, which weren't as majestic, nor the sheep, which weren't as large and fat.[61] Arabia was unwelcoming, fundamentally foreign, and prohibitively expensive. The emphasis on cost would be of paramount concern for pilgrims on a modest budget—in effect, the majority of aspirants from Turkestan. By focusing disproportionately on hardship, the series presented a vision of Arabia that evinced an abiding hostility toward pilgrimage and the central Islamic lands. This broader political context and climate makes the *Hajjnoma-i Turki* all the more important as a source for understanding the work that Mirim Khan was doing in his manuscript.

Mirim Khan would probably have agreed with the author of the *TVG* series on a number of counts: Arabia was indeed expensive and disorderly, Bedouin tribes could be terrifying, and locusts were likely disgusting. He might have even agreed that the sheep were not nearly as fat or tasty as in Turkestan—though in all likelihood, he would have expressed this in an amusing anecdote, which cast him as the clever traveler who could discern the good from the bad. The difference between the accounts was related to their broader aims: discouraging versus encouraging hajj, emphasizing versus contextualizing hardship. There was also a difference in how the authors visualized their readers: whereas Mirim Khan understood and tried to allay some of their fears, the author of the *TVG* series chose to focus on the difficult conditions in the Hijaz rather than to elaborate on the threat of disease and to advise people to delay their travel. In Mirim Khan's lifetime, and certainly by the time he had completed his pilgrimage and begun writing about it, Russia's official stance on the hajj had changed. By 1910—when the Russian Ministry of Transportation introduced direct rail service between Tashkent and Odessa for Muslims and regular steamship service from Odessa to Jeddah—the dire warnings about disease and death in the pages of the *TVG* gave way to advertisements for train schedules and state-subsidized steamers.[62] But after decades of pilgrimage travel being a contested practice that was viewed with suspicion, people were unlikely to confuse imperial pragmatism for enthusiasm or acceptance—particularly those who felt ridiculed and oppressed by rulers they understood as "infidels."

In the context of colonial rule, Mirim Khan's work, while outside the canon of great mystical poets and authors, should be read as part of a Sufi tradition that promoted mobility on the path to enlightenment. The voyage from Turkestan to Mecca was not simply a journey through physical space but a metaphysical one—a path (*tariqa*) toward the realization of Truth (*haqiqa*). As the journey changed, hardship remained par for the course. Even if it were true that "the pilgrim's path to salvation was in some years a path to a statistically probable death,"[63] this was not in and of itself a new development. Pilgrims were supposed to set their affairs in order before leaving for the journey because of the likelihood that they would not return. The major difference in the steamship era was one of scale: with the rise of mass pilgrimage, more people were subject to the risk of death, destitution, and disease than ever before. And they were not dervishes, resigned to suffering and sacrifice. To address the fears of "ordinary" people, Mirim Khan insisted that the challenges ahead were surmountable and redemptive.

The difficulties of his travels were perhaps nowhere more apparent than when the caravan was attacked during the last leg of his journey from Jeddah to Mecca. Although there were Ottoman soldiers guarding the convoy, the twenty or so troops were not sufficient to protect the group of eight hundred pilgrims. As he set the scene, Mirim Khan said it was a few hours before sundown when Bedouin suddenly surrounded them on all sides "like hunters preying on partridges." Arrows poured forth like rain during an attack that lasted for nearly two hours. As on the steamer from Sevastopol to Istanbul, Mirim Khan invoked the sense that the end of days had arrived: pilgrims huddled and said their goodbyes, readying themselves for certain death. The scene was one of utter devastation:

> Some lost two hundred *so'm* [currency]
> Some lost most of their belongings and money
> Some lost four hundred, some eight [*so'm*]
> Left with nothing but their *ihram*,
> Some women fell to the Bedouin . . .
> Others were laid bare
> Left there in thirst and hunger
> Some were struck by arrows and wounded
> Crying and wailing to God.[64]

Mirim Khan had survived—but only after metaphorically dying from fear. Then, suddenly, he cut from this scene of devastation to one of resurrection, where he was freed from his sorrows and worries and united with God. It was here that he referenced becoming possessed or mad with love, like the protagonist in Nezami's twelfth-century version of the popular story of *Leyli and Majnun*.[65] Qays, a man said to be based on a semihistorical figure by the same name, falls in love with the beautiful Leyli and becomes possessed by his affections. When he is prevented from marrying her, Qays renounces society and runs off to the desert, where he devotes himself to contemplating Leyli and composing love songs for her. Ultimately, their unrequited love kills them both, and the lovers are only united in death, when their adjacent graves become a pilgrimage site. In its various iterations across South, Central, and Western Asia, the story showed how love and asceticism overlapped and touched on the transience of life. Those with a mystical bent could read Majnun's withdrawal from society and his devotion to Leyli as the Sufi's attempt to triumph over the ego and obtain union with God. The invocation of the term *majnun*, at the moment when Mirim Khan and his travel companions met with near death, signaled to readers steeped in this cosmology the inimitable power of seeing Mecca.

The author was himself emblematic of the transformative power of the hajj. The rituals at Mecca had not only leveled the differences among the pilgrims but also had reformed Mirim Khan's polluted soul and cleansed his blackened countenance. In several sections of the hajjnoma—many of which were abridged in the lithograph version of the manuscript I consulted—Mirim Khan described the boisterous Kyrgyz, Qipchaq, and Kashgari pilgrims as stupid and shameless people with low morals.[66] Aboard a steamer to Suez, for example, he described his travel companions:

> The inside of the ship looked like the Last Judgment
> More than everyone, the Kashgaris were disorderly
> Giving themselves and one another a bad name
> They often get a thrashing
> They have no shame, these "divorced women"
> They don't understand you when you speak and distribute pearls of wisdom
> Staring at you blankly, eyes wide open, mouth agape
> Like this, your words are an affliction
> Above all, in their midst are savages
> There are among them beasts and animals.[67]

These "rabble," he said, were also completely ignorant of Islam:

> The terms, obligatory acts, the duties of the *sunna*
> He doesn't know, the fundamentals of the *sunna*
> He's not cognizant of his own state
> He doesn't know himself, or recognize God (*tangri*)
> He knows neither scholar nor man of religion,
> How can this person know how to be a Muslim (*qul*)?[68]

But Mecca's holy power changed everything—not just the rabble but also the author who looked on his coreligionists in this way. His harsh words ceased, and a renewed Mirim Khan repeatedly described the sense of parity and community that emerged:

> In their hearts, their goals were all equal
> Kings and beggars were all equal
> In this place a wealthy man cannot find contentedness
> Praying, you cannot look down on others
> No king or beggar is left out of the circumambulation (*tawaf*)
> Everyone is contented with their lot.[69]

While many contemporary hajj accounts tirelessly documented the cost of every stamp, ticket, and expenditure, Mirim Khan told his audience that as long as they had four hundred rubles, they would be fine. As they circumambulated the Kaaba, rich and poor were equal. He was cognizant of the beggars that were part of the landscape, but he never suggested that his readers were in danger of becoming destitute themselves. Instead, he argued for how they would be enriched by the experience and freed of their reliance on material possessions.

He drove these points home in a forceful section that wove together the themes of suffering, purification, and asceticism:

> After saying your farewells and leaving your cities
> Don't allow other attachments into your hearts, oh friends
> Many days passed searching for sustenance
> Many evenings were soiled by your cries about (monetary) fortune
> Without valuing their prosperity, you allowed the nights to be tarnished
> Have a strong will and don't depend on your material possessions, oh friends

> Don't sleep and dream, saying it's a long road
> Dreams and sleep will prevent you from your path
> Go ahead and break off your chains
> Don't worry about how it will be done, oh friends
> If you reach the Kaaba and whiten your blackened face
> If you brush your lips and face against the black stone
> If you pray at the gate of the Kaaba
> You will be accepted, don't let your desires remain unfulfilled, oh friends
> The *Bob-ı Atiq*, the door of God's Kaaba,
> If you become aware and pray, will accept your prayers.

And, once again, he exhorted people not to make excuses:

> Oh, you of blackened face, go there!
> Without making this and that excuse, and remaining in disgrace, my friends
> If you make seven circumambulations
> You will reach annihilation (*fana'*)
> Crying and whimpering, losing yourself
> Your bones and skin, allowing only your soul and body to remain.[70]

Mirim Khan devoted the remaining sections of his account to describing the rituals and rewards of pilgrimage and the journey home. He drew on powerful images and language to convince his audience that what they had to gain far outweighed the dangers they would face. The readers he addressed were not fanatics who could not be prevented from traveling to Mecca. They were, like him, sinners, making this and that excuse. Mirim Khan acknowledged their doubts, and then stridently urged them to rise above their fears. "There is no hajj without hardship," he told his readers, again, and again, and again.[71]

In his work on Asian mobility, David Ludden observes that "spaces that elude national maps have mostly disappeared from our intellectual life," due in part to practices that make certain spaces invisible and "expunge dissonance from our geographical imagination by invisibly burying disorderly spaces under neat graphics of national order."[72] But efforts to recreate this lost world can unwittingly lead to new elisions and effacements, presenting vast terrains without a sense of how certain cities became more than just points in a series of points on a map. As Engseng Ho reminds us, a "city could serve as a node in different circuits, being central in one but peripheral in another."[73] In the context of the transimperial routes pilgrims traversed, places like Sevastopol and Istanbul—two cities that became major hajj hubs in the nineteenth century—were vastly different depending on who you were and where you came from. Mirim Khan's text helps us to see this, via a strong and very subjective voice. Despite being a Russian national and legal subject, he felt that he was a foreigner in most of Russia but described feeling at home and among equals in Ottoman Mecca. As he ticked off the names of the cities along the way, some were simply places where he had to change or wait for trains and steamers; others were destinations. By charting his experiences, we see that cities along his route were not commensurable in any real sense and that the distances separating them from Mecca were mediated through textual strategies and mystical ideals.

Among the strategies Mirim Khan employed, his elisions and silences stand out. This was palpable when it came to Ottoman officials or governance; the soldiers accompanying the caravan on the last leg of the overland journey, for example, had failed to protect the pilgrims. Yet they escaped Mirim Khan's sharp tongue and censure—unlike the Russian officials who, in the worlds of an old Tatar who translated for them, did not recognize that they were "hajjis heading to sacred territory." This may have been because the Ottoman soldiers were not adversarial or, more likely, because the author was invested in depicting the Ottomans in a positive light. To encourage others to see what he saw, hear what he heard, feel what he felt, Mirim Khan intentionally downplayed and contextualized the negative dimensions of Arabia and the Ottoman Empire that the *TVG* series emphasized. By treating Istanbul as an extension of sacred space, he reminds us that pilgrims' views of the Ottoman Empire—its ruler and the state's perceived wealth and power—were shaped by hajj and subsequently *remembered* as part of a larger religious journey. His depictions of Istanbul and his idealization of Mecca are classic examples of how the experience of hajj led pilgrims to reinterpret their experiences.[74] Moments of dissonance in Islamic lands were expunged from a narrative forged *after* reaching the pilgrimage destination or were contextualized as an integral part of the metaphysical journey. Recognizing the significance of this sociological and religious phenomenon is central to understanding the nature of connections between Central Asian pilgrims and Ottomans.

The geography of pilgrimage was certainly altered by technology, but it was pilgrims who imbued it with meaning. Thus, while texts shed light on how people responded to the reconfiguration of routes and the changing geography of sacred space, they tell only a partial story. Mirim Khan's hajjnoma, for example, tells us very little about the boisterous Kashgaris he complained of or about those whose paths diverged from his. He describes wonders and hardships in great detail, but he does not talk about how one might go about writing a petition after being robbed or attacked by Bedouin or how travelers would find long-term lodging and support in Istanbul. In the next chapter, I turn to a closer examination of people who might have been his travel companions. Drawing on the records of a central "Uzbek" lodge, I explore how state-supported tekkes facilitated the development of Central Asian networks in the empire. That said, we leave our narrator and meet a range of pilgrims whose peregrinations come alive in the lines of tekke registers, and we shift our focus from the pages of this text to the hills of the Bosphorus and a major site of Ottoman-Central Asian interaction.

(CHAPTER 2)

SUFI LODGES AS SITES OF TRANSIMPERIAL CONNECTION

IN THE FALL OF 1905, an eight-year-old named Bekir arrived in Istanbul, about midway through a trip that would take him farther than most boys his age would travel in a lifetime. He and his father, a forty-eight-year-old hajji named Azım Han, had set out from Kashgar and crossed the dizzying mountain passes that separated his native city in East, or Chinese, Turkestan from Russian Turkestan, before reaching the terminus—or beginning, depending on how you looked at it—of the Trans-Caspian Railway. While Bekir may have been initially excited about the "fire ships" and "fire wagons" people talked about, he would never see much fire—only dark, ugly coal. As they traveled on these vessels, he would likely have experienced the seasickness and overcrowding that pilgrims frequently complained of and grown weary of being among so many people in such cramped quarters. The journey was no doubt doubly challenging for a young child, who would want to do all the things that eight-year-olds normally do and would have trouble interpreting things that make even less sense to children than they do adults. He might wonder, for example, why they had to repeatedly pay to have people stamp pieces of paper called passports. He would observe how colonial officials mistreated pilgrims and experience firsthand the strangeness of being disinfected at sanitation stations and of being placed in quarantine.[1] During the long trip, he was bound to have heard stories about people being cheated and robbed, and he would spend much time guarding his and his father's bags and being told by his father to stay close by. He was probably relieved when they arrived in Istanbul and found lodging at the Sultantepe Özbekler Tekkesi, one of the Sufi lodges that served people from Central Asia. In yet another foreign city in a foreign country, it would be home for the next couple of weeks.

When they arrived in Üsküdar, it was early November and father and son joined recent arrivals who had been coming in small groups over the course of the past few weeks. Mehmed Salih Efendi, the *postnişin* (head of a religious order), entered their names into the register of guests and added them to a running list of people whose passage he was trying to secure on the imperial caravan ships leaving for Jeddah. After tucking away a copy in one of his registers, he had sent the petition to contacts in the government and turned to dealing with other pressing problems. As part of the lodge's broader mission—later described by his brother Şeyh Edhem Efendi as "the provision of repose to dervishes and the poor" and "refuge and shelter to those among the poor people from Mavaraünnehir [Transoxiana]"—Mehmed Salih performed a number of duties that extended beyond what we might imagine as those of a Sufi shaykh. One of them was to arrange for ill pilgrims to receive medical treatment.[2] Among the recent arrivals, there was a sick teenager named Ahmet, whom he sent to a hospital for the Muslim poor called Gureba-yı Müslimin, where he would be treated for an undisclosed illness.[3]

Within days, news would arrive that the pilgrims' travel documents (*mürur tezkeresi*) and tickets were being prepared and that they could soon depart.[4] All of the men (and children) would make it in time for that year's hajj—including Ahmed, who had been released from the hospital in time to join them. While he waited for their departure, Bekir would spend his days in and around the courtyard, looking for ways to pass the time. The tekke rooms were musty and dank, and there was nothing to do indoors. The boy may have tried to help the resident servant, Hacı Mehmed, with various tasks or sit in the shaykh's receiving room and watch as he greeted guests and managed the ledgers. During the days, most of the men went out to look for work, to earn money for unexpected expenses they were quickly learning to anticipate. Some of them sold goods they had brought from home or worked odd jobs here and there as day laborers. Those who planned to stay in Istanbul longer sought employment in ateliers and workshops in Üsküdar and the old city, sometimes moving from Sultantepe to the Bukharan lodge in Sultanahmet to be closer to job prospects. When they returned in the evenings, the men gathered in the courtyard and shared stories about their days and discussed strategies for completing a successful hajj. In lilting Chaghatay they would greet each other with long lists of questions—a custom particular to Central Asians and that likely threw off Ottoman Turks. "How are you? Are you well? How is your father, son, family? Is everything in order? How was work? Did you manage not to get too tired?" they would ask. Placing their hands over their hearts, their interlocutors would answer, "Good, good, thanks to God, everything is in order," and then repeat the ritual.

On Thursdays, people gathered for the weekly remembrance of God (*dhikr*), and were often joined by others from the neighborhood and nearby tekkes. Sultantepe was a Naqshbandi brotherhood, but the dhikr incorporated rituals from other orders. Bekir would be too young to understand most of the ceremonies, which included the reading of poems by the twelfth-century mystic Ahmed Yesevi.[5] But as a boy far from home, he likely looked forward to the big cauldrons of *aş*, the carrot and mutton rice dish prepared by the resident cook for communal gatherings and that reminded Bekir of Kashgar.

Bekir bin Azım had become a hajji when he was only eight years old (unless he turned nine before reaching Mecca), crossing lands ruled by four different empires—Qing China, Russian Central Asia, Ottoman Istanbul to the Hijaz, and British-occupied Egypt. If he returned to Kashgar and lived to reach the age his father was when they set out, he would no longer be able to travel the same roads to Arabia. As empires were replaced by nation-states, borders increasingly lost their porosity and the types of transregional travel that shaped his early life—and centuries of Central Asian history—began to draw to a close. His own children would likely only know places like Bukhara, Krasnovodosk, Odessa, Istanbul, Alexandria, Mecca, and Medina from their father's stories or old texts. Undoubtedly, their father had many stories to tell. But as far as we know, he never recorded them. The only glimpses we have of his hajj are the days he spent in Istanbul in the autumn of 1905, when Mehmed Salih Efendi entered his name into a guest register he kept for the central government. We know from these sources how long Bekir was there, what kinds of people he interacted with, and how an

Ottoman tekke catering to Central Asians gave him and his father shelter and helped them reach their destination.⁶

These registers form the basis for this chapter's exploration of the Sultantepe Özbekler Tekkesi and its role in connecting Central Asians to the Ottoman Empire. If Mirim Khan's text illuminated how individual authors could give meaning to the changing journey to Mecca and reflected concerns among people from Russian Turkestan, the study of Sultantepe brings into sharper relief how the challenges of the steamship-era hajj were mitigated by Sufi lodges and the interimperial communities to which they gave shape. Drawing on the tekke's own records, this chapter employs a microhistorical approach and introduces us to a range of people who stayed there—from eight-year-old Bekir to the tekke shaykhs who ran the lodge, ensured that pilgrims got the assistance they needed, and maintained records on foreign nationals for the central government. Through an eclectic approach that includes my own introduction to the tekke, I argue that Sultantepe was a microcosm of relations between Central Asians and Ottomans. I flesh out the contours of a pilgrimage network—something often mentioned in studies of hajj but seldom presented in any detail—and show how it contributed to the formation of enduring diasporic communities in Istanbul and other Ottoman cities. Sultantepe, I argue, was not only a lodge for pilgrims in transit but also a space where people classified as foreign Muslims could forge the kinds of connections that allowed them to become locals and, sometimes, Ottomans. But before we begin to examine the flows and interactions at work, we first need to peel back some of the nationalist interpretations of Sultantepe's long history.

Locating Sultantepe in Memory and History

The first time I sat in the courtyard at Sultantepe, I was looking for information about pilgrims, not tekkes. What led me to the lodge was the work of Grace Martin Smith, a historian who had joined a circle of mystics, poets, and musicians who gathered there regularly throughout the late 1970s. In an article on Istanbul's "Uzbek" lodges, Smith described a private archive containing guest registers with detailed information about hajjis who were en route to and from Mecca.⁷ While there was no shortage of documents related to Central Asians in the Ottoman archives, or still unread hajj accounts in Uzbekistan's manuscript collections, sources with detailed information on groups of ordinary people were difficult to come by. When I finally resolved to visit and inquire about the sources Smith described, I realized en route that I had no concrete plan. My more challenging research attempts had relied on a combination of tenacity and what people in my native New York might call chutzpah—not always a formula for success in Turkey. When I got there, Ethem Bey—the son of the late shaykh Necmeddin Özbekkangay (d. 1971)—saw me standing outside and invited me in. He told stories about Sultantepe's role in the Turkish War of Independence, with which I was familiar, but was caught off guard by my interest in the tekke, the records of the people it hosted, and its role in nineteenth-century pilgrimage networks. This was my introduction to the fraught position of Sultantepe in Turkish history and of the forgotten history of Istanbul's connections to the hajj. It was almost as if the lodge had existed to fulfill a destiny of helping found the Turkish nation rather than its institutional mandate to provide lodging and support to Central Asian pilgrims.

As Ethem Bey gave me a tour of the space—including the room where the registers were still kept—I had my second introduction to the tekke. Archivists and librarians had always mediated my access to documents and manuscripts, and the sources for my research were far removed from the people and places I studied. I was suddenly cognizant of being in the space that served as one of the first sites of sustained encounter between Central Asians and Ottomans and that had shaped the trajectories of generations of people in motion. This insight made me look at the courtyard in a different way and to imagine what it would be like to sit there in the shade of the magnolia after a long day of looking for work and the relief it would provide—not only to new arrivals who had been traveling for weeks aboard crowded trains and ships but also to the tekke guests, who retired each night to crowded rooms and tents. I began to visualize how the space shaped and rooted people in Istanbul in ways that government documents alone could not account for.

That afternoon, Ethem Bey allowed me to examine two of the registers. The pages listed the names, ages, places of origin, dates of arrival and departure, and other details of guests' journeys (fig. 6). To obtain access to the sources in their entirety, however, I had to mobilize various personal and professional connections. It seemed that I was something of a liminal actor—the foreign Muslim who had to negotiate her insider-outsider status and who

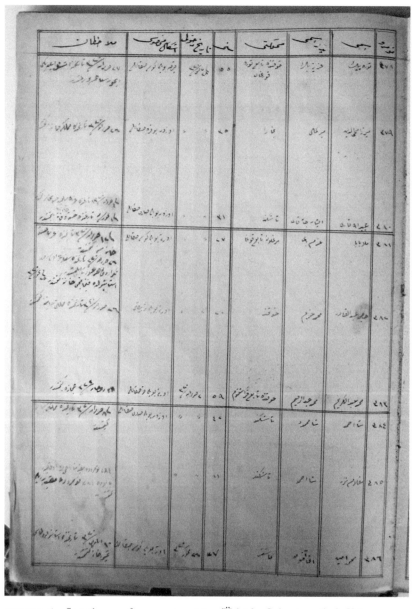

FIGURE 6. Sample page from guest register. (Üsküdar Sultantepesi'nde Kain Özbekler Dergahı'nın Nüfus ve Kayıt Defteri, fi 1 Zilkade 1316/fi 1 Mart 1315.) Photograph by author.

needed a guarantor (*kefil*) to vouch for her. During months of waiting and uncertainty over access, colleagues often asked why the registers were so important. As I pored over photographs I had taken during my visit, and others that Grace Martin Smith shared with me—four-by-six-inch black-and-white Kodak prints that I struggled to read with a magnifying glass—the answer seemed so simple: they were all about pilgrimage networks. Each entry provided a glimpse into worlds that the magnolia had survived, of times when Bukharans, Andijanis, Kashgaris, and Afghans traveled to Istanbul to see the sultan-caliph before performing the hajj. Each page was a window into the elusive circulations, interactions, and relationships that constituted and animated transregional pilgrimage networks in the last decades of Ottoman history.[8]

Sultantepe was one of several Central Asian lodges in Greater Istanbul, which included the walled city of Istanbul (Dersaadet) on the Golden Horn and the "three cities," or boroughs, of Eyüp, Galata, and Üsküdar (map 4). It was not quite a Central Asian outpost or consulate, or a "bridge between the fatherland and motherland," but one of many institutions that catered to the needs of specific groups of people traveling from abroad and that included lodges serving Tatars, Daghestanis, Indians, and Afghans. It was part of a broad network, with two other major lodges in Eyüp and Dersaadet, all of which were connected through circulations of people to tekkes in other cities, including Mecca and Medina. In Eyüp, there were two Kashgari lodges near the shrine that Mirim Khan visited. The first is commonly referred to as the Kaşgari Tekkesi and was built by Şeyh Yekçeşm el-Hac Mürteza Efendi (d. 1747) in 1745–46. It took its name, however, from Şeyh Abdullah Nidai Kaşgari (d. 1760), a Kashgari-born Sufi who traveled across Central Asia, Iraq, Greater Syria and the Hijaz before settling in Eyüp. Like Sultantepe, the Kaşgari Tekkesi was affiliated with the Mujaddidiyya branch of the Naqshbandiyya, although Abdullah Nidai Efendi is said to have been an adept of the Kasani branch of the order. Through the early twentieth century, the lodge anchored a community of Central Asians in Eyüp and hosted long-term (male and female) residents of the city.[9] A second nearby lodge, the Kalenderhane Tekkesi, was for men only and specified that all of its guests—as well as the shaykh—be unmarried. It was built in 1743 by a Sufi named La'lizade Abdülbaki Efendi (d. 1746), who was a notable member of

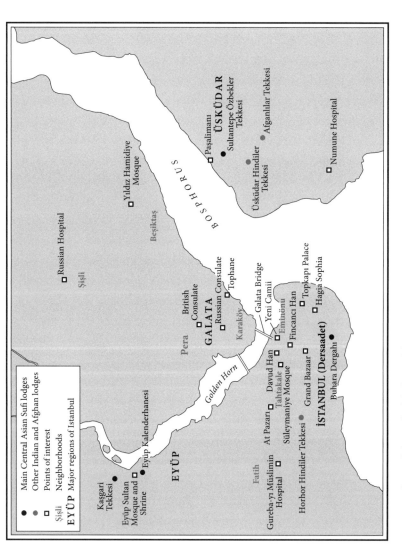

MAP 4. Central Asian Sufi lodges of Greater Istanbul, early twentieth century.

the Ottoman ulema and said to be affiliated with the Naqshbandi, Melami, and Kalenderi orders.[10] According to a report prepared by the Ministry of the Interior in 1885, the Kalenderhane Tekkesi had the highest number of dervishes in residence in Istanbul, a total of twenty-one, which was somewhat exceptional. The report suggests that it did not serve the same kinds of functions as a pilgrimage guesthouse and was primarily for ascetics.[11]

The other major lodge that rivaled Sultantepe in fame was the Buhara Dergahı on the Mehmet Paşa Hill in Sultanahmet. It was built in 1692 and was centrally located, just a stone's throw from the Hagia Sophia and within walking distance of the workshops and businesses around the Grand Bazaar and the Tahtakale neighborhood, where many Central Asian pilgrims and migrants found work. Ottoman sources describe it as "Uzbek Naqshbandi lodge" that served the people of Balkh, Bukhara, and Khoqand and similar places.[12] Under the long tenure of Buharalı Şeyh Süleyman Efendi (d. 1890), a confidante of Sultan Abdülhamid II, the lodge hosted many Central Asian dignitaries. These included the Bukharan envoy Muhammad Parsa Efendi, who was sent by the emir of Bukhara in 1867, and later Yaqub Khan (first in his capacity as an ambassador from the Khanate of Khoqand and later the Islamic Emirate of Kashgar). Süleyman Efendi exemplified a Bukharan in the upper echelons of society, who had become an Ottoman—likely without having to formally naturalize. He was a member of the Circassian Refugee Council (Meclis-i Muhacirin-i Çerakise) and the Assembly of Shaykhs (Meclis-i Meşayih) and served as an Ottoman envoy to Bukhara in 1869 and to Hungary in 1877. It is alleged that in his service to the sultan, he acted as an Ottoman double agent, providing false information to the British ambassador in Istanbul that exaggerated the sultan's pan-Islamic power and activities in India, Central Asia, and the Hijaz.[13] The shaykh presided over one of the fixtures in Greater Istanbul's growing diasporic networks and likely marshaled his connections in the service of his countrymen. The dergah was repaired twice during the Hamidian period, first by the sultan and later by a Bukharan notable named Astankul Bey. Astankul Bey's gift was used to build a mosque and room for devotional ceremonies (*tevhidhane*), which, during the height of the pilgrimage season, would provide much-needed space for additional pilgrims to unfurl a mat and pass the night.[14]

Part hostel, part urban caravanserai, and part Sufi brotherhood, the Buhara Dergahı was Ottoman in the sense that after 1826 it was administered by the

Ministry of Pious Endowments and derived its income from a combination of government subsidies and income from Islamic endowments (*waqf*). This was true of all four of the lodges, Sultantepe included. Although commonly referred to as an "Uzbek" lodge, Sultantepe was established in the early modern period, long before such national identities had taken on the meanings of the twentieth century. It served people who would later identify as Uzbek, Afghan, Kyrgyz, Uyghur, and Tajik. But in the continual processes of reinventing and rewriting Ottoman history, its purposes and origins have been shrouded in legend and folded into narratives of exceptionalism. According to a frequently cited story, for example, the tekke is said to have been built by an Ottoman sultan who was passing through Üsküdar when he saw an encampment filled with unfamiliar embroidered silk and hair tents. After riding over to inquire about the travelers' origins, the sultan learned that they had come all the way from Turkestan to see the caliph and to seek his blessing before performing the hajj. In turn, the sultan is said to have promised their leader, a Naqshbandi shaykh, that he would build a tekke for future pilgrims.[15] It appears, though, that the lodge was built not by a sultan but by a certain Abdullah Pasha, an Ottoman bureaucrat and statesman who was then the governor (*vali*) of Maraş. Over the centuries, it was renovated several times—like numerous Ottoman lodges—with direct governmental support. In 1844, it was reconstructed by Sultan Abdülmecid (r. 1839–61) and later expanded during the 1877–78 Russo-Ottoman War. At this time, a wooden structure was added to the courtyard to house the influx of Muslim refugees from the Caucasus. In the later part of the century, Abdülhamid II paid for repairs, which were acknowledged by a plaque adorning the main entrance—reminding pilgrims of the sultan's benevolence and that this was an Ottoman institution.[16]

In 1915, a report to the central government described the tekke as a "philanthropic foundation or charitable institution [*müessese-i hayriye*] open every day for the housing and maintenance of the poor and destitute of the khanates of Khiva and Bukhara and the people of Russian and Chinese Turkestan, who set out on the hajj and came to perform a pilgrimage to the seat of the caliphate and the center of the illustrious sultanate."[17] Unlike other Sufi lodges whose endowment deeds sometimes stipulated that guests could stay for only three nights, the dergah opened its doors to long-term guests, as long as they met the eligibility criteria for charitable assistance.[18] In the steamship era, the lodge served hundreds of people each year and was a major site of sustained encounter between foreign Muslims and institutional representatives of the state. In addition to providing travelers with room, board, logistical support, and community, Sultantepe (and presumably the Buhara Dergahı) helped the government monitor and regulate the mobility of foreign nationals and eased their movement through the city.

Much of the extant literature on these institutions, however, has focused on exceptional moments in their history that suit nationalist interpretations of the Ottoman era and that are often laced with Islamist undertones. In Turkey's reckoning with its Ottoman past, Sultantepe's primary function of serving pilgrims like Bekir and his father was eclipsed by the role it played in smuggling weapons and fighters to the Anatolian front during the national struggle (*kuva-yi milliye*) against the postwar occupation, later termed the Turkish War of Independence (1919–23). In her memoir of "national liberation and nation-building in Turkey," writer and political activist Halide Edip Adıvar (1884–1960) described how Şeyh Atâ Efendi sheltered her and her two small children during the tumultuous days of the Allied occupation of Istanbul.[19] Just up the street from her father's home—the house with wisteria from which her memoir took its name—Sultantepe was used as a base for transferring weapons to Anatolia and providing shelter to people including İsmet İnönü (the second president of the republic) and Mehmet Akif Ersoy (author of the Turkish national anthem) as they made their way to the front. After 1923, Adıvar and other luminaries immortalized the lodge for its service to the young nation, and the Turkish Republic's new historians reimagined its complex history along protonational and pan-Turkist lines.[20]

To resolve the tensions between Sultantepe's role in the national struggle and its history as a Sufi lodge, both Kemalists and Islamic reformists critical of Sufism emphasized the sober nature of religious practice there and its role as a "cultural center." To counter the associations between Sufism and backwardness or ritual excesses suggesting practices that might be seen as polytheistic (*shirk*), or un-Islamic innovations (*bid'a*), many Turks—including surviving family members—focused on how it represented a restrained Turkic form of Islam that was not inimical to progress. In an interview with the Turkish newspaper *Milliyet*, Atâ Efendi's nephew Ethem captured many of these sentiments:

> Before the [First] World War, the traditions of the Naqshbandi brotherhood were carried out here. They prayed, and the *hatm-i hacegan* was recited. They performed *namaz* and cooked Uzbek rice. There was a tradition of silent *dhikr*. Meaning, you sit and say your prayers in your heart. But I don't know much about these matters. We are children of the Turkish Republic. We are supporters of Atatürk.... [Even] before the Republic was founded, the brotherhood's activities here slowed down considerably. After Şeyh İbrahim Ethem Efendi, from whose lineage we are descended... the [international] lawyer and modern figure Atâ Efendi became the shaykh. The national struggle begins here in his time. It takes the shape of the *Kuvayi* [sic] *Milliye*. [Sultantepe] functions as a hospital and postal center. It is where munitions are gathered. For this reason when all the tekkes are shut down in 1925, tolerance is shown [to Sultantepe].... For the real story, consult *Nutuk*.[21]

Nutuk, "The Speech," was Mustafa Kemal's account of the national resistance movement and his rise to power, and it would become the basis for official Turkish historiography. Gesturing to *Nutuk* reaffirmed that Sultantepe was progressive and nationalist. The subtext was that, otherwise, Mustafa Kemal [Atatürk] would have shuttered its doors when he ordered the closure of Turkey's Sufi lodges in 1925. Through this selective remembering of the tekke's past and emphasis on its service to the nation, what had been a modest but important Naqshbandi Sufi lodge was reinvented as a cultural center or informal embassy, although it is never clear if it was an Ottoman one or a Central Asian one. It continues to be the focus of studies and symposia that explicitly celebrate it and Istanbul's other "Turkestani" lodges as sites that connected Turks to their ancient ethnic forebears in Asia.[22] The ahistorical nature of claims about Turkic identity aside, the nationalist and Islamist agenda (often fused) obscures the histories of the people who were building these metaphorical bridges. These were, of course, the Ottoman shaykhs and the Central Asian migrants traveling throughout the late nineteenth and early twentieth centuries, to whom we now turn.

Pilgrimage Networks

Crucial to understanding how Central Asians became integrated into the Ottoman Empire is a firm grasp of the role that networks played in connecting "foreign Muslims" to what was for them a foreign land. Although networks are often invoked in studies of transimperial mobility and pilgrimage, historians seldom elaborate on just how they work: we take for granted their importance, but we know very little about the nature of the webs of connection and circulation, the people who animated them, or how they operated on a day-to-day level. As Arang Keshavarzian writes in the context of bazaar networks in Iran, the problem often lies in the assumption that such seemingly obvious sites of political, economic, and social encounter and exchange do not need to be defined or conceptualized. Despite carrying a range of meanings over time, people assume that they have always existed and that "we all know where and what they [are]."[23]

In the context of Sufism, we might assume that networks based in Naqshbandi lodges (and other *tariqa*) followed the kinds of hierarchical organizational models that contributed to the rise of religious and political movements across diverse Islamic societies—without allowing for the existence of looser modes of belonging to Islamic brotherhoods or the possibilities of parallel and overlapping forms of association among different subsets of actors. A figure like Şeyh Süleyman Efendi, for example, might have broken bread with Ottoman statesmen and the Sultantepe shaykh, and worked with both to meet the needs of recent groups of arrivals or secure the long-term health of the lodge. He might also have written to the shaykhs of other Sufi lodges to make introductions for visitors to take up residence in other cities. At the same time, guests like Azım Han (Bekir's father), who were looking for work or housing, would likely have turned for help to someone like the resident cook. Both the shaykh and the cook would be based in the same Sufi lodge and coordinate on behalf of the people resident there, but they would often be operating at different scales. The shaykh would be no less a Sufi than one who had disciples he guided on the mystical path; the cook, no less a Sufi than a resident dervish who devoted himself purely to spiritual endeavors; and, more important, someone like Azım Han (or his son) would be no less of a member of this network than any of the other people there.

While it is widely argued that the Uzbek (along with Afghan and Indian) lodges played a significant role in the cultural, religious, and political exchanges across Asia and the Ottoman Empire, the details of how they did so are hazy. This is in part due to a focus on Sultantepe and the Buhara Dergahı as Turkish diplomatic outposts, or on the activities of dervishes and *kalender*s (antinomian, celibate ascetics) at the Kashgari lodge in Eyüp, instead of the day-to-day work that the shaykhs performed—both for pilgrims and for the Ottoman state.[24] Sketching the profile and demographics of the people who came to the lodge is an important first step in better understanding the contours of this network, which has been misunderstood as comprising primarily dervishes.[25] There was a diverse community of migrants at Sultantepe that originated primarily from Russian- and Chinese-ruled lands. Barring the occasional guest from Kazan, Khiva, or Afghanistan, most of the guests hailed from Russian Turkestan, Chinese Turkestan, and Bukhara. The majority of recorded guests were men between the ages of twenty and forty, with this age range accounting for roughly 60 to 65 percent. There were also smaller numbers of children and elderly people, including men in their seventies, eighties, and even nineties. While boys such as Bekir were given their own entries, women and girls were only recorded in the notes section and described as mothers, wives, or daughters of male guests. There was seldom information about women's ages and no entries for single women. Petitions for repatriation and other forms of aid sent to Ottoman authorities provide some additional information and indicate that it was common for families to travel together. For example, a 1911 Interior Ministry record on repatriating pilgrims to Chinese Turkestan lists fifty-three individuals by name and includes nine women. Of the nine, three were aged fifty-two, fifty, and forty, and the youngest female child, Bini, was eight years old.[26] Likewise, in March of 1914, the ministry provided assistance to a group of pilgrims from Chinese Turkestan and Bukhara, many of whom included women traveling with small children.[27] Though occurring with less frequency, there were also small groups of women with a single male chaperone, as testified by a 1910 petition from a Bukharan party that included a certain Niyaz Bibi Hatun, Edhem Han Hatun, Ayşe Bibi Hatun, and Tuba Nisa, and one male, Hacı İbrahim—all of whom were broke and stuck in Istanbul.[28]

An examination of the 1899–1906 register indicates that the average age of guests was 37.25, with 35 as the median and 30 the mode. Guests ranged in age from one to ninety. Approximately 31 percent of those registered were aged twenty-one to thirty, with thirty-one to forty-year-olds accounting for 28 percent. With less than 7 percent of guests in their teens, students

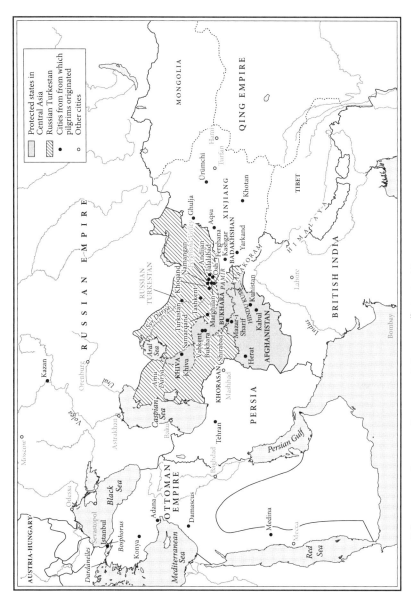

MAP 5. Major cities of origin of guests at Sultantepe Özbekler Tekkesi.

appear to have accounted for only a small proportion of those staying in this institution (which is confirmed in later entries when occupations are listed alongside age and origin).[29] The oldest guests tended to originate mainly from cities in Chinese Turkestan, and many were already listed as hajjis. For example, seventy-year-old Niyaz bin Aşir of Kashgar, who must have appeared youthful—he was described as still having a black beard (*kara sakallı*)—was a resident.[30] Between 1907 and 1923, there was a noticeable change in the profile of guests: the average age decreased from 37.25 to 34.27, the median from 35 to 25, and the mode from 30 to 25. The sharpest trend was an increase in twenty-one-year-olds to thirty-year-olds.[31] This could be because as the hajj became more accessible, people were more inclined to go in their youth. Surges in the early twentieth century might also be correlated to high cotton yields in the Ferghana Valley during this period, which in turn would have translated into a greater disposable income.

The registers also reveal a great deal of geographical diversity in terms of place of origin and that, despite its name, the tekke was not exclusively for Uzbeks. The majority of guests originated from Chinese Turkestan (which was populated by what we would now term Uyghurs, Uzbeks, and Kazakhs) and the Ferghana Valley. There was also the occasional guest from the Tatar city of Kazan or Khiva (in today's Uzbekistan), as well as a party of eight from Kuhistan (possibly the city in Afghanistan or in present-day Tajikistan) who arrived in December and January of 1902 and departed for the Hijaz within a little more than two weeks.[32] From 1899 through 1906, 42.8 percent of travelers were from Chinese Turkestan, 29.9 percent from cities in the Ferghana Valley, and 8.9 percent from Bukhara.[33] In the early twentieth century, there was a noticeable decrease in the number of pilgrims from Chinese Turkestan as compared to pilgrims from the Ferghana Valley: travelers from Chinese Turkestan (Kashgar and other cities such as Khotan, Yarkand, and Kulcha) had declined from 42.8 percent of all pilgrims in the period 1899–1906 to 29.6 percent in the period 1907–23.[34] In relation to the thousands of people traveling between the 1890s and 1910s, the number of Kashgari lodges in Istanbul, and limitless outside factors, this data cannot be analyzed in relation to any larger trends.

The guests included everyone from toddlers to ninety-year-olds, and the same diversity found echoes in the jobs and professions listed. Beyond the occasional dervish and kalender, the vast majority of lodgers were working people who had not renounced the material world and who were subject to the precarity of pilgrimage. This radically revises the view of Central Asian Muslims in the city as "dervishes … clamping to their pocket-knives and alms-cups" and begging on the streets of Istanbul. Instead, what we see are people "trying to earn some money by sharpening knives and blades, repairing kitchen wares,"[35] and seeking work as laborers and servants in a network of inns and households. The full list of occupations I have tallied—all recorded in Ottoman Turkish—includes mullah or theological student (*molla*); farmer (*dehkan, çiftci, zürra*); glazier (*camcı*); cook (*aşpez*); barber (*serteraş, berber*); cobbler (*kefşduz, kunduracı*); grocer (*bakkal*); coal dealer or stoker (*kömürcü*); chimneysweep (*çatıferaş*); baker (*nevay, ekmekçi*); carpenter (*marangoz*); butcher (*kasap*); weaver (*dokumacı*); hatmaker (*takkeci*); driver (*arabacı*); cattle merchant (*koyun tüccarı*); seal engraver (*mühürcü*); merchant (*tüccar*); ironworker (*demirci*); worker or day laborer (*amele, rençper*); plasterer (*sıvacı*); dyer, house-painter (*boyacı*); confectioner or sugar merchant (*şekerci*); wheel-maker (*çerhci*); mechanic (*makineci*); silk merchant or manufacturer (*ipekçi*); fitter (*tesviyeci*); and porter (*hammal*).

While pilgrims were primarily agriculturalists, laborers, craftsmen, and artisans, there were also a couple of acrobats (*canbaz*) who passed through over the years. The main criterion that determined who could stay was need. The mission of the lodge was to host the poor (*gureba ü fukaran*), and those who stayed for extended periods were expected to work. Moreover, we can see that the shaykhs did not tolerate wealthy guests who had the means to pay for lodging elsewhere.[36] In December of 1901, for example, when the shaykh learned that the brothers Tohta Hacı and Muhammed Said of Yarkand (age seventy and fifty-nine) were men of some "influence and wealth," he asked them to leave.[37] Likewise, Berat bin Osman of Khotan was sent away when "it became clear from an inquiry that he was a man of power."[38]

The image of the poor Central Asian dervish-as-pilgrim originates in travelers' accounts of the hajj and is consistent with the self-representation of individuals in their supplications to the sultan. Whether Central Asian pilgrims started out destitute or their poverty was a consequence of exploitation and hardship, we see that many pilgrims were of humble origins. This did not mean, however, that they were ascetics who had renounced worldly pursuits and dedicated themselves to a life of prayer and meditation. The distinction between the working poor and the indigent is important for two reasons. First, people far from home and traveling through various empires walked a fine line between having enough money for the journey, being down and out on their luck, and turning to begging. Sultantepe alleviated these risks, not only by providing room and board but also by linking foreign Muslims to local employment networks. This enabled guests to conserve financial resources and save for the remainder of the journey. Second, recognizing that pilgrims were not all mendicants is crucial for understanding the nature of imperial disputes over nationality and protection. While diplomatic battles over the right to jurisdiction of contested subjects could be waged over symbolic monetary sums and inconsequential estates, foreign consuls seldom insisted that professional beggars or penniless dervishes were their subjects. By and large, Russo- or Anglo-Ottoman disputes involved people whose labor was the real engine of industrializing empires or whose commercial contacts and mercantile activity could forge new imperial economic relationships across Asia.

A sample page from the 1899–1906 register—the same *defter* where Bekir and his father Azım's arrival and departure were recorded—shows the types of circulations that were possible for foreign Muslims. In three entries that were first entered on 13 January 1899, for example, we see the following:

Number	19
Name	Hacı Nur Muhammed
Father's name	Molla Hekim
Country	Merginan [Marghilan]
Age	37
Date of arrival	1 Kanunussani [1]314 [13 Jan. 1899]
Description	Average height, with a black beard
Comments	The aforementioned worked four months at the *dergah-ı şerif* [Sultantepe] and later, upon his own wishes, resigned. This was noted in his *nüfus tezkere* on 12 Mayıs 1315 [24 May 1899]. Subsequently, on 30 Mayıs 1315 [11 June 1899], he was asked to leave the tekke for verbally threatening Hacı Abdülhalik, because it would not be right [or lawful; *caiz*] for him to remain.

On 1 Teşrinievvel 1316 [14 Oct. 1900], he returned to the dergah.

On 22 Ramazan 1318 [13 Jan. 1901], he went to the İstanbul Dergah.

On 14 Temmuz 1318 [27 July 1902], he came to the dergah. The entry has been transferred to the last page.

[continued at end of register]

Age	37

Went to a *han* in Uzunçarşı on 3 Teşrinievvel 318 [16 Nov. 1902]

20 Mayıs 319 [2 June 1903]   Came to the dergah

[illegible] August 1903   He went to the Russian Hospital

21 Ağustos 319 [3 Sept. 1903]   Returned again to the dergah

5 Teşrinievvel 319 [18 Oct. 1903]   Went to a *han* in Uzunçarşı

21 Kanunisani 319 [3 Feb. 1904]   Came to the dergah again

4 Şubat 320 [17 Feb. 1904]   Went to Adana

4 Mart 320 [17 March 1904]   Came to the dergah

17 Mayıs 320 [30 May 1904]   Again to Adana

15 Kanunisani 320 [28 Jan. 1905]   Came to the dergah

5 Mart 321 [8 May 1905]   Expelled

25 Temmuz 323 [7 August 1908]   After the hajj, came to the dergah

22 Kanunievvel 322 [4 Jan. 1907]   Went to the Hijaz

25 Nisan 324 [8 May 1908]   Came to the dergah

27 Haziran 324 [10 July 1908] Went to a han in Uzunçarşı

Number	20
Name	Hacı Abdülhalik
Father's name	Hacı Muhammed İbrahim
Country	Merginan
Age	30
Date of arrival	15 Mayıs 1315 [27 May 1899]
Description	Short, with a light brown beard
Comments	The aforementioned worked [at the tekke] until 27 Teşrinievvel 1315 [8 Nov. 1899], at which time he cut his relations with the dergah and went to [work with] Kârı Mahmud in Uzunçarşı.

On 5 Kanunievvel 1315 [7 Dec. 1899] he returned to the dergah.

On 12 Şubat 1315 [24 Feb. 1900] he went to the Hijaz.

Number	21
Name	Hacı Muhammed Alim
Father's name	Muhammed Abdülkerim
Country	Merginan
Age	30
Date of arrival	27 Mayıs 1315 [3 June 1899]
Description	Tall, with a sparse beard
Comments	On 10 Kanunuevvel 1315 [22 Jan. 1900], he went to the Özbekler Dergahı in Istanbul.
	On 8 Şevval 1317 [8 Feb. 1900], he went to Adana.
	On 15 [illegible] 1316, he returned to the dergah again.
	On 10 Teşrinievvel 1316 [23 Oct. 1900], he went to İşan Kunduzizade as a servant.
	On 25 Mart 1317 [7 April 1901], he went to his country.
	On 26 Teşrinievvel 1319 [8 Nov. 1903], he came to the dergah.
	On 29 Şubat 1319 [13 March 1904], he went to the Fincancı Han.

While longer than most, the three entries are by no means exceptional. The reappearance of a number of hans in Uzunçarşı and Tahtakale (in Eminönü), as well as At Pazarı (in Fatih), suggests close ties between both Sultantepe and the Buhara Dergahı, as well as between the lodges and manufacturing. These connections were likely forged by Şeyh Edhem Efendi, who is said to have been the head of the Imperial School for Industry, which was established by the famous Tanzimat statesman Mithat Paşa in 1869.[39] Among the inns listed by name were Fincancı Han, Davud Han, Han-ı Halil, and Zülfikar Han. As Muhammed Alim's record indicates, people also worked as servants in Ottoman households. Other forms of short-term employment included working in coffeehouses and at the dergah itself.[40] The first register lists eight people as "işçi" (worker), and the second mentions six. Into the 1930s, there was still a resident cook (*aşpez*) and his helpers; workers who helped draw water from the well, clean the courtyard, and perform chores; and women who worked in the *haremlik*, the interior of the house, where they did laundry and helped take care of children.[41]

The entries also illustrate that the hajj was not necessarily a once-in-a-lifetime or unidirectional journey. Nur Muhammed and his friends (or enemies, given the quarrel that led to his expulsion) were listed as hajjis when they arrived. And, like many other lodgers, Abdülhalik was listed as the son of a hajji. This tells us that by 1899, there was a generation in Russian and Chinese Turkestan with parents that had traveled to Mecca and that people could afford multiple long-distance journeys. This suggests that people at Sultantepe and other lodges had direct knowledge of the city and that their connections to Ottoman lands were multigenerational. Related to this, the men's lives raise the question of whether *pilgrim* is a sufficiently expansive term. Like the nonelites that James Clifford writes of in his work on "travelling cultures,"[42] these men lived lives between and across vast spaces. We can ascertain that many Central Asians in the empire almost certainly mixed religious travel with some form of labor migration or commercial activities. As the next chapter on extraterritoriality attests, not everyone with the title *hajji* was or should be defined exclusively as a pilgrim.

Muslims had historically mixed commerce, study, travel, and religious devotion. The change was once again in terms of scale and demographics: rather than small numbers of ulema, dervishes, or diplomats, large numbers of artisans, unskilled laborers, and peasants were traveling on extended journeys and remaining abroad for long periods. The context had also changed: these travelers and migrants were now subjects of colonial empires and classified by the Ottoman government as foreign Muslims. These were the global forces that impinged on the local networks of Istanbul. Yet the fact that Nur Muhammed went to the Russian hospital in 1903 suggests that he had not renounced his Russian nationality. He could live, work, and travel freely without becoming naturalized. Throughout his time in the empire, and likely when he was between jobs, the lodge and the shaykhs there provided him with a safety net. Even after being expelled—not once but twice—Nur Muhammed was allowed to return.[43] In the absence of kinship networks, the lodge filled an important void and fostered the formation of a transimperial community rooted in Üsküdar with room for *ecanib-i Müslimin*.

We also see that the people who stayed at Sultantepe were multidimensional individuals prone to the same bursts of anger, fighting, dependencies, temptations, and bad judgment as the population at large. The tekke's doors were open to guests as long as they comported themselves well and adhered to the established norms; given the close quarters, there was a premium on maintaining order. This meant no indolence; no exploitation of the tekke's resources for personal profit; no fighting; and no drinking, gambling, or drugs. People who transgressed the rules were asked to leave, though it is not clear how culpability—or redemption—was established. Like Nur Muhammed, who had resigned from his position, fought with his friend, and continued to come and go over a decade, people could make amends. After residing in the tekke for approximately nine months, thirty-five-year-old Hacı Hasan of Marghilan, for example, was expelled in July of 1914 for playing cards in the coffeehouse (presumably gambling). He was allowed to return later that winter after "improving his conduct." A year later, Hasan was drafted into the army. But after being discharged, he returned within a year. After some time at the tekke he was again expelled for unspecified misconduct.[44] In one of the more salacious stories recorded by the shaykh, a twenty-five-year-old Khoqandi named Hacı Leyl Şah was expelled in 1902 for making sexual advances toward a woman named Emine. As the shaykh put it, "It has been understood that the aforementioned tried to seduce and take for himself the wife of Hacı Sabır."[45] After Leyl Şah was asked to leave, Emine remained with her husband, the eighty-year-old Hacı Sabır, and their three daughters Havva, Saliha, and Talime.[46]

In some cases, pilgrims came to Sultantepe with documents from other lodges—pointing to the circulations among the institutions. When Hacı Baba, a Bukharan dervish from the Eyüp Kalenderhane, arrived at Sultantepe for a "change of air," he came with a letter from the shaykh, which stated that he was leaving of his own accord and was an upright man who had never "broken anyone's heart."[47] And in early 1900, three men—Salih Hoca, age twenty of Tashkent; Abdulkadir, twenty-two of Namangan; and Ebubekir, thirty-five of Bukhara—arrived from the "İstanbul Dergahı" (likely the Buhara Dergahı) with a document that helped secure their lodging. They stayed for three days before leaving for the Hijaz.[48] A letter from the shaykh at the Buhara Dergahı in central Istanbul probably helped facilitate movement between lodges, especially during the height of the pilgrimage season. The story of connection was in these small acts: an *ilmühaber* from the shaykh signified the existence of personal ties and trust.

Hints—and instances—of violence and forbidden behavior also run through the tekke records. In addition to the verbal threats of Nur Muhammed, we see Kârı Muhammed Yusuf Hoca, a twenty-six-year-old from Samarqand, expelled in May of 1900 for assaulting a Namangani almost fifty years his senior.[49] Similarly, twenty-five-year-old Hacı Sultan of Andijan was expelled on 3 July 1909 for fighting with a certain Siraceddin, who was listed as the cook.[50] Perhaps fearing continued discord, the shaykh asked a man named Hacı Kiram of Marghilan to leave because he did not get along with his countrymen (*hemşeri*).[51] In some cases, both parties to a fight or dispute could be thrown out: on 19 June 1913, both Hacı Muhammed Salih, a twenty-six-year-old volunteer Ottoman soldier from Andijan, and Cuma Ali, a twenty-two-year-old from Khoqand, were expelled for physical assaults or fighting.[52] Guests were also expelled for drinking and drug use. Such was the case for Hacı Şakir of Marghilan. Performing the hajj had not dampened this thirty-year-old hajji's thirst for the forbidden, and he was dismissed on 20 March 1904 for coming back to the tekke drunk.[53] The thirty-three-year-old Andijani Hacı Gaib Nazar, however, was discovered to be a hashish addict, or *esrarkeş*. After spending more than two and a half years in the Hijaz (30 December 1901 through 15 June 1904), he was thrown out for smoking hashish.[54] Similarly, Hacı Muhiddin of Khoqand—who had an honorable past as a volunteer soldier—was sent away in February of 1913 for being a hashish addict.[55]

As we see from these examples, dergahs and tekkes were not the exclusive preserve of emissaries and elites or of ascetics. Rather, they served working people who were Sufis in the ways that most Central Asians were: Sunni Muslims who did not necessarily think about or primarily identify as being mystics but whose religious identities and life rituals were informed by practices inflected by the Naqshbandiyya and other brotherhoods. While episodes of drinking, cheating, fighting, and gambling may disrupt assumptions about pilgrims or pilgrimage, the people at the lodge were not defined exclusively by the hajj or the spaces they inhabited. The tekkes, too, were much more multidimensional than commonly assumed, serving both pilgrims and the Ottoman state to control and regulate foreign Muslims.

Intersections of Patronage and Regulation

Sultantepe and the city's other Central Asian Sufi lodges were heirs to a rich and evolving tradition of Naqshbandi practice and part of the warp and weft of Ottoman life. This included the political reforms that restructured the empire in the nineteenth century. The guest registers indicate that the shaykhs of these institutions were an integral part of the infrastructure of state power, responsible for counting, registering, and keeping tabs on the mobility of foreign nationals. This task became more important as travel to Mecca via Istanbul became more popular and the pilgrims in question became subjects of foreign powers outside of Ottoman legal jurisdiction.

The process of bringing the empire's religious establishment under greater central governmental control dated to the first half of the nineteenth century and began with limits on the economic and administrative autonomy of Sufi orders. Bureaucratization was incremental, beginning with the establishment in 1812 of the Directorate of Imperial Foundations (Evkaf-ı Hümayun Nezareti), which (in theory) brought the endowments of all pious foundations—including tekkes—under its control.[56] Ten years after the 1826 "auspicious incident" that marked the abolition of the Janissary corps and the Bektashi order, the Porte instituted practices such as requiring shaykhs to register and document all students, dervishes, and guests, subject to the inspection of the central government. They included sartorial reforms (such as requiring Sufis to wear garb particular to their order) and requirements that dervishes carry identity papers. The decree also restricted the appointment of shaykhs to only one position at a time. More stringent requirements were also placed on the granting of certificates of authoritative knowledge to disciples (*ijaza*; Ott., *icazet*) and on the appointment of shaykhs to tekkes. These requirements were part of a broader project "to render more visible and calculable an ever-increasing number of micro-level, daily social practices and institutions," which extended across a spectrum of private and public spaces that included hotels.[57]

Similar reforms continued into the second half of the nineteenth century with the establishment of the Assembly of Shaykhs (Meclis-i Meşayih) in 1866. The foundation of this governing body "marked the formal bureaucratization of the orders and increasing rationalization of the conditions for Sufi practice, [and] meant that more and more aspects of the life of the orders would be subject to explicit calculation, according to the emergent criteria of reason and performance, as targets of 'policy.'"[58] Consequent to these reforms, the shaykhs of Sultantepe, the Buhara Dergahı, and the Kaşgari Tekkesi had effectively become Ottoman bureaucrats,[59] who were expected to aid in managing foreign Muslims. Indeed, the shaykhs cooperated with Istanbul municipal authorities, as well as with the Russian consulate in Istanbul, in order to regulate the mobility of guests. In 1901, for example, the Russian consulate's registry office (*kançilarya*) contacted the shaykh about a certain Hacı Abdulkayyum, whom they were looking for in relation to an investigation of another Russian subject.[60] And in 1899, the shaykh annotated the entries of two men, ages twenty-five and nineteen, stating that they had been turned over to the Russian consulate and sent back to Samarqand. Although their ages would suggest that they were too old to be runaways, the shaykhs noted that one of their fathers had asked Russian authorities for help.[61]

If the registration of guests was part of a broader effort to bring the religious establishment under central control and to increase the legibility of foreign nationals, it had also become crucial to the regulation of public health. The prevalence of water- and air-borne illnesses such as cholera and tuberculosis among pilgrims was an ongoing cause for concern, particularly in the imperial capital. The postnişin was quick to send guests showing signs of illness to Gureba-yı Müslimin,[62] which was one of the city's first endowed hospitals and had a ward for the treatment of infectious diseases. Part of the hospital's mission was to treat Muslims far from home, but there were only two hundred beds. According to the Istanbul director of police, Lütfi Pasha, in 1909 there was a demand of fifteen to twenty people for treatment each day, but only three to four available beds. Because many of the patients were from distant places and physically incapable of going home, Lütfi Pasha said they should be given priority in admissions since left untreated they posed a threat to public health.[63] In the first register alone, there are at least twenty-three documented individuals who were sent to the hospital, which demonstrates how the tekke shaykh mediated between local hospitals and Ottoman ministries that would dispense sultanic charity. For those who recovered and returned to their homelands, receiving free treatment at what was then a state-of-the-art hospital was surely part of what would become their narrative of the hajj and their experiences in Ottoman lands. Just some examples include the thirty-three-year-old Abdülnazar of Shahrisabz (near Samarqand), who went to the hospital twice before leaving for the Hijaz.[64] Like Abdülnazar, others returned from the hospital, recuperated a bit longer in the tekke, and continued on their journeys. This was the case for the seventy-year-old Cöre Bay of Shahrisabz, who arrived on 8 January 1900 and was sent to the hospital on the twenty-eighth. Cöre Bay was sent back on 25 February, returning on 12 March before leaving for Kütahya on 8 May 1900.[65] Similarly, Hacı Ahmed was treated at Gureba-yı Müslimin before leaving for Konya and ultimately the hajj. He had first arrived on 23 June 1900 and left for Konya on 23 July 1900. He returned about three months later, received medical care, recuperated for two months, and then left for the Hijaz.[66]

For those whose journeys were cut short by death, the shaykhs arranged for burial and notification of relations. After the death of a certain Hacı Abdülcelil of Marghilan, who died a week after arriving at the tekke in July of 1901, the shaykh cobbled together the funds required to lay him to rest. He noted that they had combined the money found on his person (21.5 kuruş) with fifty kuruş obtained from the municipality and an unspecified amount of sultanic charity (*sadaka-yı hazret-i padişah*). The shaykh spelled out that he was recording the details of the burial because he had not been able to find any relatives of the deceased.[67] Similarly, Hacı Molla Hüseyin of Andijan did not have any relations when he passed away at age forty-two, six days after arriving at the tekke on 14 September 1901. The shaykh took care of his funeral, and Molla Hüseyin was buried in the adjacent cemetery.[68] The tekke, which was supposed to be a place of temporary stay on his way to Mecca, had become his final resting place.

Sultantepe also absorbed destitute Central Asians who were in transit and often unable to return to their homelands. This, combined with the sultan's system of gifts and alms distribution to pilgrims (and later the more bureaucratized version of alms distribution under the Committee of Union and Progress), formed the basis of an informal, albeit imperfect and underfunded, system of social welfare. Although registers are not available for similar lodges in Istanbul, petitions to the Ottoman Empire from Central Asians reveal that many destitute travelers and pilgrims benefited from the shelter and provisions provided by these institutions while they were continuing on their journeys or waiting for responses to their appeals for governmental assistance. I explore these petitions at length in Chapter 4, but here I want to underscore how assisting pilgrims with travel arrangements, providing requisite Ottoman documents, facilitating health care, assuming responsibility for burial, and, most important, providing free room and board in a foreign city were what made transimperial mobility possible for many people. From their arrival to departure, whether for Mecca or the eternity of the other world, these intimate encounters shaped lodgers' experiences in the Ottoman Empire. Beyond providing people with a place to rest their heads for the night, these government-subsidized institutions mitigated the costs—both financial and psychological—of a taxing journey and offered a brief respite.

As much as they were part of a growing structure to monitor the movements of people in Ottoman space, the tekkes were also integrated into a system of gift distribution through which certain conceptions of power—mainly the paternal benevolence of the sultan—were manifested and legitimized. During the reign of Sultan Abdülhamid II, the sultan allocated 24 percent of his imperial philanthropy to the Hijaz (the other main focus being the capital, at 41 percent).[69] These funds were mainly used for providing relief to the poorest pilgrims through subsidies, grants, and accommodations in a new Ottoman guesthouse; they were also used for the upkeep of pious endowments.[70] This gift giving was directed not only at Ottoman subjects but at the subjects of other states and was designed to deliver political messages to a wider public about the sultan's benevolence and power.[71] It was not only texts such as *Hajjnoma-i Turkiy* that circulated this message beyond Ottoman domains. Each time the shaykh welcomed a guest, helped a traveler obtain documents or tickets, or helped to write a petition, he did so as an Ottoman official and bolstered the carefully cultivated image of the sultan. There were also physical reminders of sultanic patronage, such as the plaque commemorating Sultan Abdülhamid II's renovation of the tekke, which would greet guests as they came and went.

The tekke's role in regulating the trajectories of foreign Muslims looked a lot like Islamic charity, and it was likely experienced and understood as sultanic benevolence. The types of social welfare the state provided was rooted in Islamic tradition but promoted as part of the "orchestrated performances of sultanic generosity."[72] Though modest structures, the tekkes played an important role in improving the overall Ottoman image through temporal measures such as getting pilgrims on steamers and providing them with support in a foreign and often hostile city. This function should not be underestimated: Russian ambassador Nikolai Ignat'ev had proposed funding similar structures that would be administered and financed by the tsarist state.[73] Although the Ministry of Internal Affairs in St. Petersburg vetoed his proposal, Ignat'ev was clearly on to something. In its continued patronage of the tekkes, the Ottoman state was probably also aware of the important role these structures played in offsetting the pilgrims' negative experiences and, perhaps more importantly, lessening the burden on the various ministries that faced an onslaught of petitions from pilgrims asking for help. Even as these state-run institutions kept tabs on itinerant foreign Muslims for the government, their regulation of guests' mobility was carried out with a light hand and resembled sultanic patronage rather than policing.

As Cem Behar reminds us, Istanbul was "a world in itself," and that always seemed tremendous. If for natives of the city and internal migrants, it was the neighborhood (*mahalle*) that fostered local identities and cohesion, the same was likely true for foreigners.[74] Central Asians would be familiar with the three boroughs of Istanbul—Üsküdar, Eyüp, and, perhaps to a lesser extent, Galata—and then with the main lodges at Sultantepe, Eyüp, and Sultanahmet, as well as the commercial workshops and inns around the waterfront of the old city. The tekke would constitute the locus of the neighborhood, each one an economic and social unit unto itself—even as it maintained ties to the government, other Sufi lodges, Central Asian households and businesses, and Ottoman hospitals and charitable foundations through the figure of the shaykh. These lodges were entrenched as religious institutions within local communities and reached beyond Greater Istanbul via the continual movement of hajjis traversing Central Asia, Mecca, and points in between. They played a key role in integrating these travelers into Ottoman life, making it possible for them to experience the kinds of category-transcending interactions that would allow them to envision themselves as subjects of the sultan.

Looking beyond the paper trail of the central government archive—where Central Asians often come into view as problems for the state—and employing a microhistorical approach allows us to more fully grasp how networks took shape and connections were forged. Reading between the ledger lines highlights the importance of making the geography of Islam and Islamic institutions a central object of our analysis, particularly in an era of rapid global change, when old sites like Sultantepe began to shoulder new burdens. Whether they were there for a matter of days or returned repeatedly over the decades, migrants found a space and a community that helped them navigate the changing norms and terrain of a foreign country.[75] A major dimension of this change was in the arena of legislation designed to demarcate the boundaries between the rights of Ottomans and foreigners and limit the reach of the Capitulations. As we turn to the impact of colonialism and nationality reform on pilgrimage and migration, it is important to remember how these state-supported institutions were a counterpoint to fraught interactions that were part of the steamship-era hajj. From Eyüp to Tarsus and Jerusalem, Mecca, and Medina, shaykhs served travelers with common ethnic, linguistic, and communal affiliations from a range of polities, regardless of their legal nationality. And members of the communities in question activated these bonds when they needed guarantors for legal transactions involving naturalization, land sales, or marriage. By connecting new arrivals to employment, health care, lodging, spiritual life, and social activities—the constituent elements of a (trans)regional network—they were building blocks for diasporic communities anchored in a familiar religious ethos. This sense of belonging made possible by such sites was particularly important in a rapidly changing international legal order. To use Mirim Khan's turn of phrase, they were the kinds of places capable of lifting the dust from pilgrims' hearts.

{ CHAPTER 3 }

EXTRATERRITORIALITY AND THE QUESTION OF PROTECTION

WHEN HACI MİRZA BİN REHİM DIED, in the winter of 1910, his Russian passport did not signify very much to the Ottoman authorities handling his funerary affairs. The fifty-four-year-old was en route to Gureba-yı Müslimin Hospital when he succumbed to pneumonia, taking what would be his last voyage. He was then buried, his old clothes sold, and the proceeds—along with 16.5 kuruş found on his person—sent to the Ottoman Treasury (Beytülmal).[1] Perhaps because of the small sums involved, local officials (in this case, police) did not think it worth the effort to contact the Russian consulate. Or they may have believed that the hajji was subject to Ottoman jurisdiction. Since the early 1890s, the Ottoman Foreign Ministry had maintained that it was the sole protector of Bukharans in the empire, even as it conceded tsarist jurisdictions over people from formally colonized territories in the Caucasus and Central Asia. The problem—and there were several in this particular case—was that Mirza was not a Bukharan (and thus not a subject of the emir or under Ottoman protection). He was from Turkestan, a colony established in 1867 with lands conquered from Khiva, Bukhara, and Khoqand (and therefore a subject of the Russian Empire). Not surprisingly, soon after his death, the Russian consul in Istanbul contacted the Ottoman Interior Ministry and asked for the transfer of his "estate." Attempts to assert this form of consular jurisdiction over the dead, for sums large and small, had become commonplace by 1910, and the Ottoman Interior Ministry instructed local Istanbul authorities to comply with the request. They were apparently not aware that the hajji's affairs had already been settled in a manner local officials saw as consonant with customary practice. It took several weeks and much correspondence among multiple bureaucracies to understand that there was nothing to turn over to Russia.

If the investigation into Hacı Mirza's estate had continued, or had concerned larger sums or property, the question of his nationality would likely have become more complicated still. Whereas the Russian consul's note to the Foreign Ministry alone might lead us to believe he was a pilgrim, in fact, the hajji was a long-term resident of Istanbul. Beyond the paper trail that made its way into the imperial archives, the Sultantepe registers provide brief glimpses of an earlier phase of his life, when he arrived at the tekke—already as a hajji—in January of 1907. From Sultantepe, he had moved to the "Eyüp Dergâhı," returned briefly about a year later, and then left for a han in Üsküdar.[2] If he had lived in the empire five years without making any claims to foreign nationality—Bukharan, Russian, or otherwise—he would have fulfilled the residence requirements of the 1869 Ottoman Nationality Law and could arguably be considered an Ottoman subject. But, as far as we know, these questions were never raised during his lifetime, and the issue of his nationality came to the fore only when the pilgrim-turned-Istanbul-denizen died. It was then that he was drawn into the "nationality games" that sought to reclassify bodies and fix fluid identities in the comparatively more rigid categories of empires and international law.[3]

The indeterminate nature of Hacı Mirza's legal personhood and the fragments of his story are characteristic of many incidents that made their way into the Ottoman archives. The confusion over how to categorize him in death sets the stage for this chapter's examination of understudied convergences of hajj, migration, and the politics of nationality and protection. Although many cases over contested subjects involved more than did this poor hajji's estate, the handling of his affairs highlights the competing understandings of belonging that emerged in the Hamidian period and persisted throughout the Young Turk era. The catalyst for these developments lay in the realm of geopolitics and international law, as hajj overlapped with new legal spaces for the regulation of interstate relations. The extension of British and Russian imperial rule into Asia was joined by attempts to leverage that power through mobile Muslim subjects in Ottoman lands, setting in motion tensions among Central Asians, the Ottoman state, and foreign consuls that were captured by what an Ottoman Foreign Ministry official termed the "protection question." This was the question of whether Afghans, Bukharans, and Chinese Muslims in Ottoman lands had legitimate claims to Russian and British legal nationality and, by extension, capitulatory privileges. It was a question prompted not only by foreign consuls but also by hajjis who engaged with the law and threatened to become a new protégé population.

In tracing the Porte's attempts to answer the Central Asian protection question, this chapter makes two contributions to our understanding of foreign Muslims' status in the empire and of the role of the caliphate in late Ottoman history. First, it shows the seminal role that the Foreign Ministry Office of Legal Counsel played in articulating the idea that the Ottoman caliph was the sole protector of Bukharans and other Muslims from informally colonized lands. Rather than a pan-Islamic initiative to augment Ottoman prestige or advance the cause of Muslim unity, I demonstrate that this was a clear instance of using international legal arguments to defend Ottoman sovereignty—ultimately by depriving certain Muslims from privileges derived from foreign subjecthood. Related to this, the chapter elucidates how the Ottoman Foreign Ministry envisioned the caliphate as part of the structure of power and drew on it to curtail the expansion of consular protections to people seen as taking on "borrowed nationalities." These were colonial subjects whom Ottoman legal jurists saw as employing various ruses solely for the purpose of obtaining rights and protections enshrined in international agreements and treaties.[4] Second, this chapter demonstrates that imperial competition over nationality and protection often limited the opportunities for legal maneuvering among Muslim subjects of European protectorates (rather than formal colonies). I argue that competing jurisdiction and sovereignty did not necessarily produce opportunities for people who were savvy enough to exploit the legal order. Rather, the Porte's assertion of caliphal protection often limited the legal strategies available to Central Asians. Beginning in the Hamidian era, the Foreign Ministry sought to determine the rights of Muslims based on the type of polities from which they originated. As a result, a foreign Muslim from Bukhara was effectively accorded a different legal status from that granted an ecnebi from Tashkent, because each had a different status in the sultan's domains that was derived from international law.

Becoming Ottoman, Foreign, and Protected

Despite the rhetoric about Islamic unity during the late Ottoman era, in the realm of governance, the question of where Muslims were from became increasingly connected to questions of legal nationality and jurisdictional sovereignty.[5] Although the Ottomans did not have the power to dismantle the system of extraterritoriality, they engaged with the international legal order to guard against Muslims who sought to infringe on their sovereignty. Studies of extraterritoriality have traced how people responded to these changes, particularly how they tried to maximize subjecthood rights and to exploit competition over foreign protection and legal jurisdiction. The growth of European consular courts, for example, made practices such as affiliation switching and "forum shopping"—when individuals within legally pluralist systems switched legal identities (i.e., their nationality) and forums in order to maximize benefits—increasingly common.[6] But learning how to navigate these changes necessitated a steep learning curve for ordinary people and government officials alike and did not always end in success. While extraterritoriality was a boon to Muslim colonial subjects traveling, trading, or residing in the sultan's domains, this new form of patronage and protection often came at the expense of the Ottoman Empire and pitted foreign Muslims and the Ottoman government against one another. The story of a Bukharan migrant named Celal bin Hekim sheds light on some of these emerging rifts.

Sometime in the early 1860s, Celal left Bukhara and traveled vast distances before settling in the Red Sea port city of Jeddah. Over the course of the next three decades, he worked as a *bedelci*, an agent for people who paid to avoid (or were exempt from) military service.[7] Such a job would involve large outlays of money, extensive travel, and strong local and regional connections. During his residence in the empire, Celal "benefited from all the rights of Ottoman nationality"—making it all the more galling for Ottoman authorities when, after getting into trouble with the law, he asserted that he was a Russian subject and exempt from Ottoman jurisdiction. Unsure how to proceed—since this was still a relatively new development among Bukharans in the Hijaz—the provincial government forwarded the case to Istanbul, where the Foreign Ministry would decide whether this Bukharan living as an

Ottoman had any valid legal basis for claiming Russian nationality.[8] What, Ottoman authorities wanted to know, was his "real" nationality (*asıl tabiiyet*)? The answer had important implications: if he was an Ottoman, Celal would be subject to shari'a law; if Russian, he would be exempt from detention or trial in the Hijaz and placed under tsarist jurisdiction. But what if he was a Bukharan subject? Were subjects of the emir—a Russian vassal—entitled to the same rights and protection as subjects of the tsar? According to legal advisers in the Ottoman Foreign Ministry, the answer was a firm "no." Protectorates such as Bukhara, they insisted, were semisovereign, and their subjects were ineligible for European capitulatory privileges or protections.[9]

Whereas Central Asian Muslims living in the empire had historically been subject to Ottoman law and enjoyed the rights of the sultan's subjects, to the consternation of the Porte, this began to change in the 1880s. This was when Britain and Russia started to offer Afghans and Bukharans "protection"—a term that could mean anything from consular patronage of travelers in need to the provision of legal immunity and commercial privileges (*imtiyazat*) that had historically been the purview of European Christians. As Sarah Abrevaya Stein explains in her study of extraterritoriality in the Ottoman twentieth century, "In the absence of strict and coherent rules, clear directives, or fixed ambitions on the part of the states involved—and in light of so many border changes and migrations—protection was a plastic entity shaped by the competing dreams and nightmares of the parties involved."[10] For the Ottomans, this nightmare was a recurring one, populated by growing groups of people that included Muslims. As I discussed in my introduction, the rise of extraterritoriality was an outgrowth of the expansion of the capitulatory regime after 1856, when revocable sultanic grants (*ahdname*) to European powers were enshrined in bi- and multilateral treaties and given the force of international law. Originally intended to encourage European merchants to do business in the empire by promising that their subjects would not be subject to Islamic law, the capitulatory regime began to encompass Ottomans who obtained certificates or deeds of protection (*berat*), as well as Muslim subjects of steadily expanding colonial empires. Extraterritoriality gave foreign nationals and protégés immunities from prosecution and litigation in Ottoman courts and helped them avoid conscription and police searches—thus directly undercutting Ottoman sovereignty within its domains.[11]

While histories of the capitulations have focused primarily on their use and abuse by European powers and their non-Muslim protégés, the figure of the *berath*—and the manipulation of extraterritoriality—crossed ethnic, religious, and class lines. Over the course of the nineteenth century, capitulatory powers were generous in their granting of protection, particularly to people in regions where they wanted to advance their political and economic power. The British, for example, regularly gave Central Asians and Afghans traveling through India identity papers, which granted them the benefits of British nationality, and Russian consular staff would give Bukharans Russian subjecthood, even though they were legally subjects of the Bukharan emir.[12] Beyond those who were given official deeds of protection and registered by consuls as their subjects, people like Celal, who had spurious claims to European nationality, began to behave like European protégés.

This form of protection marked a new phase in the expansion of extraterritoriality, much of which occurred during Celal's time in the empire. In the three decades since he had first migrated, the world around him had changed dramatically. Bukhara had become a Russian protectorate, he a foreign Muslim in Ottoman lands, the hajj a mass phenomenon, and Jeddah a bustling port city that brought a steady stream of Bukharans and other Central Asians to the Holy Cities. Laws, too, had changed. The expansion of colonial power and revolutions in mobility that brought so many of his countrymen to the Hijaz coincided with an extensive period of Ottoman political and administrative "reordering" known as the Tanzimat (1839–76), during which the Porte sought to secure territorial integrity against nationalist movements and European intervention. Two major decrees, the 1839 Rescript of the Rose Chamber and the 1856 Reform Edict, outlined centralizing measures and promised all Ottoman subjects equal rights and protections under the law. The reforms undermined centuries of legal distinctions between Muslim subjects and Christians and Jews, and they introduced the legal category of "Ottoman," which included subjects of all faiths. The reforms also sought to cultivate an imperial identity among the empire's heterogeneous population, institute more direct forms of control over Ottoman subjects, and curb the proliferation of deeds of protection among Ottoman Christians by granting them equal rights and opportunities. These decrees were soon supplemented by legislation that formalized naturalization procedures. According to the 1869 Ottoman Nationality Law

(*Tabiiyet-i Osmaniye Kanunnamesi*), any person born to an Ottoman father was a subject, but one could also become an Ottoman through residence. Those born in the empire to foreign parents could become naturalized within three years of reaching an unspecified age of majority (article 2), and foreign nationals could become naturalized after fulfilling a five-year residency requirement (article 3). The fourth article allowed for Ottoman nationality to be granted to exceptional individuals who had not fulfilled the terms listed in articles 2 and 3 and were deemed "worthy of special permission." The final, ninth article stated that each individual living in the empire was considered an Ottoman and subject to Ottoman law, and that anyone claiming to be a foreign national had to provide evidence to this effect.[13]

While long treated as a citizenship law, the Tabiiyet-i Osmaniye Kanunnamesi was primarily a nationality law. As recent scholarship has shown, it built on an 1863 regulation that forced protégés to choose to naturalize as foreign subjects or submit to Ottoman territorial jurisdiction. When many protégés responded by naturalizing with a foreign state *and* retaining their Ottoman residency and nationality, the Porte sought to resolve this by enacting stricter laws.[14] Per the 1869 law, all non-Ottomans—Muslim and non-Muslim alike—were excluded from Ottoman subjecthood and legally categorized as foreigners (*ecanib*, sing. *ecnebi*). The word *ecnebi*'s historical association with Christians, however, led Ottoman officials to distinguish non-Ottoman Muslims and refer to them as *ecanib-i müslimin*.[15] "Foreign Muslim" became an unofficial but capacious subcategory that included migrants and travelers from colonies, protectorates, and European spheres or zones of influence in Asia and Africa, as well as pilgrims and long-term pious residents of the Holy Cities (*mücavirin*).

Although the Tanzimat reforms did not have an immediate impact on Celal's everyday life, more consistent implementation of an 1867 law prohibiting foreign Muslims from acquiring property in the Hijaz may have given him incentive to become legally naturalized. Since there was no cadastral survey, taxation, or conscription in the Hijaz, there were few drawbacks to becoming an Ottoman subject.[16] Celal likely knew that doing so would not foreclose the possibility of his later claiming foreign nationality. Many Muslim migrants from North Africa, Bukhara, and Afghanistan whom he may have done business with or met while traveling through Alexandria and Istanbul had managed to secure French, Russian, or British nationality or protégé status and were now enjoying the attendant legal and financial advantages. In the Hijaz, many migrants had previously become Ottomans in order to buy land. Perhaps sensing that he might benefit from holding a Russian passport, Celal decided to register at the Russian Consulate-General in Istanbul during a trip to the city in 1890. When he was detained the next year for a legal matter involving a slave (*bir esir köle maddesi*), his decision seemed prescient.

The Russian consulate in Jeddah had only recently been established, in 1891, and the consul was eager to exercise his authority by helping people like Celal.[17] Like Great Britain, Russia was trying to foster loyalty among colonial Muslim subjects and to establish a foothold in the Hijaz by providing subjects with protection—in what we might term another "competitive scramble" for protégés.[18] That Russian authorities differentiated among colonial subjects within Russia's imperial territories—and would have been loath to recognize Bukharans as Russian nationals in the metropole—did not deter them from ignoring these differences when the subjects in question were in Ottoman lands. In the case of Bukhara, the subjects of the emir retained Bukharan subjecthood and "were treated as foreigners in nearly all respects when they crossed the border between the emirates and the empire proper."[19] If Celal was aware of these realities, he may have thought it worth trying his luck. What he did not seem to anticipate was that, after a decade of similar attempts by other Muslims facing prosecution, the Ottoman Foreign Ministry had started to formulate policies regarding the rights of Bukharans and Afghans to Russian and British protection, which would prevent him from evading Ottoman justice.

When the Office of Legal Counsel received the report from Jeddah, the contempt of legal advisers nearly leapt off the page. Not only had Celal left long before Bukhara became a protectorate, but they noted that he had happily taken advantage of being an Ottoman subject for thirty years. According to article 9 of the 1869 Ottoman Nationality Law, everyone living in the empire was presumed to be Ottoman and subject to Ottoman law. And anyone claiming to be a foreign national had to provide evidence to this effect. Even if he was from parts of Bukhara that had been formally annexed to Russian Turkestan—which would have rendered him a colonial subject rather than a "protected subject" (*mahmi*)—the foreign ministry insisted that he had no valid claim to Russian nationality, since he had migrated when the emirate was completely independent. The Hijaz governor, acting in concert with the Ministry of Foreign Affairs and the Citizenship Affairs Bureau in Istanbul, thus rejected the evidence of Russian nationality that the consul in Jeddah had provided: a copy of an 1890 Russian certificate stating that the fifty-seven-year-old, hazel-eyed Bukharan of midheight was born in Russia.[20] Celal's scheme had failed.

The emergence of an international legal order privileging the laws of "civilized" nations (over those of "barbaric" and "quasi-" or "semicivilized" ones) had pressed authorities in polities as varied as China, Japan, and the Ottoman Empire to find ways to limit the power of foreign consuls and extraterritorial courts and to rein in the privileges of European protégés.[21] And, just as the French balked at recognizing colonial Algerian subjects as French nationals when they crossed the border into Tunisia, Ottoman officials were frustrated by exempting foreign Muslims from Ottoman jurisdiction, particularly when many of them originated from colonies where they would be subject to shariʻa law.[22] The Ottoman Foreign Ministry was keenly aware that Central Asians did not have recourse to the types of rights and protections in St. Petersburg and London that they had started seeking in Ottoman Iraq and Arabia and that it would have been unimaginable for Russian authorities to intervene on Celal's behalf in Bukhara. Even though they were classified by European international legal jurists as a semicivilized power, the Ottomans sought to work within the extant system to curtail the expansion of extraterritorial privileges to individuals with borrowed nationalities and to end the abuse of the Capitulations. The twist was that they did this by countering that Muslims from protectorates were protected by the caliphate.

The path to this decision is outlined in an 1886 case involving an Afghan migrant in Baghdad who, after thirty-five years of living as an Ottoman, had tried to become a British national. A few years prior to Celal's unsuccessful experiment with affiliation switching, Hacı Habib had tried something similar in Ottoman Iraq, where the British held sway over an extensive system of extraterritorial courts that served mostly Indian pilgrims to Shiʻi shrines and the diasporic communities that had formed in the vicinity of these holy sites. Shortly after Kabul was brought under the protection of the British empire, Habib decided to obtain British nationality.[23] Although the details of the case are unclear, two possibilities are that he was facing some form of legal action or that he had a son eligible for conscription into the army. While first-generation migrants were not liable for military duty, cases involving *muhacir* in other parts of the empire suggest that second-generation migrants were not exempt from conscription.[24] Or he may have wanted to embark on a business venture that would be facilitated by extraterritorial privileges.

Britain's readiness to extend jurisdiction to another group of Muslims—the large community of Afghans in an important frontier region—was a worrisome development for the Porte and prompted it to try to definitively quash this trend.[25] The task of figuring out how was given to legal advisers in the Office of Legal Counsel (Hukuk Müşavirliği İstişare Odası), a bureau within the Foreign Ministry staffed by senior legal experts who advised the government on matters related to international law. With attacks on its jurisdictional sovereignty throughout the empire, and still recovering from the disastrous 1877–78 Russo-Ottoman War (which had ended in great territorial losses in the Balkans), the bureau searched for ways to make international law work in its favor. From its inception circa 1883, it considered a host of complex issues related to extraterritoriality and issued legal opinions that informed policy making in other organs of government such as the Council of State.[26] During the Hamidian period, the Office of Legal Counsel emerged as a major institution, responsible for guiding the central government through a plethora of issues related to sovereignty, jurisdiction, and international law. It continued to do this work after the revolution that ushered in the Young Turk era.

After researching customary law and dominant international legal norms, Ottoman legal advisers maintained that Afghans who had left their country prior to its "annexation" could not claim British nationality ex post facto and that these migrants preserved their "original" or "real" nationality (*muhaciret halinde ahali-i merkume tabiiyet-i asliyelerini muhafaza ederler*). In formulating this opinion, they drew on a landmark 1881 Foreign Ministry decision that stated explicitly that "Bukharan and Afghan migrants living and traveling in the empire cannot be considered Russian or British subjects if they are not from *nevahi* [administrative units] annexed to Russian Turkestan or India," and that the only protection to which these peoples were entitled was that of the Ottoman state (*Devlet-i Aliye himayesi tahtında bulunmaları lazım gelir*).

This was the first formal iteration of the state's position that Afghans and Bukharans were not eligible for capitulatory privileges and that they were protected by the Ottomans. While this ostensibly settled the case in question, the Office of Legal Counsel next issued a more general opinion regarding Muslims who had left their countries long before annexation and settled in the Ottoman Empire. After years of residence as de facto Ottomans, they wrote, these migrants were subject to article 9 of the 1869 Ottoman Nationality Law and, as such, had "absolutely no right to the protection of a foreign state." This meant that Hacı Habib could not claim British protection, for he had left Afghanistan when it was completely independent and established permanent residence in Iraq. His only protector was the Ottoman state, and he was under the exclusive protection of the caliph.[27]

The bureau next considered whether foreign Muslims who were *not* Ottomans (naturalized or in accordance with article 9) and who "originated from states and tribes that, while under Russian and British protection, more or less retained their independence and autonomy," could claim the nationality or protection of either empire.[28] Not surprisingly, the answer was, again, "no." Engaging contemporary international law, the bureau held that protectorates were semiautonomous states and that their subjects were *mahmi* ("protected"; i.e., people who were subjects of protected states rather than subjects or legal nationals of empires). All existing treaties and capitulatory privileges applied exclusively to "real" (*asıl, sahih*) European nationals, not to these protected subjects, who, as the Office of Legal Counsel noted, should not to be confused with European protégés.[29] Legal advisers held that since the 1869 Ottoman Nationality Law had started to diminish the numbers of Christian protégés, the Porte would not tolerate the rise of a new innovation in the form of Muslims claiming protégé status—a decision that was particularly important given the rapid spread of European protectorates. As Will Hanley has argued in his study of nationality, "the growth of European imperialism meant that the new influx of non-European foreigners, protected under the capitulation treaties, took the place of the imagined fifth column of protégés." The suspect status of the protégé was now "transposed onto the new group of colonial subjects."[30]

The Office of Legal Counsel based the 1881 decision on the idea (which gained traction when the French informally colonized Tunisia later that year) that protected states and protectorates were semisovereign. According to international law, in both Afghanistan and Bukhara, sovereignty was divided between the protecting state and the local emir. Unlike the colonies of Turkestan and India, Afghanistan and Bukhara were semisovereign states and technically "independent." As a result, individuals from these countries were only subjects of their respective emirs. According to the Office of Legal Counsel, unless they had "exceptional documents" granting them the rights of British and Russian subjects, Afghans and Bukharans in the empire were subject to Ottoman laws and jurisdiction. The legal opinion did not explain, however, what constituted an exceptional document. Given the propensity of officials to provide British passports to Afghans and Bukharans traveling via Karachi and Bombay, they likely meant another form of identification. In articulating this position, the Porte was motivated to quash the proliferation of extraterritorial rights to Muslims—particularly in parts of Syria where it was actively settling Muslim refugees and migrants (*muhacirin*). Failure to do so would only invite further foreign intervention, which was already a significant problem in Iraq and threatening to spill over into the Hijaz. Their principal concern was about preventing Muslim protégés and their consular representatives from eroding Ottoman sovereignty in strategic frontier provinces—not, as historians have suggested, primarily about Muslim loyalty to the caliphate or guarding the sultan's prerogative to patronize pilgrims.[31] Because of the very real danger of British and Russian (and French, Dutch, et al.) manipulation of the status of "protected peoples" in the empire, the Foreign Ministry did not recognize them as legitimate holders of nationality or citizenship rights of European states. And just as feelings of loyalty or jealousy did not drive state policy, neither did they direct people living in cosmopolitan settings where acquiring Russian or British nationality could mean the difference between making a living and not being able to compete with European protégés. Ottoman protection did not offer comparable privileges.

Hacı Habib, like Celal, did not get very far with his claim. The Foreign Ministry would not allow Habib to switch roles and perform as an Englishman on the Ottoman stage. But, he had prompted the articulation of a major Ottoman legal decision: Afghans and Bukharans (and later subjects of Chinese Turkestan) were prohibited from claiming rights in the Ottoman Empire that they could not enjoy at home—whether "home" was an emirate they had left prior to its annexation or an imperial protectorate or territory where the local population did not have the rights of imperial citizens. The idea that protectorates were independent—which the French employed to maintain their rule in Tunisia—served as the scaffolding for the Porte's position that Bukharans and Afghans were not entitled to the same rights as Russian and British nationals, as well as colonial subjects of Russian Turkestan and British India. While it would prove difficult to enforce, this differentiation informed Ottoman policy through World War I.

Despite the nomenclature employed by the Ottoman government, "the protected" were not so protected. First the 1869 law had categorized them as foreigners and excluded them from enjoying certain rights that had previously been customary among Sunni Muslims, and now the Porte did not recognize them as nationals of any state other than the protectorates from which they originated. Again and again, the Office of Legal Counsel would argue that subjects of protected states did not have the rights of people who were legal nationals of the imperial power originally granted capitulatory privileges. However, the protected states in question—Afghanistan, Bukhara, and Chinese Turkestan—had no power to independently conduct foreign policy or negotiate international agreements with the Ottomans.[32] And while the Office of Legal Counsel was adamant that individuals such as Habib had no rights as foreign nationals, it did not elaborate on what it meant to be a foreign Muslim "under the exclusive protection of the Ottoman caliphate" or how this argument fit into the framework of international law. Were these persons subjects of the caliph but not the sultan? If so, what did that mean when the caliphate and sultanate were invested in one person and one state and there was no dedicated Ministry of the Caliphate?

The conferral of legal nationality and protection was consistent with contemporary imperial praxis and part of a broader strategy to extend power along pilgrimage routes and exploit hajj networks and patronage for political capital and legitimacy. This was not always a cynical move, and European imperial subjects abroad (and at home, in the case of heirs to the estates of relatives who died while traveling or on the hajj) often benefited from this novel extension of patronage. Increasingly, pilgrims relied on these protections to complete what was still a long, costly, and dangerous journey.[33] But as Ottoman statesmen feared, the benevolence of the Great Powers—in the case of Central Asians, primarily Russia and Britain—was primarily strategic; mobile Muslim migrants and pilgrims constituted a promising path to project authority into Arabia, which constituted a holy landscape for their large populations of Muslim colonial subjects and a site of growing interimperial competition. From the perspective of the government in Istanbul—as well as provincial authorities in Basra, Baghdad, Damascus, and Jeddah—Russian and British attempts to establish jurisdiction looked a lot like legal imperialism. To borrow a term from Lauren Benton's work on the Atlantic world, ongoing consular support of claims to Russian and British nationality and the conferral of protection was a means of casting "shadows of sovereignty" into lands beyond the territorial borders of these expanding colonial empires.[34]

The Protection Question

The Porte communicated its position on subjects of Bukhara and Afghanistan to Russian and British consular authorities repeatedly but met with mixed results. In the case of Afghans, the British ultimately relented in 1891 "and backtracked on London's earlier position of an absolute right of protection over Afghans in Ottoman lands"—likely since they had effectively established their jurisdiction over Indian Muslims in most of the empire.[35] Perhaps hoping for similar success, Russia tried several times to formalize the basis for tsarist jurisdiction over Bukharans, beginning in 1895, when the Russian ambassador to Istanbul notified the Ottoman Foreign Ministry that the Bukharan emir had requested Russian protection from the government and that henceforth Bukharans would "enjoy the protection of Russian consuls" and "the protection assured by international law" (i.e., the Capitulations).[36] The note presented the issue as a *fait accompli* and did not provide an explanation for why the emir's purported request should entail the extension of capitulatory rights to all Bukharans in the empire. Was there a valid legal basis for the extension of the Capitulations? Had other great powers (*düvel-i muazzama*) been notified?

This sparked a lengthy Ottoman investigation (which was repeated almost verbatim in 1911) about the validity of this assertion and the vague meaning of protection. In a series of missives, the Foreign Ministry wrote to Ottoman diplomats in St. Petersburg, Paris, Berlin, London, Rome, and Vienna, asking if Russian authorities had sent them similar notifications. The responses made clear that Russia had notified only the Porte, reaffirming concerns about the dangers of budging on the question of Bukharans' rights to foreign protection. The majority of consuls noted that there were few Bukharans in these cities but suggested that the notice had more to do with undermining Ottoman sovereignty than anything else. The correspondence also made clear that the only obstacle to recognizing Russian protection was the danger of allowing Central Asian Muslims to benefit from privileges and immunities that had been awarded to Russian legal nationals. This included both non-Muslim Russian subjects (i.e., in Ottoman eyes, Europeans) and colonial subjects of Turkestan. While the Foreign Ministry did not oppose the provisioning of financial or logistical consular patronage to pilgrims and travelers in need—and was generally silent when Russian consuls paid for pilgrims' steamship tickets back home—it did not want to establish a legal precedent allowing Muslim colonial subjects to benefit from the Capitulations. Ultimately, the Foreign Ministry concluded that Bukharans were not "real subjects" (*véritable sujets*) and should not be covered by any treaties signed with Russia or any other Western powers. In fact, this was very similar to what had transpired vis-à-vis the British and Afghans, when in 1890 the Ministry of Foreign Affairs asked for a copy of the treaty between the British and the emir of Afghanistan and proceeded in 1891 to ask its consuls abroad whether other powers recognized British protection. In the British case as well, the Office of Legal Counsel found that the treaty alone did not give British consular authorities any right to extend protections to subjects of the emir in Ottoman lands.[37]

In addition to reaffirming the Office of Legal Counsel's earlier differentiation between real (i.e., colonial) subjects and mahmi, the 1895 inquiry made clear that "the question of protection of Bukharans, Afghans, and Chinese Muslims," as the file was labeled, had crystallized as a major issue in need of resolution. But, not surprisingly, a solution was not forthcoming. Russian consuls continued to push forward with their claims and, increasingly, to insist on the right to adjudicate the legal affairs of deceased Bukharans and Kashgaris. Perhaps owing to the lack of an international legal precedent or recognized agreement that gave them this authority, attempts to protect Muslims from Chinese Turkestan, in particular, were articulated in the language of Islamic law and custom. As the Ottomans invoked international legal norms to counter extraterritoriality, tsarist officials were drawing on discourses about the correct implementation of Islamic law, which was consistent with colonial legal practices, where Islamic law was reified in an intercolonial international legal jargon. The logic of the Capitulations—which was to exempt Christian European subjects from "irrational" and "uncivilized" Islamic law—was now fully subverted, as was any pretense that protection was primarily about integrating subjects in the colonies.[38]

"Speaking shari'a" to the Ottomans—in the Hijaz no less—informed a 1908 attempt by the Russian consul to establish jurisdiction over the estate of a deceased Kashgari.[39] That December, Hijaz provincial governor Mehmed Kazım Pasha wrote to Istanbul and told the Ministry of the Interior that the Russian consul had objected to his handling of the death. According to Mehmed Kazım, local authorities followed customary practices from "days of old" and absorbed the deceased pilgrim's estate into the treasury. But the Russian consul claimed that the pilgrim was under Russian protection (*taht-ı himaye*).[40] In a clear-cut yet misguided instance of invoking Islamic law, the consul berated provincial authorities for acting against shari'a and insinuated that the heirs of the deceased man included orphaned children—perhaps in an attempt to bolster his argument by emphasizing the special status of orphans in Islamic law. "It might be the case that when their father died," he wrote, "far from home and in the path of God . . . orphans back home were suffering and in need."[41]

That might very well have been the case, but Mehmed Kazım Pasha was not moved. Nor were Ottoman legal advisers, who paid no heed to the admonitions about Islamic law and focused instead on how to address the consul's latest initiative to expand the reach of his authority in the Hijaz. This was part of a much broader trend, whereby colonial powers sought to prevent the Sharifate's treasury from simply taking the inheritance of deceased pilgrims while also extending their authority vis-à-vis subjects and protégés in Ottoman lands. For more than three decades, Ottoman authorities had been dealing with similar cases involving British, Dutch, French, and Russian consuls and their subjects and were familiar with scripts about estates, indigence, and orphans.[42] In this instance, the Office of Legal Counsel quickly countered that the Russian consul had no authority to intervene in the affairs of Kashgaris (or Afghans, suggesting that this was a simultaneous development). He advised the Foreign Ministry to find another way to handle such cases in the future so as not to invite foreign intervention.[43] It is not clear what the value of the estate was or if these monies made their way from the Hijaz treasury to the central government's coffers. If they did, unclaimed funds likely offset the considerable financial burdens related to repatriating non-Ottoman subjects.[44]

What Russian consuls and authorities seem to have recognized, but that is often downplayed in histories that stress accommodation and imperial integration, is that hajj patronage was inextricably tied to the broader Anglo-Russian rivalries and competition for power that shaped tsarist policies in Qajar Iran and Xinjiang/Chinese Turkestan. As one historian of extraterritoriality notes in the context of North Africa and the Middle East, imperial competition in other places could transform the legal status of individuals far beyond particular colonial frontiers.[45] Thus, establishing the right to regulate the estates of Chinese Muslims may have been a way for Russia to forge new patron-client relationships in East Turkestan. After the conquest of Khoqand, David Brophy has shown how the tsar extended the right of protection to subjects of Russian Turkestan—as well as to subjects of the emir of Bukhara, who were active in trade—in order to further Russian economic and political interests in Qing-ruled territories. In particular, Russia's interest was the inland oasis "treaty ports" of China's northwest frontier province of Xinjiang, where there were many émigrés from Russian Turkestan. Indeed, the traveling cultures of Central Asian Sufis, ulema, soldiers, and merchants shared similarities with other prominent groups like the Hadrami diaspora. Instead of the ports of the Indian Ocean, they extended from the oases of Transoxiana and the Ferghana Valley into Altishahr, the Indian subcontinent, the Arabian Peninsula, and other Ottoman lands. In Chinese Turkestan, "Andijanlik" (Andijanis) maintained a geographical identity distinguishing them from natives—even when they dominated trade or became the local rulers. Throughout the centuries, these groups maintained their ties to Andijan, a city just beyond mountains and deserts and ruled by a different khan (and later a tsar), while shaping and becoming an inextricable part of politics, society, and the economy of Chinese Turkestan. According to Brophy, "thousands of Andijanis ... who until recently had thought of the Russians as a hostile empire and Russian merchants as rivals, suddenly found themselves subjects of the 'White King'" and sought to benefit from this status by claiming Russian nationality. This included treaties with the Qing, such as the 1881 Treaty of St. Petersburg, which provided Russian subjects with freedom of movement throughout Xinjiang and exemptions from Qing duties on the traffic and sale of their goods. As they struggled to differentiate "Russian-subject Andijanis from Qing-subject Kashgaris," Qing authorities faced problems in "policing subjecthood status that took on epidemic proportions."[46]

This broader perspective reminds us of the global dimensions of extraterritoriality: We can surmise that Russia's interest in providing protection to Qing (and later Chinese) subjects in Ottoman lands was linked to Anglo-Russian competition for influence in Xinjiang. Regulating the estates of deceased Kashgaris or offering them extraterritorial protections in the Hijaz may have been a strategy to augment Russian influence among a mobile diaspora that had desirable footholds in and strong connections across Xinjiang, India, and the Hijaz. At the same time, observing how Andijanis, Kashgaris, and Bukharans obtained Russian (or British) subjecthood in other imperial contexts reminds us that this was not a sign of conferring political or religious legitimacy on any one sovereign.

Competing Jurisdiction in the Hijaz

For the international legal advisers in the Ottoman Foreign Ministry Office of Legal Counsel, who studied, read, wrote, and opined on extraterritoriality, it must have seemed that anyone who could get a foreign passport and papers did so. In Alexandria, it was the Maltese, the Algerians, the Tunisians; in Baghdad, it was Indians and Afghans; in Ottoman cities with foreign consulates, it was seemingly everyone. Throughout the long nineteenth century, the Foreign Ministry tried to block potential protégés in myriad ways and bring an end to the dual system of justice and rights for foreign nationals that had become the Ottomans' *bête noire*. Heightened mobility and "fluid and pluralistic notions of sovereignty and nationality" escalated the reach of these problems, since people in motion—pilgrims and pious residents included—acted as conduits for extending extraterritoriality.[47] More than anywhere else in the empire, the need to stymie the expansion of the Capitulations was most pressing in the Hijaz. Although custodianship of the Haremeyn—"the jewel in the crown of the caliphate" (*gevher-i iklil-i hilafet*)—was the cornerstone of the dynasty's claims to Islamic legitimacy, Ottoman authority in the province was tenuous. On the one hand, the sultan shared power with the sharif of Mecca, continuing a system of dual sovereignty that dated to the sixteenth century. On the other hand, by the time the governor of Egypt, Mehmed Ali Pasha, put down the Wahhabi revolt of 1811–18, and the government in Istanbul was able to reestablish Ottoman power vis-à-vis the ambitious Pasha in the 1840s, the Porte was faced with new pressures. In addition to growing European involvement in hajj regulation, the Porte faced its own dilemmas in managing pilgrims' mobility. Like European powers that were hesitant to institute quotas or enforce visa regulations for fear of a backlash among their Muslim subjects, the Ottomans had to make difficult calculations about restricting mobility and the right to purchase land in the sacred cities where they were stewards.

The broader context for imperial anxiety was Britain's schemes to prop up the sharif as an alternative sovereign and to insist that the province was not exempt from the Capitulations. Despite formal pledges to guarantee Ottoman sovereignty at the end of the Crimean War (1853–56), the British worked to undermine the sultan's authority and extend the Crown's jurisdiction over Indian pilgrims and long-term residents of the city. Thus, even as the Porte continued to financially sponsor foreign Muslims who were pious residents of the Holy Cities, concern was mounting in Istanbul about how wealthy foreign Muslims might aid in the expansion of European power.[48] Ottoman statesmen in both the Hijaz and Istanbul recognized the connection between ownership of land and sovereignty as early as the 1860s and sought ways to prevent non-Ottoman Muslims from amassing greater wealth. One of the earliest fields in which the government sought to limit the rights of non-Ottomans was property holding. In 1861, the Council of Ministers in Istanbul warned the emir of Mecca and the governor of Jeddah that mücavirin should not be permitted foreign protection and that Jawi and Indian Muslims should only be allowed to settle in the cities if they agreed to abide by shari'a law. The council was explicit that long-term pious residents could not seek any form of outside protection and recommended that "in light of the requirements of international law, it would not be feasible to not recognize [their] nationality at all."[49] These concerns began to shape legislation on property holding, and in 1867, the Porte passed a law that prohibited foreigners from buying immovable property. The Law on the Rights of Foreign Citizens to Own Land (*Tebaa-yı Ecnebiyenin Emlake Mutasarrıf Olmaları Hakkında Kanun*) actually formalized the rights of foreigners to purchase real estate throughout the empire, but it made an exception for the Hijaz because of sensitivities about foreign intervention.[50]

But despite repeated directives from the Ministry of Foreign Affairs to enforce regulations on land sales to non-Ottomans in Mecca, Medina, and Jeddah, provincial authorities resisted from 1867 through the 1910s. Even if officials within the ministries of the Interior and Foreign Affairs, and in organs of state such as the Council of Ministers, feared that foreign Muslims could become "stalking horses for European political subversion and extraterritorial control," the actions of local authorities suggest that not everyone in the Hijaz was convinced of an imminent threat.[51] Where the government in Istanbul saw potential chinks in their armor against the Capitulations, local authorities and notables saw Muslims who were a feature of the religious, social, and economic life of the cities. They did not abide by blanket categorizations of Bukharans and Kashgaris—many with ties to Mecca and Medina that went back generations—or suddenly view them as foreigners.[52]

As a result of the divergence of views about their status, it was relatively easy to circumvent the law. Bukharans and Kashgaris continued to purchase and endow land with the aid of local judges and officials who allowed them to act through guarantors and Ottoman legal proxies. They also obtained the requisite Ottoman identity papers and became naturalized, often without giving up foreign nationality. The first signs of noncompliance became evident in the early 1880s, when the Porte learned that between 1877 and 1879 the governor of Medina (Medine Muhafız ve Kumandanı) had approved the sale of twenty-four houses and one mill, and Meccan officials had authorized the sale of 90 houses and 290 parcels of land to foreign Muslims.[53] An ensuing investigation made clear that shariʿa court judges and other officials who derived income from fees associated with transferring and endowing real estate were largely to blame for infractions of the law. The Council of State issued a strong statement reiterating the need for the prohibition and calling for the punishment of officials who flouted the law. But it did not order the confiscation of the illegally acquired properties. In a telling—and common—refrain, the council expressed concerns that doing so would not "suit the glory of the exalted caliphate."

Instead, the council asked for a register listing all of the properties in question and recommended further deliberation on the proper course of action.[54] There is no evidence that the properties were ever seized.

The Council of State's concerns about the caliphate amounted to an admission that maintaining the prestige of this institution could trump the law—only adding to the inconsistency of official policy on land sales. Furthermore, throughout this period, the Porte was likely turning a blind eye to foreign capital when Ottoman statesmen supported the projects in question. A transaction from this period involving no less than an adviser to Sultan Abdülhamid II sheds light on what we might describe as the normality of irregularity. Between 1876 and 1877, the Bukharan-envoy-turned-Ottoman-statesman Buharalı Şeyh Süleyman Efendi played a role in the construction of a Sufi lodge in Medina. Süleyman Efendi was the postnişin of the Bukhara Dergahı in Istanbul and a confidante of the sultan, who had recently returned from a diplomatic mission to Bukhara and served on the Muslim Refugee Commission. The shaykh had high-level contacts in Mecca and Medina and appears to have played a role in legalizing a Sufi lodge that was likely built with foreign capital. In concert with a local proxy in Medina, a Bukharan merchant named Buharizade el-hac Ali İshak Efendi (whose nationality was unclear), he built a nineteen-room structure that would provide accommodations for indigent pilgrims and dervishes from Balkh, Bukhara, Khiva, Khoqand, and Kashgar. At some point, however, the two men ran out of funds and asked Sultan Abdülhamid II to pay for the final phase of construction. The request and related correspondence repeatedly emphasized that Süleyman Efendi had purchased the land with his own money ("kendi nam ve hesabına olmak üzere," "kendi malından"), suggesting that this may not have been the case. In all likelihood, a proxy named Muhammed Zakir Bey was the actual buyer, and Süleyman Efendi was helping to legalize the sale.[55] The financing, however, was murky and may have been connected to fund-raising efforts in Russia that alarmed tsarist authorities. In 1876, a Medinan resident (described as a mücavir) was arrested in Russia for raising funds for a Sufi lodge and was also accused of being an Ottoman spy.[56]

The Porte depended on foreign philanthropic funds to finance construction of lodges and to replenish housing stock for the growing numbers of pilgrims and migrants. If Central Asians could no longer buy land or property, who was going to meet the housing needs of the thousands of people traveling from the region each year? The Hijaz Provincial Assembly posed this question in 1882 when a wealthy Kashgari, Abdurresul Efendi, expressed interest in building a philanthropic institution in Medina (most likely a Sufi lodge), where he also hoped to reside. In correspondence with Istanbul, the provincial assembly officially acknowledged the rationale for the 1867 prohibition but contended that individuals from Kashgar and "similar places" should not be regarded as foreigners. This was because they did not have relations with or subjecthood in "a foreign state," were subjects of a Muslim sovereign, and were not seeking to profit at Ottoman expense. Kashgaris were indirectly contrasted with pilgrims from Dagestan, India, and Java, whose nationality was said to be "unknown" (*meçhul*).[57] In fact, their nationalities were clear: they were colonial subjects and were also among the larger and wealthier groups of foreign Muslims in the Hijaz.

As an interim measure, the assembly proposed that Abdurresul Efendi and other Kashgaris be permitted to buy and sell land acquired within the last two years. The challenge to Istanbul authorities was based on the view that foreignness emanated from being under non-Muslim (read Christian) rule. The assembly's position suggests that even though the short-lived Emirate of Kashgar had collapsed after the death of Yaqub Beg in 1877 and subsequently been re-incorporated into the Qing Empire, the annexation may not have been considered permanent. Or, members of the assembly may have distinguished it from more direct forms of colonial rule such as in India and Algeria. As Brophy has argued, "whether in Istanbul or Kazan, Muslims looking on at the Qing did not see there an oppressive empire that could be compared to the threat that Russia or Britain posed to the Islamic world."[58] From the Ottoman perspective, there was some truth to this, since the Qing did not have diplomatic representation in the empire or capitulatory concessions. But by the 1880s, Russian consuls had started to intervene not only on behalf of Bukharans but also Muslims from Xinjiang. The Porte insisted, therefore, on at least nominal compliance. And this was what it got.

A high profile 1902 case highlights how foreign Muslims continued to buy and endow land with the assistance of local proxies. The case involved a long-term resident of the Hijaz named Mir Bedreddin bin Sadreddin, who was described as the shaykh al-Islam of Bukhara. More likely, he was of a noble Bukharan lineage of chief judges.⁵⁹ According to the Medina governor, Mir Bedreddin had purchased land in Mecca worth 4,150 lira and then endowed it for some unspecified purpose. When Istanbul authorities learned of the sale, they were concerned about how such a highly placed foreign figure was able to evade the law. According to the governor of the Hijaz, Mir Bedreddin had been given Ottoman identity papers (*tezkire-i osmaniye*) on 17 April 1901, but the Citizenship Affairs Bureau had no record of his naturalization. The Interior Ministry next inquired on what basis the shaykh had been given the said papers. This time, Hijaz authorities responded that Mir Bedreddin was a long-term pious resident and that his request for Ottoman identity papers had been approved "in the recognized way"—that is, through the provision of an oath and guarantee by an honorable community member. This was through the Bukharan pilgrimage leader Şeyh Ahmed.⁶⁰ The Hijaz governor's office also claimed it had no knowledge of Mir Bedreddin's position (which, given Şeyh Ahmed's involvement, seems unlikely) and that he had since left Mecca and died.

As the inquiry unfolded, all signs pointed to a cover-up. It seemed that Mir Bedreddin had never been naturalized and that his agents—two local Central Asians named Hoca Abdülhadi and Molla Ustan—had obtained the identity papers of another Bukharan with the same name and then used them to purchase the land. Every reported method of legalizing the sale had been unlawful. But while there was no question in Istanbul that the illegally obtained *tezkire-i osmaniye* was null and void, there was also no consensus on how to proceed, and the case went all the way to the grand vizier. The case's ultimate findings are unclear; nevertheless, it is important for showing that someone named Mir Bedreddin had attained (albeit illegally) Ottoman identity papers and become naturalized, cautiously covering all his proverbial bases to legalize the purchase. Medina authorities had not required him to renounce his foreign nationality or seen his official position in Bukhara as an impediment to buying land. The evidence suggests they were content with routine Hanafi legal provisions such as having an oath and guarantee from a prominent member of the community.

Thus, while the 1882 Council of Ministers decision has been held up as evidence of mounting suspicion of Central Asians, "the state" periodically turned a blind eye to proxies acting on behalf of Muslim foreign nationals in the Hijaz and to regular infusions of cash from abroad. For example, in roughly the same period that Istanbul launched an investigation into the Mir Bedreddin case, the emir of Bukhara, Abd al-Ahad (r. 1886–1910), established an endowment in Bukhara consisting of 128 shops and a commercial building complex (*saray*), which would fund "a large group of prayer reciters, teachers, guardians and holders of other duties in Medina."[61] Given the designated uses for the income, the funds were likely administered by the Ministry of Imperial Endowments (Evkaf-ı Hümayun Nezareti) and would not have been clandestine. In fact, between 1896 and 1913, the emir established several lodges in Mecca and Medina and was not alone in pursuing such charitable endeavors; records from the Ottoman archives show that Central Asians who had settled in the empire (both mücavirin and permanent migrants), as well as notables from Bukhara, Kashgar, and other parts of the region, were actively involved in funding new construction such as Sufi lodges for pilgrims. This casts doubt on the contention that "in the matter of charitable gifts to the holy places the sultan showed . . . jealousy"[62] and may only apply to Indian and other foreign nationals who were seen as potentially destabilizing because of the relative power and threat posed by the British in the Red Sea and Indian Ocean world.

Provincial authorities often responded to these top-down directives with indifference, foot dragging, and, sometimes, direct challenges to the idea that Central Asians—and other Sunni Muslims—were "real" foreigners. A recurring response was that Central Asians had deep roots in the Holy Cities and that they were not aligned with foreign powers who were working against the interests of the Ottoman state. These cases suggest that real estate transactions involving proxies and multiple agents were the norm. The problem was not simply a struggle between the center and Meccan or Medinan peripheries, or divergence between law in theory and law in practice—though there were elements of both at work. On a broader level, there was continual inconsistency vis-à-vis foreign Muslims, both in the implementation of laws meant to prohibit them from buying land or making large gifts and in the punishment of transgressions. Well-connected Ottoman statesmen like Süleyman Efendi worked within the power structure to facilitate projects financed by mücavirin and Muslims abroad (fig. 7). The level of threat associated with Muslim foreigners was based on factors in need of fuller study, including their economic and political power in the Hijaz, their ties to high-ranking Ottoman officials, the level of their economic integration into European trade networks and global capital, and the extent to which they sought foreign support in other parts of the empire.

In lieu of a clear legal boundary between Ottomans and non-Ottomans (that applied to all foreign Muslims equally), what emerged was a series of ad hoc arrangements with different groups of foreigners, based in part on how they had been incorporated into colonial empires and the perceived threat they posed to the Ottoman state. Since the 1870s there had been efforts to standardize practices, but the foreign ministry's position on mahmi had not helped matters much. Central Asian "protected peoples" were doubly excluded in legal terms: first designated as non-Ottomans by the state, then labeled mahmi who did not bear the rights of European nationals or protégés, including capitulatory rights. A "protected person" from Bukhara or Kabul was neither a real colonial subject nor an Ottoman. And whereas a

FIGURE 7. The Bukharan shaykh Süleyman Efendi (front row, third from left) during an Ottoman diplomatic mission to Budapest in 1877. Nadir Eserler Library, Istanbul University, 91313-53.

subject of Russian Turkestan or British India could purchase land (barring the Hijaz), these protected subjects (mahmi) were legally prohibited from acquiring immovable property throughout the empire.

Yet the Porte's position that some foreign Muslims were exclusively protected by the caliphate—with no clear explication in legal terms of what this meant—may have reinforced the notion that being a Sunni Muslim was integral to membership in the empire. Whichever way the Porte chose to classify Central Asians, many Ottoman subjects still considered them to belong to communities that transcended legal nationality.

The Dead Ends of Protection

Although many migrants quickly learned to work within the interstices of imperial mobility and nationality regulations and to live as dual nationals in Ottoman and Russian territories, these strategies were not always available to people from protectorates or empires that did not have diplomatic relations with the Ottomans. Rather than overstate the potential for negotiation in a search for subaltern agency (which implies that the parties were on equal footing), the unfolding of the Central Asian protection question impels us to recognize that these liminal subjects could not uniformly benefit from extraterritorial rights and battles over jurisdiction without recourse to various ruses. Throughout the four decades or so that the Porte was actively engaged with the question of legal nationality, it continually ran up against obstacles in defining who was or was not an Ottoman. As a consequence, for all of the individuals who achieved favorable results in the legally plural order, many faced uncertain outcomes and dead ends.[63] The stories of Celal and Hacı Habib, in particular, attest to the limits of their power to negotiate or exploit Russo- and Anglo-Ottoman legal and jurisdictional ambiguities. This limitation also applied to the men and women who could not renounce their Russian subjecthood, as well as to people whom Ottoman statesmen did not recognize as legal nationals of any empire—Russian, British, or Ottoman. The claim of being protected by the caliphate could even result in the denial of rights via Islamic law; in the 1908 dispute over the deceased Kashgari pilgrim's estate, for example, the man's legal heirs—who may or may not have included orphans—never received their share of his wealth.

Another side of the protection question was that those who wanted to become Ottomans were often prevented from doing so because European consuls would not consent or recognize their naturalization. Even when Ottoman government officials provided proof of Ottoman nationality, Russian authorities challenged the legality of their naturalization—what I term nationality conversion (*tebdil-i tabiiyet*)—and insisted on their rights to protection, even in death. Despite the assumption that the tsarist state was eager to expel its Muslim subjects—an idea shaped in large part by the mass migrations in the second half of the nineteenth century—this was far from the truth. As Eric Lohr and James H. Meyer have shown, tsarist officials required their subjects to first renounce their subjecthood in Russia before obtaining Ottoman nationality. This meant that Central Asians who decided to naturalize after arriving in the sultan's domains had to travel to distant Russian cities and file expensive paperwork in order to "legally" become Ottomans—a costly and laborious enterprise that few were likely to undertake.[64] Effectively, as Will Smiley argues in the context of Russian fugitives from war, these would-be Ottomans were unable to break free of the bonds of their Russian subjecthood—even in death—especially if they had amassed property in the Ottoman Empire.[65] A full discussion of Russia's insistence on preserving subjects falls outside the scope of this book, but the salient point is that Russian reluctance to accept Ottoman naturalization rendered the Porte increasingly cautious about allowing Central Asians to buy land and to obtain Ottoman identity papers without prior approval from Russian consular officials. Many long-term residents of Mecca and Medina, for example, could not opt out of being foreign Muslims and were left in legal limbo.

This is apparent in a 1913 incident during which the Medina governor lamented that he had been waiting for a response from the Jeddah Russian consul for more than a year about Central Asian residents who wanted to become Ottoman subjects. In an impassioned letter to Istanbul, he voiced his frustration that Russian consular officials did not recognize Ottoman naturalization procedures and explained that, as a result, local Muslims were complaining about delayed real estate deals and housing problems. Although the residents in question had tried to become naturalized through legal means, their attempts were blocked by the Porte's insistence that they furnish proof that Russia had relinquished them as subjects.[66] This seemed to contradict a 1912 Council of State decision, which "determined that in order to apply for Ottoman citizenship, foreign subjects did not have to apply for permission from their own country."[67] As in the 1882 case involving Abdurresul Efendi of Kashgar, the view from Medina was that Bukharans and other Central Asians who had resided in the empire since "days of old" should be permitted to buy land. The governor cited the practice of allowing Tunisians to do so, contingent upon their swearing oaths that they would not seek foreign protection in any future disputes and that failure to abide by these oaths would result in confiscation of their property and immediate exile.[68] But his letter suggested that even these measures were unnecessary and that resolving the matter was urgent for the local population, public improvements, and nothing less than the progress of the country.[69] Officials in the central government, however, did not agree.

Later that year, the secretary to the minister of foreign affairs communicated to the Interior Ministry that certain pilgrims and long-term residents were claiming and reverting to foreign nationality. To avoid "serious dangers," he admonished his colleagues to enact strict precautions in granting Ottoman subjecthood. The measures he prescribed, however, differed little from procedures laid out in the 1867 regulations on foreigners' property rights, the 1869 Ottoman Nationality Law, and numerous legal opinions and decrees that had been issued since the 1880s. This was, in effect, old news. It was now the Foreign Ministry that lamented its situation. Authorities held that each country should be able to determine independently who could become an Ottoman and that the state had never recognized Russian procedural requirements for naturalization. But the point was moot: tsarist consuls continued to intervene on behalf of Muslims they considered their subjects, and for more than three decades the ministry had not been able to effectively challenge their claims. With the possibility of another war with Russia on the horizon, the Council of State reiterated its concerns that allowing foreign Muslims to purchase property could cause them to act against Ottoman interests.[70]

Despite the council's insistence, however, Hijaz authorities—particularly in Medina—pushed back. They pledged to follow the decree but questioned its logic and insisted that Central Asian residents were not foreign.

"Whether they themselves or their father and grandfathers married and established families here," wrote the Medina governor, "they had become part of the people [ahali]." In earlier times, he added, these Muslims had been able to purchase land and real estate; there was "no reason" why they should be exempt from doing so now.[71] The issues of protection and nationality had become as much an intraempire issue as an international one, as local communities asserted their own understandings of belonging and what it meant to be a foreigner against those of the metropole. It was the same dynamic that informed the handling of Hacı Mirza's "estate" by local officials in Istanbul, who noted the Russian passport and then continued to treat the hajji in death as they would a Muslim local, not a Muslim foreigner. Given that the most mundane affairs could result in diplomatic interventions, the Porte was left continually vulnerable to Russian and British infringements on its sovereignty.

Despite decades of trying to defend Ottoman sovereignty by working within the system of international law,[72] the Porte met with only limited success in preventing the expansion of extraterritoriality. And even as legal nationality became increasingly important, it was by no means universally clear what this term meant. For the mücavirin waiting throughout 1913 to become Ottomans, nationality was about settling, buying land, and living a pious life in Medina. For officials at the Porte, it was a legal status tied to concerns about jurisdictional sovereignty. For people desiring to transact real estate deals or judges and provincial administrators in the Hijaz, it was not always apparent what was at issue: why were people from Bukhara, Afghanistan, and Kashgar not able to enjoy rights their forefathers had—especially if they were under the protection of the caliph? Contestation, confusion, and diplomatic struggles had resulted in a type of legal limbo in which "protected peoples" bore the burdens of colonial pressures and jurisdictional disputes. As the Central Asians in Medina waited to be naturalized, they had no national identity to use to their advantage in any legal forum and no clear sense of what it meant to be protected by the caliph. Was there a passport or a consul that would serve them? If asked where they were from, they would likely have said "Bukhara the Noble" or the "City of the Prophet," inspiring intense frustration among Ottoman legal jurists. In trying to navigate the international legal order, foreign Muslims and Ottoman statesmen alike were joined in an increasingly arduous pursuit that often led to one dead end after another.

If it was during Abdülhamid's reign that the sultan put forward claims to spiritual leadership (*riyaset-i ruhaniye*) over all Muslims irrespective of their subjecthood,[73] it was also under his rule that the central government began in earnest to differentiate among Muslims in the empire. Beyond the Tanzimat-era reforms that sought to create a firmer boundary between Ottoman subjects and foreigners, the Hamidian government marshaled the expertise of legal jurists in the Foreign Ministry Office of Legal Counsel to limit the rights of informally colonized people. While cloaked in the language of "caliphal protection," the Porte was drawing on European legal norms to limit abuses of the Capitulations that undermined Ottoman sovereignty. Not surprisingly, the Porte's answer to the protection question was riddled with problems—and generated new questions. Since the sultanate and caliphate were invested in a singular entity, what did it mean to be excluded from Ottoman nationality but under caliphal protection? Between 1880 and the First World War, the Porte returned to this question again and again. The reasons ran the gamut from a partial loss of institutional memory after the Young Turk Revolution to intransigence from Russian and British consuls. Another major problem was the lack of consensus within Ottoman society about what it meant to be an Ottoman and a foreigner. Were foreign Muslims truly foreign? Should hajjis in the empire be treated like other ecnebi?

The Porte was in a tenuous position because of its pursuit of two incongruous objectives: seeking legitimacy through the caliphate—an institution that in theory did not recognize divisions among the umma—and limiting the rights of Muslims whose legal actions threatened Ottoman sovereignty. As we have seen, the tensions inherent in these endeavors limited both the government's and foreign Muslims' range of action and threatened to compromise the glory of the caliphate. The central government often was unable to fully implement reforms, and Central Asians who were denied both Ottoman and European legal nationality faced a narrowing of choices. Those who wanted to enjoy the rights of Ottomans (such as landholding) had to officially renounce their foreign nationality and become Ottoman subjects. Yet, given the reluctance of foreign powers such as Russia to relinquish subjects, attempts at Ottoman naturalization could result in a protracted state of liminality that paralleled the pilgrimage but was a product of larger geopolitical struggles.

At the same time, a point worth underscoring is that nationality was not a sign of political loyalty or allegiance: migrants often maintained their Russian nationality for as long as they could because it offered comparative advantages. The Andijani merchant in Chinese Turkestan who acquired or kept Russian nationality was operating under the same logic as a compatriot in Arabia. Likewise, imperial Russia's conferral of extraterritoriality and protection to Bukharans and Kashgaris in Xinjiang was informed by similar strategic objectives. Yet it is primarily in the context of Ottoman and Russian historiographical debates that such legal strategies are read through the prism of religious patronage or of allegiance to a sovereign, whether sultan or tsar. This is partially due to the interconnections of hajj and migration, but it is also related to directions in scholarship that seek to reinterpret European powers' relationships with their Muslim subjects. Even a brief examination of similar dynamics in the imperial frontier zones of China reminds us that many of the Central Asians traveling to Ottoman lands were part of an extraterritorial world that extended across East, Central, and Western Asia, and in which practices such as affiliation switching had become widespread. Likewise, Ottoman efforts to defend their jurisdiction over this contested population were not driven by a unique interest in Kashgaris (or Afghans, or Bukharans) per se—or their heirs abroad—but by the imperative of maintaining their sovereignty when and where possible. But as we will see in the next chapter, the Foreign Ministry's assertion of caliphal protection raised new questions about the empire's responsibilities toward mahmi, particularly in the arena of petitioning and patronage, and that were left to ministries charged with "domestic" politics to figure out.

{ CHAPTER 4 }

PETITIONING THE SULTAN

FOR THE GOVERNMENT OFFICIALS at work in the Istanbul Municipality (Şehremaneti) and the Ministry of the Interior, the hajj had no season, no beginning, no end. Part of the job of managing the affairs of the city—and of the empire at large—involved regulating the affairs of hajjis year-round. When Haşim and Muhammed, two Bukharans residing in one of Istanbul's Uzbek lodges, were down on their luck, they sent a petition in December of 1905 asking for help from the Ottoman government; their petition was forwarded to the Municipality.[1] When a Russian vessel carrying passengers suspected of having cholera was headed to Istanbul in 1907, the Ministries of the Interior and Police worked with municipal officials to quarantine the ship in a Black Sea cordon on the approach to the city. For months thereafter, they had to deal with problems related to pilgrims who did not make it to Mecca in time, some of whom wanted to wait in Istanbul until they could go on hajj the following year.[2] When husband and wife Berat Hacı and Niyazi Bibi were robbed by Bedouin in 1910, they petitioned the grand vizier and asked to be repatriated to their native Kashgar. Although they had made it as far as the capital, they were living a wretched life in "the corners of inns" and asked for the state's mercy.[3]

Government officials worked assiduously to get Haşim and Muhammed a monthly stipend and to send Niyazi Bibi and Berat Hacı back to Kashgar, even though they were not Ottoman subjects. Everyone from scholars and dervishes seeking patronage for their pious endeavors and pilgrims who needed to replace their passports, to women abandoned by husbands who would not provide for them, seemed to be asking the Ottoman government for material support. In part, these were demands on the sultan in his role as caliph, but they extended far beyond what the sultan was charged with as Custodian of the Haremeyn. The preponderance of petitions from those whom the Porte had designated as mahmi—particularly subjects of Qing and Republican China—suggested that there was more to the dynamics of petitioning than traditional forms of Islamic hajj patronage. While both petitioners and their patrons employed the language of Islamic benevolence and charity, pilgrims also drew on new tropes and harnessed the rhetoric of protection to make demands on the sultan-caliph. The Ottoman central government in turn recognized its expanded duties toward these groups and realized that in articulating its "caliphal protection," it had become responsible for sponsoring indigent people whose presence—particularly in the imperial capital—invited foreign intervention and posed challenges to maintaining imperial order. If the cost of providing this material support was high, the cost of not responding would be higher: in addition to compromising the prestige of the Ottoman caliphate, it would exacerbate threats to public health and order that were of great concern throughout the Hamidian and Young Turk eras.

By approaching petitioning and Ottoman patronage in the context of extraterritoriality, this chapter explores how the Foreign Ministry Office of Legal Counsel's articulation of "spiritual authority" led Bukharans and Kashgaris to turn to the proverbial door of the state and call on it to realize its assertion of being their protector. I argue that the state was compelled to provide for these Muslims because it had entered into an implicit contract. Although the petitioners were not subjects of the sultan in the sense of Ottoman nationals (and had been classified as foreigners), they were nonetheless subjects of the caliph (*kul*). And, in the case of mahmi, they had become a new kind of caliphal subject. If the Ottoman state was going to deny them the rights of both Ottoman and European nationals—and then assert its jurisdiction over their affairs—Central Asian protected persons would respond by engaging with the state on its terms. The chapter also considers how patronage reinforced the government's claims to being a protector and leader over people who were excluded from the polity as subjects. Petitioning the sultan-caliph reified the relationship between sultan and mahmi and contributed to the making of spiritual subjecthood through a mechanism we might understand in terms of legal posturing—that is, practices by which people referenced procedures and precedents to obtain certain legal ends and by which they strengthened specious or loose relations between subjects and sovereigns.[4] The idea of being a spiritual leader or sovereign was then realized (not always willingly) through the provision of material support to people who were not legal Ottoman nationals but who were protected by the caliphate.

Petitioning Outside the State-Subject Model

Historians have defined petitions as demands or requests for a favor or the redress of an injustice in the form of a written letter to an established authority. The granting of favors and distribution of justice were important elements of the ruler's relationship with his or her subjects, particularly in states where rights emanated from the sovereign rather than from participatory government. People turned to the sovereign for a number of reasons: to complain about abuses by officials, to settle private disputes, and to request various kinds of assistance. Petitions could also serve as authoritative documents that strengthened legal cases—for example, part of a barrage of documents meant to impress and even intimidate in sharia courts. In this sense, they had a performative dimension and could convey the impression that a litigant possessed the requisite legal knowledge and resources to win a case.[5] As sources for social and political history, petitions provide insight into visions of justice and morality and how people understood state power and sought to use it for their own ends. Guided by what supplicants and their intermediaries hoped would be winning strategies, petitions are by their nature dialogic and can be read as sites of encounter and negotiation between a sovereign and his or her subjects. Though often mediated by a petition-writer (*arzuhalci*) (fig. 8), the sheer repetition of certain phrases sheds light on both mundane social problems and larger political issues, even if this can sometimes prove to be problematic for historians seeking to reconstruct "authentic voices."[6]

Intermediaries notwithstanding, there are two main actors in the arzuhal: the sultan (and his government) and the subject (*kul*) or servant (*bende*). The kul is the main agent and uses the medium to initiate a request for sultanic intervention. He or she begins by addressing the sultan with formulaic

FIGURE 8. Ottoman petitioners and petition-writer (*arzuhalci*). Undated, but believed to be early 1900s.

honorifics, such as *şahenşah-i alem* (king of kings of the world) and the *alempenah* (refuge of the universe). The implication is that this majestic, benevolent, and just ruler has great responsibility and is charged with, among other things, providing alms (*sadaka*), assistance (*iane*), respect (*hürmet*), kindness (*şefkat*), and mercy (*merhamet*) to his subjects—irrespective of their provenance.[7] On the page and in the text, both the sovereign and the subject's roles are largely preordained. Consonant with the idea of the Ottoman circle of justice, the subject prostrates him- or herself as a member of the sultan's flock whose responsibilities include working the land, paying taxes, serving in the army, and praying for state and sovereign. In return, the sultan is charged with maintaining order and prosperity, dispensing justice, and helping the supplicant overcome hardship. The appeals end with pro forma language repeating the sultan's right to rule as he sees fit and the implication that his ruling will be—should be—equitable. There are often hints by the petitioner that failure to act justly will threaten the implicit social and political contract keeping the Ottoman dynasty in power. We might read these subtle threats as pointing to the presence of a third actor beyond the bounds of the page. In the context of petitioners from foreign Muslims, for example, the agents of the request often intimated either that the sultan's failure to right a particular wrong would broadcast his lack of power to observers or, conversely, that his benevolence would be shared with coreligionists as evidence of Ottoman might.

Indeed, petitioning was not the preserve of Ottomans and was common among foreign Muslims throughout the life of the empire. Like Ottoman subjects, Central Asian supplicants used similar language and presented themselves as the sultan's kul. They long enjoyed state support of their sojourns through the empire, most of which were organized around religious pursuits. As Nurten Kılıç-Schubel writes in her study of the Kubravi shaykh Kamal al-din Husayn Khwarazmi (d. 1551), many Central Asian pilgrims took the northwestern route through Istanbul to Mecca because of the "extraordinary protection and care accorded [them], particularly the scholars and shaykhs among them, by the Ottomans."[8] These pilgrims—which in Khwarazmi's case included a retinue of approximately three hundred people—were granted favor in the imperial court and hosted by dignitaries within the government, before continuing their travels to Mecca. Sultans of the early modern period directed officials to assist them along the way, provided decrees of passage (*yol emri*), and furnished monetary provisions to cover their trips. Such practices continued into the nineteenth century, and the state provided stipends and gifts to visiting diplomatic and political envoys who often traveled to Istanbul for work and continued to Mecca and Medina before returning to khanates and emirates in Transoxiana, the Ferghana Valley, and Kashgar. In what was a typical example from the first half of the nineteenth century, in 1848, the Porte awarded the Khoqandi prince (*hanzade*) Sadık Bey and the khan's sword-bearer (*silahdar*) with an imperial gift of two thousand kuruş to complete the hajj.

The tradition of Ottoman patronage also extended to people outside these elite circles to include ulema, dervishes, students, and scholars. Bukharans, Khoqandis, and Kashgaris came to the empire with their own petitioning traditions and combined this with local knowledge to tailor their appeals to the Ottoman state.[9] In one of the more straightforward examples of this tradition, two dervishes named İsâ and Mulla Kul petitioned the sultan in 1842. As they made their way across the empire, the two men asked the sultan to direct the customs controller (Emtia Gümrüği Emini Beğ Efendi) to provide them with transportation to the Hijaz on a customs ship departing from Alexandria. Upon receipt in the palace, Sultan Abdülmecid complied with their request. He scrawled two and a half lines at the top of the petition and instructed the customs controller to provide passage aboard a ship leaving for the Egyptian port city.[10] Similarly, in May of 1843, two Bukharans named Ahmed and Musa petitioned the grand vizier for transport on a vessel leaving Alexandria and requested the allocation of alms from what they termed "the Muslim treasury." The petitioners wrote:

> my Sultan,
>
> My illustrious, gracious, merciful master,   may His Excellency be blessed
>
> The petition of your *kul*, poor [members] of the Bukharan Naqshbandiyya who long to see the *beytülşerif* (Kaaba), but lack the strength and power [to do so], are for alms (*sadaka*) from the Muslim imperial treasury (*beytülmal-ı müslimin*) to be given to your poor subjects, and for an imperial decree to be sent to the Customs Controller directing him to arrange our passage by sea on a vessel and the payment of our expenses.[11]

While it is not clear if the grand vizier arranged for the payment of alms, with the approval of Sultan Abdülmecid, he directed the customs controller to transport the men to the Hijaz. As in the case of the two dervishes from 1842, the brevity of both the petition and the state response indicated that there was nothing unusual about the request, including the idea that Bukharans conceived of the Ottoman treasury as the "Muslim treasury."

As in the modern era, many of the people seeking aid from the Ottomans were travelers who blurred the lines between pilgrimage and migration. The Bukharan Naqshbandi shaykh Ahmed, for example, wrote to Sultan Abdülmecid in 1851 and described himself as a poor alim with a household of ten women and children. The family was living in the Yeni Camii mosque complex. With winter on the horizon, he asked the sultan for royal charity (*sadaka-yı mülûkane*)—specifically, for six months of salary and housing in Istanbul, ostensibly until they could continue their travels to Mecca.[12] Judging by the shaykh's handwriting and word choices (for example, he used the Turki verb *bormoq* instead of the Ottoman *varmak* for "to reach [a place]"), he had clearly penned the letter himself. The petition made its way through the government, and the minister of police was directed by an imperial council of judicial ordinances (Meclis-i Vala) to corroborate the shaykh's claims. This entailed contacting the Buhara Dergahı, where the head of the lodge confirmed that the family was in need and deserving of imperial benevolence (*şayan-ı atıfet-i seniye*).[13] After receiving this information, the council approved a two-month allowance of eighteen hundred kuruş and gave instructions for the provision of lodging in Istanbul and, later, for their passage to Alexandria.[14]

The flowery Persian and Chaghatay prose of ulema and the occasional requests of dervishes for free or reduced passage on Ottoman vessels was giving way in the second half of the nineteenth century to hundreds of petitions from a much wider demographic that expressed entitlement to Ottoman aid. A September 1912 petition from two Kashgari natives is fairly typical. In a joint appeal to the grand vizier, Seyyid Naci bin Hacı Kasım and Gaffar Hacı bin Baki asked for free passage to Jeddah. They explained that after reaching Istanbul, they had checked into the Fincancı Inn in the old city and that while they were out inquiring about the departure time of their ship, the inn burned down in one of the city's frequent fires. According to the men, "It was impossible to rescue anything, everything was completely burned and when we returned, we found the inn in ashes."[15] They also stated that while they had originally had enough money to make their journey, they had converted some of their cash into goods that were destroyed by the fire. They were indeed luckier than their fellow countrymen Hacı Mahmud, Hacı Haşim, and Hacı Yusuf, who had petitioned the grand vizier five days earlier after losing their cash, passports, and possessions, and barely escaping with their lives in the same conflagration.[16] After all the obstacles and suffering they had experienced during their three-month journey to Istanbul, Naci and Gaffar were reluctant to go home without first performing the hajj. They asked for free passage to Jeddah from "their" Islamic Ottoman government (*hükumet-i islamiye-yi osmaniyemiz*). The appeal was successful: the Ministry of Religious Endowments helped them get new passports and funded the rest of their journey.[17]

While Bukharans and Naqshbandi adepts would continue to possess a form of cultural capital, the language and strategies for crafting an effective petition would change. First, beginning in the Hamidian period (and continuing after the Young Turk Revolution), petitioners began to draw on pan-Islamic rhetoric of the state. Second, they began to address the imperial government's concerns about public health and order, as well as its preoccupations with its image. Third, petitioners alluded to the state's responsibilities toward mahmi given the sultan-caliph's self-declared role as their protector. More than just the "refuge of Muslims," the sultan was often described as a "protector" (*hami*). These shifts were accompanied by a marked change in state discourse: Ottoman statesmen increasingly described supplicants as deserving of charity, mercy, and benevolence and indicated that their presence in the city constituted a problem. This was in contrast to poor but educated men of religion who merited the sultan's respect and reverence. In concert with the protection question that occupied the Foreign Ministry, Ottoman statesmen in the Interior Ministry and Istanbul Municipality were occupied with the question of how to manage and meet their demands and needs— and move them through the capital.

Patronage and Order

As I pointed out in the opening of this chapter, it is important to keep in mind just how present the hajj was in the day-to-day affairs of administration, particularly in Istanbul; pilgrimage was not an event happening in a distant province or something limited to a season but an open-ended form of migration that continually brought people into the city. Hajjis traveling to and from Mecca and Medina were everywhere—in the capital's streets, guesthouses, mosque complexes, and lodges—and when they had problems, their problems became the state's problems. Thus, when individuals like Seyyid Naci and Gaffar Hacı turned to the government for help after losing all their money and possessions, the governmental response was not one defined exclusively by "the hajj." The Porte knew that if they were not able to find accommodation in a tekke or another guesthouse, these poor travelers would likely end up on the streets of Istanbul. And if they did not find the funds to continue to Mecca, they would haunt the city streets indefinitely.

In this sense, the Ottoman central government's responses to pilgrims—and patronage—became connected to domestic reforms. Just as nineteenth-century measures to regulate mobility shaped record-keeping practices at Sufi lodges, modernizing reforms aimed at more effective policing of major cities like Istanbul affected the experiences of the urban poor, Ottoman and non-Ottoman alike. From the 1860s onward, reform-minded Ottoman statesmen sought to promote public order and peace (*asayiş*) and public security and safety (*emniyet*) through various measures that targeted vulnerable populations. As Nazan Maksudyan elaborates in her work on orphans and destitute children, "the beautification and sterilization of urban centers" were hallmarks of Tanzimat ideals of progress and civilization. To achieve new metrics of order, the central government undertook major reforms in the affairs of children, the poor, and migrants, which were aimed at simultaneously removing the groups in question from public space and "reforming" them (*ıslah*) by making them "into skilled and productive laborers."[18] Orphanages were but one example of institutions that sought both to train children in certain fields and to discipline productive Ottoman subjects. Vagrants and beggars were another target, and in 1890, the central government instituted a new law, the Regulations on the Prohibition of Begging (*Tese'ülün Men'ine Dair Nizamname*), that distinguished between legal and illegal beggars, with the criterion for illegality being based on ability to work.[19] Although the law did not equate beggars and vagrants, the former were increasingly seen as a sign of a social ill. Whereas begging had historically been considered a profession, complete with its own guild and laws of conduct, the regulation essentially criminalized urban poverty and framed it as something to be eradicated in the name of progress. The law was not enforced until the opening of the Darülaceze on 31 January 1896.[20] This "house of the poor," however, was only for those who could not work. Many internal male migrants who resorted to panhandling were considered able-bodied but unwilling to engage in productive labor and defined as a threat to public morality and safety. Migrants from outside the city were to be sent back to their places of origin rather than to the new institutions for Istanbul's indigent.[21]

Part of the impetus for these measures was the aftermath of the 1877–78 Russo-Ottoman War and the influx of refugees into Istanbul, whom "urban professional elites [regarded] as the chief source of crime and pauperism in the cities."[22] People who were not yet integrated into the social fabric of the empire presented problems for effective policing, particularly for a state that had declared bankruptcy and was dealing not only with extensive migration from Russia but also with internal migration to the capital from economically depressed parts of the empire.[23] A common theme in the late nineteenth-century press and in government sources, for example, was how the ugly sight of refugees and beggars on the Galata Bridge—a thoroughfare that connected the mosques and markets of the old city to the European quarter of Pera—was detrimental to the empire's image and pointed to signs of moral degeneration.

Central Asian pilgrims were certainly not vagrants but, from the perspective of reform-minded Ottoman statesmen and bureaucrats, they posed various obstacles to ordering society: on the one hand, they were foreign nationals who could not simply be removed from public space like Ottoman subjects (when the Ottomans tried, they often faced Russian and British consular challenges); on the other hand, their exposure to contagious diseases made them a potentially dangerous population that could wreak havoc on dense population centers like Istanbul. By 1866, when the first international sanitary commission was formed, pilgrims' bodies had already started to become sites of regulation, surveillance, and biomedical controls. Among the European powers involved in hajj regulation, institutional and discursive processes combined to attach stigma to pilgrims and to "pauperize" them as conduits of backwardness and disease.[24] Although Ottoman elites had to a marked degree internalized orientalist discourse in many fields, the state's assumption of custodianship of the hajj prevented it from attaching the same level of stigma to a religious practice recognized as a duty incumbent on Muslims of sound body and mind.[25] But even as they recognized the sanctity of hajj, state officials often referred to poor pilgrims in paternalistic language that emphasized their indigence and helplessness. This was no doubt influenced by petitioners' use of phrases to emphasize their poverty (*fakir ü sefil*, *fakir ü garib*, *perişan*, *biçare*) vis-à-vis the paternal figure of the sultan.

In response to the spike in pilgrims traveling via the Black Sea, which picked up annually as imperial Russia's investment in rail and steamer lines intensified in the 1900s,[26] the Porte began to impose restrictions on passengers who wanted to disembark in Istanbul. It did this not only as a result of concerns about disease but also as an attempt to prevent disorder. While this book is not focused on quarantine, a brief foray into how it touched on Istanbul in 1907 will enable us to better understand, first, challenges for the Ottoman state that stemmed from being at the crossroads of Russian-sponsored hajj routes and, second, the ways that the regulation of disease became inextricably connected to concerns about maintaining order within the capital.

That year, cholera epidemics in Russia prompted the Porte to issue a special decree to quarantine multiple Russian vessels in the Ottoman Black Sea port of Sinop, where ships and pilgrims would be disinfected and wait five days before sailing through the Straits and directly to Jeddah.[27] When a major outbreak of cholera occurred at Sinop, however, a temporary sanitary council (*sıhhıye meclisi*) was tasked with rerouting vessels to other quarantine stations and facilitating the transportation of Russian Muslims from Odessa. The commission comprised members from the Ministries of the Interior, Health, and Police, as well as the Muslim Refugee Commission.[28] In response to wider concerns about public order, it issued direct orders that no pilgrims should be allowed to go to Istanbul. They were to be kept under police surveillance and sent directly to Jeddah after clearing quarantine,[29] without mixing or interacting with residents of Dersaadet, "the gate of felicity." But while the passengers were supposed to remain at Anadolukavağı—a sleepy village on the Asian shores of the Bosphorus—for no longer than five days, communications between the various agencies about finances delayed their processing. Like many other passengers held up in quarantine stations that dotted the approach from the Black Sea, they would be stuck in what must have felt like the middle of nowhere.

While the Ministries of Health and the Interior were supposed to cover the expenditures for quarantine, neither had allocated sufficient funds for this in their annual budgets. As a result, the quarantine station staff sent telegram after telegram to the Ministry of the Interior, warning that the window for making it in time for that year's rites was drawing to a close.[30] On 9 December 1907 (3 Zilkade 1325), officials at Anadolukavağı telegraphed the Interior Ministry asking for permission to arrange immediate transport for the pilgrims to Jeddah. One day later, they telegraphed again, stating that they had not yet received an answer. "We have been so bold as to again ask for the necessary measures to be taken," the note stated, "since pilgrims are complaining." The next day, the Interior Ministry wrote to the offices of the grand vizier, communicating pilgrims' discontent and the urgency of making immediate arrangements for their transport. Finally, by 18 December, authorities at Anadolukavağı reported that they had dealt with the last of the pilgrims. Most of them had been there much longer than five days, not because of disease but disorganization.

The cordon established that winter extended along the straits connecting the Black and "White" Seas (the Ottoman for Mediterranean) on the approach to Istanbul. In addition to Anadolukavağı, similar scenarios were playing out at the Kavak quarantine station, another small village on the Bosphorus where pilgrims would be trapped amid great beauty—stuck between the seas that they hoped would take them to Mecca. On 7 January 1908, the Istanbul Municipality wrote to the Interior Ministry about a family that had been quarantined there, after arriving on the Russian vessel *Lazarev*. It was already the third of Dhu al-hijjah, and fewer than five days remained until the start of the hajj (which started on the eighth day of the month). Passengers delayed in Istanbul would not make it in time and would likely be sent back home. Among those who remained at Kavak, a man named Hacı Said Efendi asked the government to grant him and his family (his wife and two children) permission to wait out the year in Istanbul. Hacı Said specified that he would stay with Tesbihci Mahmud Efendi, a prayer bead (*tesbih*) producer or seller, in the Uzunçarşı neighborhood. The family waited twenty days while the Interior Ministry deliberated. Ultimately they were given permission to go to Istanbul on the condition that a medical examination indicated that they were all in good health. A photo from the 1870s of quarantine captures the heaviness that sepia tones seem particularly adept at reflecting (fig. 9). It is the melancholy of a place where people wait in limbo, their plans for spiritual transformation tested and sometimes thwarted by cholera epidemics and the institutions designed to prevent their spread. Hacı Said Efendi and his family would experience this as they looked out at a similar vista on the Bosphorus for nearly a month, uncertain about their next steps, even as it became increasingly clear that they would not make it to Mecca in time for the hajj.

In 1907, the central government collaborated with Russian authorities in another case that highlights the experiences of uncertainty pilgrims faced. In this instance, the Porte was trying to transport four hundred people from Dagestan and Bukhara who were stranded in the Red Sea port of Yenbu. "A large number of hajjis arrived from Medina the Illuminated to Yenbu," the Hijaz governor wrote in March of 1907. "But because there are not enough ships, there is exceptional crowding in the country." The governor implored Ottoman officials to reach out to the Russian consulate in Jeddah to aid in

FIGURE 9. Quarantine station at Anadolukavağı, Istanbul, c. 1870s.

their transport.³¹ In November of the same year—more than seven months later—Ottoman statesmen in the capital were still making arrangements for these pilgrims to complete the journey home.³²

The management of these incidents laid bare the extent of governmental anxieties about hajj traffic from Russia. The continual influx of foreign Muslims en route to and from Mecca fed into a larger problem of potential threats to order and complicated the management of mobility since the people in question could not be policed like Ottomans. Russia's investment in the Black Sea routes coincided with—and undermined—major reforms that sought to control public space and to increase Ottoman subjects' productivity. The problem would become more pronounced after the Young Turk Revolution, when, as the work of Nadir Özbek has shown, the government endeavored to separate the provision of social welfare from the person of the monarch and to present such services as part of the responsibility of a modern state. In May of 1909, the government had taken a harder line toward begging and passed legislation on vagrants and "suspect individuals" (*serseri ve şüpheli eşhas*). The definition of what constituted begging was not only broadened, but for the first time in Ottoman history, begging among the able-bodied was directly equated with vagrancy and defined as a potential criminal act. According to the 1909 law, vagrants would be sent to their homelands or a suitable location on their first arrest and imprisoned for a second offense. Almost immediately after the passage of this legislation, the Directorate of Public Security began sending vagrants to the port cities of Izmir, Thessaloniki, and Beirut, as well as a number of destinations in Anatolia. These newly criminalized men were put to work, with the idea that it would redeem them as productive members of society.³³ The Unionist government "attempted to redefine social welfare by shifting the emphasis from the 'overpersonalized' monarchical forms to 'public assistance' which was believed to hold 'bureaucratic,' 'modern,' and 'secular connotations.'"³⁴ One step in this direction was the creation of a new Administration of Public Assistance (Müessesat-ı Hayriye-i Sıhhıye İdaresi). In 1910, a new law "rearranged the customary 'poor relief payments' of the central state [*muhtacin maaşı*] on a more bureaucratic, allegedly more efficient system."³⁵ Previously, these payments had been distributed as gifts from the sultan to the poor and needy. The government also issued new laws abolishing traditional forms of poor relief that were financed by religious foundations.

My point is not that pilgrims were regarded en masse as derelicts and vagrants but that the government was increasingly preoccupied with controlling internal migration and keeping undesirable people out of Istanbul and other major cities. And many pilgrims fell into this category. Not only could the Porte *not* regulate the numbers of people traveling annually on the hajj (as in the modern Saudi quota system), but for all the reasons we saw in the last chapter, it also could not "redeem," relocate, or transfer foreign nationals using the methods it employed vis-à-vis its own subjects. Although the Ottomans had limited control over the hajj routes or the number of foreign nationals traveling through the empire, they could help move pilgrims out of urban centers like Istanbul by responding favorably to their requests for repatriation. Providing assistance to indigent pilgrims—whether helping them continue on the road to Mecca or to make the journey home—was another way to remove them from public space. In this sense, repatriation was similar in some ways to deportation, which foreign consulates and imperial powers used regularly to remove potentially problematic subjects. In a March 1910 Council of Ministers fiscal allocation to fund the "transfer" of six hundred Ottomans, Afghans, and Moroccans who had just completed the hajj, it was telling that the government used the term *sevk*—a word often used in the context of undesirable Ottoman populations.[36]

An Ottoman Burden

If colonial powers associated pilgrims traveling abroad with issues related to sanitation and security such as cholera and pan-Islamism, by the early twentieth century, Ottoman anxieties about foreign pilgrims traveling through the sultan's domains were driven by a mixture of fears of disease, disorder, and challenges to sovereignty. As I demonstrated in the previous chapter, it was the latter that drove the Office of Legal Counsel to formulate its position on the status of mahmi in the empire. The assertion of caliphal protection had far-reaching implications for the state's obligations toward Bukharans and Chinese Muslims. By denying their right to foreign nationality, the Porte assumed responsibility for protections that pilgrims could otherwise receive from consular representatives. The enunciation of "caliphal protection" was truly a double-edged sword, since there was no way to limit *only* the expansion of the Capitulations. Combined with the domestic pressures to remove itinerant people from public space, this position essentially forced the government's hand in responding favorably to appeals from people it claimed to protect under the auspices of the caliphate. The asymmetry of the situation derived from the fact that, unlike Ottomans, the caliph's spiritual subjects did not pay taxes and were not subject to conscription. If they promoted the pan-Islamic power and authority of the sultan-caliph, this would only compound the problems the Porte faced: what Ottoman bureaucrats and statesmen wanted was fewer, not more, pilgrims.

The multiple reasons driving Ottoman patronage—including a real sense of Islamic duty toward pilgrims in need—all come together in a rich file of petitions and related government correspondence from the early 1910s. In late April of 1911, more than a full four months after completing the hajj, a group of down-on-their-luck travelers wrote to the Interior Ministry. "To the exalted, illustrious Ministry of the Interior," they began,

> It is the request of your humble servants
>
> Your subjects [*kul*], are people of Chinese Turkestan. Last year we left our country [*memleket*] and went directly to see the holy Kaaba. As we began to make the journey to our memleket, we arrived by ship the other day in Istanbul. We are five individuals from the same town . . . but among us Hacı Ruzi bin Hüdaberdi has 60 kuruş, and Hacı Ömer bin Tohta has 125, Hacı Muhammed bin Hüdaberdi has 108 kuruş, Hacı Emin bin Islam has 40 kuruş, and Hacı İsa ibn Salih doesn't have 10 paras to his name. Altogether, the five of us have only 335 kuruş. It's clear that the five of us are in need of a considerable amount of funds to go home. We, your subjects, had a considerable amount of money when we set out, but it was not enough and we have since fallen into despair. We request from the state that you send your hajji subjects back to our country, or to Andijan, which is a forty-day journey overland to our village in Khotan. Along with the inhabitants of our village we will always, and until the end of our days, pray for the constitutional government and for the health of the padişah of the *millet* if you could at least send us poor hajjis as far as Andijan. And to command belongs unto him to whom all commanding belongs.

Your five hajji servants, who have fallen into poverty, from the people of Turkestan and China

Hacı İsa ibn Salih, Hacı Emin ibn İsa, Hacı Muhammed ibn Hüdaberdi, Hacı Ömer ibn Hüdaberdi, Hacı Ruzi ibn Hüdaberdi[37]

Their appeal was typical of the dozens the ministry received between 1910 and 1912, as well as the years before and through the First World War. The supplicants described how they had been robbed by bandits and Bedouin and tricked by hustlers, ticket agents, and brokers who profited at the expense of foreigners. Still others had the misfortune to alight at inns that fell victim to Istanbul's frequent fires, losing all their belongings and passports. Sometimes the petitioners didn't specify how they had come to be destitute but simply described themselves as such. What was important was that they positioned themselves as the sultan-caliph's subjects, indicating engagement with the Porte's claims to be their protectors. But the lack of a dedicated ministry of the caliphate meant that their requests were directed to central government offices such as the Interior Ministry.

If we begin with the first governmental source related to petitions such as Hacı İsa's, we find a draft of a letter from the Ministry of the Interior to the navy. It begins by summarizing that each year, pilgrims from distant lands such as Russia and Bukhara arrive in Istanbul and pass the night in the courtyards of mosques and inns. To provide them with "protection" (*himayet*), the Ministry of the Interior explained that it planned to appropriate a structure that could accommodate three hundred people. The structure in question was a school building in Ahurkapi owned by the navy. In the meantime, as an emergency measure, pilgrims were being housed in tents outside the city center.[38] In the margins of the draft, someone at the ministry added that these provisions were necessary, not only for the "protection" of the pilgrims but also for the protection of the state: a key phrase that was incorporated into the final draft was that the matter "concerned the country's health and general welfare." Many of the pilgrims had been exposed to cholera, and their deplorable living conditions were conducive to its spread. They therefore needed to be prevented from interacting with the Ottoman population.[39]

When the navy responded that the military building was unavailable, the hunt for suitable accommodations continued: on 2 September 1910, the Interior Ministry drafted another letter to the Istanbul Municipality explaining the situation. Once again a note was added to the margins, stating that "the aforementioned pilgrims could not as in the past be allowed to sleep in the courtyards of mosques and inns . . . because this was not in accord with the laws of protecting public health or sanitation (*kavaid-i hıfzu'l-sıhhıye*) and that their continued residency in such places was not permissible "from the perspective of the country's current state of public health."[40] The pilgrims were referred to as "foreign hajjis," and the ministry indicated that the police were tracking their whereabouts and numbers.[41]

As the Ministry of the Interior was trying to find a location to house the pilgrims, it continued to receive petition after petition. Hacı İdris of China claimed that Bedouin stole all his money while he was traveling from Mecca to Istanbul,[42] and Hacı Halime had lost not only all her money but also her husband (he had been murdered by Bedouin).[43] They and many like them asked for the caliph to help them travel to Odessa, from where they would continue to their cities of residence. Upon receiving their requests, the Porte forwarded them to the Istanbul Municipality. But there seemed to be no end. On 23 April 1911, the municipality explained to the Interior Ministry that it simply did not have funds budgeted for such expenses.[44] While it was clear that they would continue to receive such petitions, they couldn't continue to allocate money "out of nowhere." The municipality forwarded four more supplications, leading to extensive correspondence between the Interior Ministry, Office of the Grand Vizier, Ministry of Pious Endowments, and Police—making clear that this was a problem of domestic governance and public security. Someone at one point tried to arrange for the Chinese Muslims to board a ship from the Baltic that was sailing to China, again suggesting a deep unfamiliarity with the geographies in question.[45]

Eventually, the matter went to the Council of Ministers, which appropriated money from a fund for "unexpected expenditures" to cover petitioners' travel to the Black Sea port city of Odessa and then to Andijan via the Trans-Caspian Railway. From this city in the Ferghana Valley, the Chinese Muslims could travel "with ease" the rest of the way. The Porte would arrange their steamship and rail fare and arrange passports for those who needed them. It would also provide pilgrims with bread and pocket money. This arrangement would also suit the honor or fame of the government (*şan-ı hükumet*).[46] For outside observers who weren't privy to the internal wrangling and negotiations that all of this entailed, it might have seemed like proof positive that the Ottomans were trying to act as the patrons of these pilgrims and win their hearts. And there is no doubt that it was probably a godsend for the destitute pilgrims. Yet, as we know, the Interior Ministry was primarily motivated to maintain order in the capital. Allowing these pilgrims to continue to sleep in the courtyards of mosques and inns in the center of the city was "not appropriate," and arranging to send them back to Asia was necessary for maintaining the public good (*maslahat*).

In addition to concerns about public health and order, the government had to intervene owing to concerns about maintaining a positive image. As one Interior Ministry official wrote, "It is necessary to send these destitute Turkestani pilgrims who don't have the means to make the return to their homelands and sleep in mosque courtyards and here and there in a wretched state, as in previous instances, to their homelands, since it is not allowable to have them in such a wretched state in the seat of the caliphate, and in full view of friend and foe alike."[47] These foreign pilgrims, many of whom slept and congregated in what we would now consider tourist attractions in the center of the city, were often described as presenting an ugly image and bothering more desirable foreign travelers and the local population.[48] As these fears found echoes in the press, petition writers began to employ them in regular tropes. For example, in an appeal to the grand vizier, we see the request for assistance framed in terms that captured the government's concerns: "Your servants are subjects of the Chinese state, and while we were traveling through the vicinity of Sevastopol, our money was stolen by Russian bandits. With the aid of some [of] our countrymen, we were able to find refuge in the court of the sultan (Istanbul).... For a long time now we have been sleeping in and around inns, and this constitutes quite an ugly spectacle for friends and foes (*yar ü iğyar*). Thus, we request that you kindly send us for free as far as the port of Jeddah."[49]

As Selim Deringil has observed, the formulaic statement of "not looking good to friend or foe" was a reference to foreign consuls and missionaries.[50] Governmental concerns about the sight of these travelers was echoed by another official at the Interior Ministry, who explained to the Istanbul Municipality that wretched groups of Central Asians were stranded in Sultanahmet, Hagia Sophia, and Eyüp. He asked how much money the municipality could allocate for their transport to Chinese Turkestan.[51] As the author put it, the sight of these impoverished travelers in central neighborhoods demonstrated in clear language to the omnipresent foreign (probably European) visitors in Istanbul how Chinese Muslims were being hosted in the center of the Islamic caliphate.[52]

This was the same official we met in my introduction, who believed that the poor and destitute Chinese (*bu fakir ve sefil Çinliler*) should be regarded as a delegation of envoys (*heyet-i murahhas*), whose hearts should be satisfied vis-à-vis the caliphate.[53] The same official later advocated proposals for stemming the flow of such "delegations." Abandoning his pan-Islamic sentiment in favor of pragmatism, he wrote:

> Like last year, this year too, a great number of poor pilgrims have applied, group after group, to the Interior Ministry for their free passage, invoking various touching stories of suffering. Even if it is desirable, in keeping with the governmental policies of Islamic unity, to secure the contentment of these pilgrims, in reality, neither the Municipality nor the Interior Ministry have the funds to continually send group after group even as far as Odessa. . . . Because it is undesirable to reject their touching claims, and because we cannot leave them in such a wretched state, we should send them back, with the aid of the police.

To prevent such problems in the future, he suggested that unless they could prove that they had enough funds, pilgrims should not be allowed to disembark in the imperial capital.[54] This would also help stem the rising numbers of supplications from people who had just arrived in the city and were asking for state support.

By the 1910s, Ottoman officials had learned to anticipate requests from hajjis seeking repatriation but were distressed by the increase in supplications from those who had not yet made it as far as Mecca. In 1911, a petition from several Kashgaris who were already in dire straits prompted considerable concern in the Ministry of the Interior and a police investigation into the petitioners' circumstances. The police determined that the petitioners had arrived in Istanbul some twenty-five days earlier and then run out of money. They were forced to leave the inn where they were staying (the Şeyh Davud Han, in Tahtakale) and had started to sleep in the courtyard of the Yeni Camii Mosque in Eminönü. The Istanbul Municipality had then moved them to tents on the outskirts of Istanbul, near a hospital in Demirkapı. There, the pilgrims were getting by with whatever money they took in as alms.[55]

Shortly thereafter, an Interior Ministry official drafted a letter to the grand vizier; if the number of crossed out lines and rewritten sentences is any indication, he was particularly vexed and having trouble articulating the crux of the issue. The only solution for preventing this type of situation, he asserted, was to impress on people traveling from the region that, according to the Hanafi school of Islamic law, it was not required for the poor to fulfill this pillar of Islam. But in this case, he explained, they could not send these petitioners back to China without allowing them first to perform the pilgrimage. Since it was already too late to secure their passage to Mecca in time for that year's rites, the government was in the unenviable position of having to support them for a full year until the next hajj, send them to Mecca, and then provide them with sufficient funds to make the journey home. He suggested that at least thirty thousand kuruş be allocated and recommended that the petition be passed on to the Ministry of Finance, where it would be settled—but not before reiterating that it would be unsuitable to send the pilgrims home without allowing them to perform the hajj.[56] The Porte had earlier also expressed the belief that this would not be permissible from the perspective of "the unity of Islam" and the "glory of the caliphate."[57] There was no money in the budget for such an expense, but money would once again be found. The ensuing aid was no doubt presented to petitioners as an act of imperial benevolence and generosity befitting the Ottoman caliphate, even if this was only one of many considerations facing the Unionist government.

Effectively, the tension between imperial interests and the patronage of petitioners was resolved through measures that fit within a pan-Islamic framework but were taken with an eye toward maintaining order in the capital. Contrary to the idea that imposing hajj-related mobility controls (beyond quarantine) was out of the question, the Ottomans were very ready to do just that. Whereas historians frequently reproduce colonial claims about not being able to impose restrictions on the hajj, the sole Muslim empire looked for ways to do so. There was too much at stake for unchecked mobility: jurisdictional sovereignty, public health and order, and the material burdens on a bankrupt empire engaged in multiple wars and conflicts. If it was the sultan-caliph's sacred obligation to ensure that pilgrims were able to fulfill their hajj, it had also become the sultan-caliph's burden.[58] Pilgrims, for their part, made requests and demands of the state and pragmatically used an Islamic vocabulary that prompted the Ottomans to action. But the pilgrims' actions were also pragmatic in nature. They were savvy enough to play on Ottoman fears about public health and order and were astute participants in the system the Ottoman state presented them with. They actively sought to improve their experiences traveling through Ottoman lands by asking for the Porte to make good on being their "exclusive protector."

Both sides often seemed at a loss. If destitute pilgrims wrote heartrending petitions describing their plight, Ottoman statesmen wrote equally moving memoranda depicting their unenviable positions as their protectors. Ultimately, they provided pilgrims with whatever funds and assistance they could muster. Despite the wide variety of motives driving their patronage and repatriation, the Ottoman central government provided thousands of pilgrims each year with material aid that allowed them to complete their journeys. And when these hajjis finally returned to their homes, the connections between the religious journey and patronage may have prompted them to focus on the positive aspects of the pilgrimage. We can imagine, for example, how Hacı İsa and his companions, on returning to Khotan, told stories about Istanbul's beauty and how "their Islamic government" had arranged for them to take a steamship to Odessa and then a train to Andijan. If they had kept their word, they were probably including the Ottoman sultan in their prayers and asking their compatriots to do so as well.

If Ottoman legal jurists conceived of the caliphate as a means to counter extraterritoriality or to assert power over Muslims abroad, it is safe to say that they did not anticipate the material consequences and the ways they would be called to account by people who were not their subjects. Petitions for material support were the logical outgrowth of Ottoman rhetoric of spiritual sovereignty and caliphal protection, which led to the emergence of rights discourses invoking the caliph's "spiritual" responsibilities to protect pilgrims. This was an unanticipated development for officials tasked with managing demands made by foreigners they were effectively trying to exclude from Ottoman nationality and whom they increasingly viewed as potential threats to public order and health. Thus, while the state repeatedly came to the aid of destitute pilgrims, the reasons behind these acts of munificence were varied and complex and the way in which aid was arranged haphazard. Although Ottoman officials recognized their "spiritual responsibility" toward petitioners, they also sought ways to escape this burden. The very same minister who had in 1910 written about the need to protect the Chinese Muslims was faced with the reality that neither the Istanbul Municipality nor the Ministry of the Interior had the funds to continuously send travelers as far as Odessa, let alone China. The only solution for preventing the poverty that seemed to have become integral to their experiences in Istanbul was to have the police prevent them from disembarking in the city's ports, unless they could prove that they had enough funds to cover five to ten days in the city and to complete the pilgrimage.[59]

As we have seen, since at least the Hamidian period, Ottoman statesmen placed a premium on projecting the image of a well-ordered state. The establishment of poorhouses and the criminalization of vagrancy and begging were all part of these efforts. Pilgrims—many of whom the Ottomans failed to actually protect from exploitative pilgrimage guides and Bedouin tribes—were part of another population that needed to be policed and moved out of public space. The proposed solutions were therefore to prevent their interaction with the domestic population by temporarily housing them in government-sponsored structures outside the city center, preventing them from disembarking in Istanbul, and arranging for their departures.

One official proposed yet another solution: to find ways to prevent them from coming to Istanbul in the first place. Since they did not have the power to stem the tide of pilgrims arriving from Chinese Turkestan, a more pragmatic approach might be to make contact with Kashgari ulema and have them explain to Muslims in the region that religion does not require (*farz*) the poor to perform the pilgrimage. The author cited Hanafi law but then noted that many Chinese Muslims followed the Shafi'i school. Thus, he reasoned that the matter required further deliberation until a more permanent solution could be found.⁶⁰ A permanent solution, however, was difficult to envision since custodianship of the hajj and concerns about public order meant that the state was responsible for the welfare of pilgrims whom they had no power to actually prevent from traveling to the empire and whom they claimed to be the exclusive protectors of.

The central government thus continued to patch together funds from various ministries and the treasury and to work with the Russian consulate in Istanbul to make arrangements for Russian subjects to travel to Odessa and then on to Andijan and Kashgar. In fact, to move people through chokepoints like Istanbul and to repatriate Muslims from across Russian- and Chinese-ruled Turkestan, the Ottoman government frequently cooperated with Russian authorities. In September of 1912, the grand vizier claimed to make "one last" appropriation of funding (which had reached more than thirty-five thousand kuruş) and explained that the Council of Ministers (Meclis-i Vükela) had decided that going forward, arrangements should be made in the budget of the Ministry of Pious Endowments for this type of spending.⁶¹ It is not clear if such a line item was incorporated into the budget for 1913. By 1914, the number of pilgrims arriving had started to decrease, and many of those who were already in Ottoman domains were not able to return to Central Asia, at least via Istanbul, because of the outbreak of the First World War.⁶² Some of these pilgrims would settle down and become integrated into diasporic communities of Central Asians concentrated in cities like Istanbul and Medina, ultimately becoming Ottomans.

{ CHAPTER 5 }

FROM PILGRIMS TO MIGRANTS AND DE FACTO OTTOMANS

> The entire old East was in these streets. Turkestanis with their scant, round trimmed beards, prominent cheekbones, their faces strained by asceticism and piety, their hands clasped in their long-sleeved shawl robes, having come in who knows which year's hajj caravan—just like storks separated from their flock—ended up staying in a corner of this city [İstanbul]. Chinese Muslims, married in Ayvansaray or Hırka-i Şerif [Mosque] and becoming heads of households, their limbs by custom still finding our clothes strange, [mixed with] people of the Caucasus in black kalpaks, their waists tightened with belts with silver buckles, [and] Yemenis, wrapped in white cloaks, their figures reminding old hajjis of Arafat . . .
>
> Ahmed Hamdi Tanpınar, *Beş Şehir (Five Cities)*

IN THE BUSY COMMERCIAL DISTRICTS that lead from the Süleymaniye Mosque Complex down to Mahmutpaşa—where many Central Asians found lodging and work at Istanbul's inns, workshops, and coffeehouses—there are still businesses for hajj and umra services, with names that evoke Bukhara and Turkestan. Despite a recent surge in labor migration from Central Asia—bringing men and women to take care of Istanbul's elderly and to work in its service industries—the connections between places like Bukhara, Greater Istanbul, and Arabia no longer make much sense, and for most city dwellers, the existence of Bukharan hajj businesses is probably little more than a curiosity, if that.

But during the early life of famed novelist Ahmed Hamdi Tanpınar (1901–62), the connections between Central Asians and the hajj were still clear. As he wrote in his essay collection *Beş Şehir,* Turkestanis were part of the diverse Muslim cosmopolitan community that populated Istanbul and connected it in one's imagination to distant places—an "old East," Arafat—and to the hajj (fig. 10). Into the mid-twentieth century, when one visited the city, it would be commonplace to see Bukharan and Kashgari hajjis gathered by the steps of Yeni Camii, near the hans where they worked and bachelor houses where they resided or near the lodges of Üsküdar and Eyüp Sultan, where they had forged small communities. At the end of empire, Central Asians and Indians would be gathered in and around the Zawiya al-Uzbakiyya (Uzbek Sufi Lodge), just off the Via Dolorosa in Jerusalem—the route that led Jesus to his crucifixion. In the midst of the Arabic being spoken in the busy streets, one would likely hear Turki, Persian, and Urdu and notice the code switching that is a feature of conversation among multilingual people. In Tarsus, migrants from the Ferghana Valley would be milling about the Türkistan Tekke, a Sufi lodge established long before steamship routes eclipsed the overland roads leading through Anatolia into Greater Syria. In Medina, Bukharans could be found at any number of the guesthouses established between the early modern and modern era, one just off the Prophet's Mosque.[1] In each setting, their distinctive silk and velvet hats and robes (*doppi, chopon*) would give away that they originated from somewhere else, their accents in Turkish and Arabic hinting that they were not quite Ottoman.

FIGURE 10. Central Asians wandering among shops in Eminönü, İstanbul. *Hac, Kutsal Yolculuk* (İstanbul: Denizler Kitabevi, 2014).

Unlike Muslim migrants and refugees (*muhacirin*) who fled persecution and war in the Balkans, Caucasus, and Crimea and sought shelter in the sultan's domains, the nature of nineteenth-century Central Asian migration was, as Tanpınar suggested, ad hoc. Bukharans, Andijanis, and Kashgaris did not arrive en masse, and were not processed by special refugee commissions, and resettled in Rumeli, Anatolia, or Arab provinces, where they were expected to become productive and loyal citizens of their adopted homeland.[2] Rather, they were travelers like Nur Muhammed (who we met in Chapter 2)—people who came in small waves and stayed behind after completing their pilgrimage and who straddled the fine line between Ottomans and foreigners that the Porte began to draw in 1869. Their stories are often scattered and lost or overshadowed by accounts of people at the center of diplomatic struggles over nationality and protection, the masses of problem subjects whom the central government sought to repatriate, and pan-Turkists who reshaped how the Turkish Republic understood its historical connections to Central Asians.

This chapter looks at the hajjis who stayed behind after completing the hajj and became Ottomans. I begin by working back from the onset of the First World War—when the abrogation of the Capitulations sparked a rush of applications for legal naturalization—and investigate two forms of pilgrimage-related migration and paths to Ottoman subjecthood. In the first part of the chapter, I examine the process of granting nationality to long-term residents and denizens—referred to in governmental sources as *telsik* (a new term that appeared for naturalization)—and argue that the abrogation of the Capitulations facilitated the formalization of a type of extralegal belonging that had emerged after 1869. I call this status de facto subjecthood and use it to refer to persons who lived for all intents and purposes as Ottomans, even though they were not Ottoman legal nationals. My analysis entails distinguishing between foreigners perceived as outsiders and foreigners as people with non-Ottoman legal nationality.[3] While this is a distinction that often gets lost in translation, it is important for understanding how Central Asians became integrated into Ottoman societies and why they were able to bypass—not necessarily via subterfuge—legal restrictions on the rights of ecnebi. De facto subjecthood existed not simply because people exploited legal loopholes but because the central government could not achieve consensus on what it meant to be a foreigner and was not willing to enforce many of its own regulations.

Tracing the connections between hajj and migration sheds light on a fuller range of Asian mobilities and challenges the commonly held view that Central Asian migration to Ottoman lands was driven primarily by ethnicity. There is a reason why Bukharans, Turkestanis, and Kashgaris settled in cities along hajj routes like Istanbul, Damascus, Jerusalem, Mecca, and Medina rather than "Turkish" cities. This becomes clearer in the second part of the chapter, as we move to the Holy Cities and examine an understudied form of state-sponsored migration and subsidized residence termed *mücaveret*. The experiences of Central Asians in the Hijaz raise questions about nationality and imperial belonging in "exceptional" provinces that impel us to reconsider what it meant to be a Muslim foreigner or to become Ottoman in a polity that was legitimized by the caliphate *and* ruled through difference.

De Facto Ottomans

For the Andijani native Hacı Sahib, who migrated to Istanbul in the early 1900s, becoming Ottoman was a process that was a long time in the making. Sometime before or after completing the hajj, he had settled in Eyüp—perhaps hesitant to return to the Ferghana Valley, which was still shaken by the 1898 uprising and subsequent Russian reprisals.[4] Once the hajji accumulated sufficient capital, he opened a prayer-bead business and married an Ottoman woman, Fatma Tevhide Hanım, the daughter of a local coffeehouse proprietor. Together they had two little girls named Naime and Nebiye. As he built a new life in the Ottoman capital, Hacı Sahib held on to his Russian identity papers and passport, *ne olur ne olmaz* (just in case).[5] Like many of his countrymen, Hacı Sahib may have made the calculation that he could one day stand to benefit from foreign nationality. If he were to expand his business, for example, capitulatory privileges would allow him to compete with European protégés in ways that Ottoman subjects could not. Given that he could already live and work in the empire without becoming Ottoman, this was the path of least resistance since he otherwise would have to take a costly trip to Russia to legally (per Russia) renounce his subjecthood.[6]

It was only in the days after 9 September 1914, when the government of the Committee of Union and Progress (CUP) unilaterally abrogated the Capitulations, that Hacı Sahib seems to have questioned the wisdom of maintaining his foreign nationality. That fall, people in the city began decorating their homes and businesses with flags and banners and turning out to large public rallies to celebrate independence from the onerous capitulatory agreements that had long plagued the empire.[7] When the CUP entered the war on the side of the Central Powers on 29 October, the government's marshaling of patriotic and antiforeign sentiment only increased. Ottomans throughout Istanbul began to mobilize against foreigners, who were increasingly seen as "dangerous insider[s] in cahoots with non-Muslim traders against the beneficial emergence of a 'national economy.'"[8] Although it was unlikely that his neighbors or associates regarded him as an insidious outsider, maintaining foreign nationality was becoming a liability rather than an advantage. With two young children and a wife who probably did not want to move from Istanbul to a distant village in Turkestan, he submitted a petition to the Interior Ministry asking to be naturalized. The documentation included a sworn statement that he renounced any future rights to foreign nationality. The process of seeking naturalization—*telsik*—was followed by a fairly straightforward investigation: Ottoman authorities consulted with intermediaries such as tekke shaykhs in Eyüp and established that the hajji had fulfilled the five-year residency requirement of the 1869 Ottoman Nationality Law and that he was a reputable man with a sound business. His application was swiftly approved: he and his daughters—who had automatically taken the nationality of their father at birth—became Ottomans.[9]

They were not alone. From Basra to Beirut and Mecca and Medina, the onset of the war prompted a sudden spike in Central Asians seeking "nationality conversion" (*tebdil-i tabiiyet*) and what they described as "refuge" (*dehalet*). The government received so many requests from foreigners of various nationalities that in early 1915 the Foreign Ministry Nationalities Bureau issued a standardized form that people could fill in with their personal details. When Hacı Seyyid Murad, a Bukharan subject residing in Damascus, began the process of changing his nationality in January of that year, he entered his information into a preprinted form. And when Murad Şah, a graduate of the Beirut Teacher's College, became naturalized in 1916, he was asked to answer a list of questions: Which state was the applicant a national of? How long had he or she resided in the empire, and whereabouts? Did s/he have a spouse or any children? Had they been recorded in the population register? Was there any reason to prevent Ottoman naturalization? Did the person in question have any foreign papers?[10]

Often, government officials charged with matters related to nationality turned to authorities at the Central Asian Sufi lodges to answer these questions, revealing how the tekke shaykhs acted in the capacity of neighborhood headmen (*muhtar*). Beyond religious figures, they were "guarantor[s] of the identity, moral integrity, and social and marital status" of members of transimperial communities and helped ensure that foreign Muslims became "full legal entities" through their intercession.[11] Indeed, this process built on a long tradition at Sufi lodges, and records from Sultantepe include formulaic pledge letters from Central Asians who became Ottoman subjects and who swore that they would not revert or make future claims to foreign nationality.[12]

In response to the surge in naturalization applications, the Interior Ministry issued guidelines in July of 1915 for processing telsik cases, which, like the forms issued earlier that year, presumed that applicants had resided in the empire long enough to marry, have children, and buy homes and businesses.[13] Worth keeping in mind is that while the 1867 land law permitted foreigners to acquire real estate, it made an exception for foreign Muslims in the Hijaz. It also stipulated that foreigners had to be subjects of states that had signed individual protocols with the Porte. Effectively, Bukharans and other subjects of protected states were prohibited from buying land throughout the empire because they were from "semi-sovereign" or "independent" Muslim states whose rulers could not conduct foreign policy or sign international agreements.[14] While they were permitted to marry Ottomans, the 1869 law stipulated that their spouses were supposed to lose their Ottoman nationality. Yet case after case suggested that these restrictions were not enforced and highlighted how commonly exceptions were made for Sunni Muslims who were, in theory, ecnebi. Rather than outsiders, potential troublemakers, or seditious subjects (*muzır*),[15] they seemed to be widely accepted into Ottoman communities as locals.

The parallels in the story of Hacı Sahib and a Bukharan subject named Murad bear this out and suggest that these types of naturalization requests represented the formalization of subjecthood for Central Asian migrants who were already living as members of Ottoman religious and social communities. Like Hacı Sahib, Murad Efendi lived in the empire for years before applying for Ottoman nationality. He had arrived in Istanbul circa 1902 and married an Ottoman woman, the daughter of a Sufi shaykh. The couple had two daughters, Saime and Şükriye, and eventually built a house on land that Murad had purchased near Sultantepe. For more than a decade, he resided in Üsküdar without taking any action to renounce his Bukharan nationality or to legally acquire Ottoman subjecthood. This changed in January of 1915, when Murad petitioned the Porte and expressed his desire to become an Ottoman subject. The state undertook a short inquiry, during which time the Interior Ministry arranged to contact the Sultantepe shaykh about Murad Efendi's character. The telsik file did not mention that Şükriye had retained her Ottoman subjecthood or raise any questions about his purchase of land. After the shaykh confirmed that he was indeed a man of honor and good repute, Murad's naturalization was approved, and he became an Ottoman.[16] The question is, what was he—and Hacı Sahib, Naime, and Nebiye—before?

Prior to legally obtaining Ottoman nationality, it seemed, many Central Asians were for all intents and purposes living as subjects of the sultan-caliph. Just as the acquisition of British, French, or Russian nationality did not make Maltese, Algerians, or Bukharans (or Ottomans) into Europeans, it did not suddenly render them foreigners beyond a narrow legal sense. This was especially true among Muslim foreign nationals originating from Central Asia, who came to the empire primarily in the context of hajj-related migration. The fact that these migrants originated from various polities with different standing in the international state system would have made it difficult for most people to distinguish who was a colonial subject or a subject of a semiautonomous state. Moreover, as in other Ottoman contexts, "many foreigners, once registered with a consulate, never practiced legal foreignness again. In their social behavior, they did little to distinguish themselves from locals."[17] Unless they had to go to court or needed travel and identity documents, foreign nationality was not a defining feature of day-to-day life and would not necessarily be public knowledge.

What was interesting about these individuals was that unlike people living between the Russian and Ottoman Empires—whom James Meyer describes as maintaining a kind of dual citizenship—these migrants do not appear to have "exploited ambiguities regarding their citizenship status to receive consular assistance and other benefits available to Russian subjects in the Ottoman Empire" or to have sought to "play the two states against one another."[18] Their stories are illustrative of people who maintained their foreign nationality in Ottoman lands without necessarily manipulating the extraterritorial order. This included those who held on to their foreign nationality *and* volunteered to fight for the Ottomans.

During the long period of mobilization between 1911 and 1918, which began with the Italo-Ottoman War in Libya, continued with the Balkan Wars, and culminated with the entry of the empire into the Great War, the Sultantepe registers provide insights into stories of Bukharans and subjects of Russian Turkestan who volunteered to join the military. In distinction to those who were "taken into" the army—who had ostensibly become naturalized and were conscripted—the shaykh annotated entries of individuals who volunteered to fight.[19] For example, in February of 1913, fifty-five-year-old Hacı Yusuf of Marghilan (a town in Russian Turkestan) arrived at Sultantepe on his way to the Hijaz. While his intention was to go to Medina and take up pious residence, for some reason Yusuf changed his mind and volunteered to join the army—presumably forces fighting in the Balkans. Like another hajji who had left for the front a few days prior to his arrival, the shaykh noted that Yusuf had set out for "the field of holy war." It was only after falling ill and being discharged that he returned to Sultantepe and went, as originally planned, to Medina instead.[20]

There were numerous similar cases. For example, a Bukharan named Hacı Osman volunteered in 1915 and wrote to tell the shaykh that he was fighting in an irregular band or battalion in the Black Sea region (a "çete taburu" in Lazestan). His entry stated that Osman had also endowed a large iron pot to the tekke for its kitchen.[21] Another hajji named Yusuf—also from Marghilan—would join a battalion and write that he had become a siege artilleryman.[22] The registers did not list either man as an Ottoman subject, and there is no indication that they had been asked to sign oaths renouncing their foreign subjecthood before going to the front. This was consistent with a 1904 admission by the Council of Ministers that although Muslim migrants (muhacirin) were required by law to cut off ties to their states of origin (meaning, to renounce their citizenship or legal nationality), the law had not yet been applied to Bukharans.[23] Ottoman sources also suggest that there was a tradition of Bukharans (likely meaning Central Asians, more generally) serving in the military without becoming naturalized and that this was owing to governmental concerns that any formal renunciation of Russian subjecthood before enlisting would invite foreign consular intervention.[24] A case from May of 1913, in which the Russian embassy in Istanbul sent two notices to the Ottoman Foreign Ministry about a Bukharan subject, "Hadji Abdul-Kadir Mollah Maksoudoff Aksakal," who had enlisted in Mersin, suggests that this was a problem the Ottomans would want to avoid—particularly in the context of the desperate need for soldiers in the long period of mobilization.[25]

Stories of volunteer enlistment again demonstrate irregularity in the application of nationality laws and raise questions about the extent to which the Ottoman-foreigner dichotomy informed the experiences of Central Asians. They also raise the question of why foreigners would fight for the empire. To answer this question, it is instructive to distinguish between legal nationality and subjecthood and to recognize that between 1869 and 1914, there was more flexibility in the notion of subjecthood than there was in legal nationality. As we have already seen, one could be subject to the sultan-caliph and under Ottoman protection—but not an Ottoman legal national. Moreover, having, using, or acquiring a particular nationality was not an indication of allegiance to that state, of integration into its citizenry, or of the kinds of belonging and patriotism we associate with citizenship and nation-state nationalisms. Distinguishing among subjects/citizens and nationals, foreigners, and foreign nationals sheds light on why it was possible for someone like Hacı Yusuf to volunteer to fight in an Ottoman war: if being or having a legal nationality did not require the kind of loyalty associated with citizenship, it also did not preclude people from fighting on behalf of empires they felt cultural or religious affinities to. This was especially true for colonial subjects, whose assumption of legal nationality while abroad was primarily strategic.

More mundane examples from this period offer additional insight into these questions, particularly the possibilities for Central Asians to live in the empire and flout or circumvent intertwined restrictions on land tenure and marriage. Beyond marriages for love, foreign nationals often entered into marital unions for the sake of land. As we saw in Chapter 3, two years prior to the promulgation of the Ottoman Nationality Law, the Law on the Rights of Foreign Citizens to Own Land permitted foreign nationals to purchase real estate throughout the empire. But, as previously discussed, the law explicitly prohibited foreign Muslims from purchasing land or real estate in the Hijaz, and land sales elsewhere were only authorized to subjects of states that had signed individual protocols with the Porte. These were agreements with sovereign states authorizing the sale of land only on the condition that purchasers would be subject to the jurisdiction of Ottoman courts in all property-related matters and not their consular courts. What this meant for informally colonized Muslims was that the 1867 law effectively extended beyond the Hijaz. This was because semisovereign states like Bukhara and Afghanistan could not conduct their own foreign policy and enter into international agreements. And because the Porte did not have diplomatic relations with the Qing or Republican China, all Muslims from Chinese Turkestan were technically prohibited from buying land.

Foreign Muslim nationals also faced restrictions on marriage. According to the 1869 Nationality Law, Ottoman women who married foreigners were to lose their subjecthood and take the nationality of their husbands.[26] A notable exception was the prohibition on marriages between Ottoman women and Persian men, which was an integral part of state efforts to retain subjects and maintain control in the provinces of Mosul and Baghdad. In an important amendment to the Nationality Law, the Porte decreed that Ottoman women who married Persians would retain their subjecthood, as would any children born of their unions. Their children would not inherit their father's nationality or be eligible for the extraterritorial protections of Persian subjects or British nationals and protégés. Moreover, male children would be liable for conscription. The central government was seeking to hold on to subjects in regions where the growth of the British consular court system and protection regime (mainly Iraq) threatened Ottoman sovereignty, and there were simultaneous concerns about large-scale conversions among Sunnis to Shi'ism.[27]

In a comparatively understudied phenomenon, the Porte began to prohibit marital unions between foreign nationals and Ottoman women in the Hijaz, which were contracted in order to circumvent restrictions on buying immovable property. Unlike Basra, Baghdad, or Mosul, the central government did not have the same anxieties about conversion to Shi'ism, but it was concerned about the proliferation of diplomatic rows over disputed estates. Even though the Capitulations did not extend to the Hijaz, European consuls aggressively pursued cases involving the estates of people with Ottoman nationality. A 1912 incident involving the estate of an Indian mücavir named

Abdulgani Mir, in which the British claimed this resident of Taif as their subject, serves as a good example. Although the deceased was born in the Hijaz—thus, an Ottoman by both birth and residence—in death, the British contested his nationality and started a protracted dispute. The incident typified the rise in legal quagmires "created by conflicts involving the subjects of local rulers, recognized protégés, resident expatriates, recent immigrants, [and] familiar strangers under shifting or uncertain jurisdictions."[28]

Given the economic and political power of the robust Indian, Hadrami, and Jawi merchant communities—which by the 1880s owned approximately one-eighth of real estate in the province and enjoyed "a virtual monopoly over every sector of productivity and commercial resources in the region"—the Porte had cause for real concern. As M. Christopher Low demonstrates, foreign land ownership was viewed by many within the government as "the starting point on a road leading inexorably toward intervention, autonomy, and eventually independence."[29] Against the backdrop of escalating European intervention in Mount Lebanon from the 1860s on, the British occupation of Egypt in 1882, and British intrigues to support a rival caliph in Arabia, the root of this fear was that foreign Muslims with entrenched economic power would pave the way for the creation of a Muslim protégé class and open up the province to the Capitulations and, ultimately, European machinations.

As authorities in Istanbul investigated ongoing violations of the 1867 law and sought measures to prevent land sales, they realized that in addition to methods such as acting through local proxies, foreign nationals were contracting marriages with Ottoman women to legalize real estate transactions. In response to a query from the Council of State about the permissibility of such unions, in 1889 the Foreign Ministry Office of Legal Counsel issued a legal opinion on the issue. The opinion reiterated that foreign Muslims could not purchase immovable property and stressed that women who married foreigners should lose their Ottoman nationality. "Whether in the Haremeyn or in Jeddah," the opinion stated, "Ottoman women who marry Indian or Javanese foreigners are to be considered nationals of the state to which their husbands belong." Legal counsel added that whereas women who knowingly or "outright" married foreigners were to be immediately and "without hesitation" counted as ecnebi, those whose husbands became foreign nationals after the marriage was contracted did not automatically lose their nationality. This signaled tacit acknowledgment that acquiring foreign nationality was often surreptitious and that the women in question might not be aware of their partners' change in legal identity until such time that their spouses tried to activate the attendant benefits or privileges. But in both cases, the central government's position was that "from the moment they changed their nationality," women lost the right to any real estate or land they owned. And in the case of their death—allowing for the fact that it might have stayed in their possession, and thereby recognizing widespread failures of enforcement—their property could not be transferred to their spouses.[30]

As in most frontiers and borderlands, marriages among foreign men and Ottoman women were common and served as a path toward economic and social integration. The Porte was not prohibiting marriage itself but trying to limit its use as a means for casting off Ottoman subjecthood (in the case of Iraq) or for acquiring immovable property. But in this it was not consistent. In Istanbul, these marriages were not only tolerated among foreign Central Asian men but also sanctioned. In a 1905 case involving a Bukharan visitor to the city who wanted to marry a local woman, the Interior Ministry (in consultation with the Foreign Ministry) stated that "according to the recognized way, it is lawful for marriages between Ottoman Muslim women and Sunni men found in foreign nationality."[31] The man in question, Hacı Kurban bin Abdulgaffar, could wed an Ottoman woman without any obstacles or pledges to renounce foreign nationality. There was no discussion of his future wife being denaturalized.

The decision is important for two reasons. First, despite the fact that many Central Asians *actively* held on to Russian nationality when they came to the empire, the ministry's phrasing (the use of *bulunan* to mean "found in") suggested that it viewed foreignness as something that was imposed or that was a condition of the annexation of Bukhara. Rather than a typical passive Ottoman construction, the phrasing highlighted abiding ambivalence within the central government about Bukharans as foreigners. It was this *imperial* tentativeness and inconsistency that allowed Ottoman women (including Fatma Tevhide Hanım and Murad Efendi's wife) to maintain their nationality after marrying Central Asians—not a subversion of the legal order. Second, given the widespread mobility of Bukharan and other Central Asian hajjis, inconsistent enforcement of denaturalization in different provinces and cities meant that legal restrictions were to a large extent moot. One thing the state was very aware of was the extent of foreign Muslims' mobility: throughout the period studied here, the central government played an important role in facilitating Central Asian migrations (not only pilgrimages) to the Holy Cities. This was not only through indirect support of Sufi lodges but also via direct patronage of individuals who wanted to live in the noble sanctuaries of the Haremeyn. These short- and long-term pious residents moved regularly between the spiritual and political capitals of the empire, their movements opening up important questions about the diverse actors and motives that determined belonging and legal nationality at the fin de siècle.

Guests of God and the Sultan

Mecca and Medina were inhospitable places, what cultural anthropologist Engseng Ho might call improbable cities (figs. 11 and 12).[32] They were arid and remote, with limited economic opportunities, and surrounded by Bedouin who depended on looting pilgrim caravans for their livelihood. Yet from the earliest period of Islamic history, they attracted Muslims who wanted to pursue lives of piety in the vicinity of the most sacred precincts of their faith. Mecca "the Honored" was where the Prophet Muhammad first received revelation, and where he had given his last sermon at Arafat. Medina "the Illuminated" was the city where the first Muslim community was forged and home to the resting place of the Prophet and his namesake mosque, Masjid an-Nabawi. The names of the two major cemeteries—the "Exalted Heaven" in Mecca and the "Eternal Heaven" in Medina—captured the umma's regard for the soil of the two cities, which promised pathways to paradise rather than material comforts of this world.

The Muslims drawn to the Holy Cities were referred to as *mücavir* (plural, *mücavirin*) and were specifically distinguished from Muslim refugees and migrants known as *muhacirin* and, later, *mülteci*. Whereas the latter were permanent migrants who would become Ottomans, mücavirin were in theory guests of the Holy Cities. In reality, many of them settled down and made Mecca—and, in the case of Central Asians, primarily Medina—home. They effectively constituted diasporas with entrenched economic, social, and religious interests, which were linked to their homelands. Medina, for example, was funded by numerous Bukharan pious endowments. Bukharan ulema had a long-standing presence in the city "at least since the 17th century," and "enjoyed an excellent reputation in particular as religious scholars and teachers."[33]

Mücavirin were also distinguished from indigenous inhabitants, whom the commander of the Egyptian hajj caravan claimed in 1901 did "not surpass the number of fingers on a hand."[34] İbrahim Rıfat Paşa's observation raises the question of who was local in the Haremeyn, if most of the cities' inhabitants were not natives, and what it meant to be an Ottoman in such a setting. Insofar as recent studies of the hajj mention these local nonnatives, they tend to conflate them with pilgrims or to present a flat picture of them as wealthy foreign nationals and members of merchant diasporas. But the phenomenon of pious residence was also common in cities along the road to Mecca, such as Jerusalem, where Indians and Central Asians settled for "months or years at a time, for the sake of business, tourism, or studying in the madrasas."[35]

These communities did not begin and end with the wealthy South and Southeast Asian mercantile families that dominated regional trade networks and burgeoning hajj-related industries. We know that they included many middling religious scholars and poor Sufi adepts, students, dervishes, and shaykhs. Because of the absence of a cadastral survey in the province,

FIGURE 11. A street in Mecca. *Hac, Kutsal Yolculuk* (İstanbul: Denizler Kitabevi, 2014).

however, it is difficult to arrive at more than a cursory demographic sketch of mücavirin as a whole and their numbers among Central Asians, in particular. Historians have culled demographic information for the Hijaz primarily from European sources and estimated that between 1840 and 1870 the urban population of Jeddah was between twenty thousand and thirty thousand persons, while Mecca was home to about forty thousand to eighty thousand people, and Medina eighteen thousand to forty thousand. The total Hijaz population of roughly eighty-five thousand increased to 160,000 by 1908. This figure does not include pilgrims, villagers in the surrounding towns, or nomads, which William Ochsenwald puts at close to four hundred thousand. He estimates that circa 1883, there were approximately twenty thousand mücavirin in Medina, among a total population that likely did not exceed forty thousand.[36] According to Yıldız Palace records from the same year, there were three thousand Bukharans in Mecca and another ten thousand Indians and Jawi,[37] for a total of twenty thousand long-term residents.[38]

Provisioning the Hijaz was a caliphal duty "essential for the legitimacy of the Ottoman sultans who, unable to trace their lineage back to the Prophet Muhammad, based their claim to the Caliphate on their custodianship of

FIGURE 12. Medina the Illuminated. *Hac, Kutsal Yolculuk* (İstanbul: Denizler Kitabevi, 2014).

the Two Holy Sanctuaries of Mecca and Medina."[39] The cost of ensuring that the Sharif of Mecca recognized Ottoman sovereignty was the regular infusion of cash and subsidies via the annual imperial gift or purse, the *surre-i hümayun*. Annual payments were sent with the official caravan from Istanbul and included allocations to the sharifs, Arab natives, Bedouin, and ulema. They also included payments to mücavirin. The central government specifically earmarked funds for long-term residents who were seen as deserving of not only charity (*sadaka*) but also honor and respect.[40] As İbrahim Rıfat Paşa noted in *Miratü'l-Haremeyn*, a form of imperial philanthropy once called "Rum sadakası" had originated shortly after Sultan Selim's conquest in the early sixteenth century. Funds from the Egyptian treasury were paid to mücavirin and grain distributed to the inhabitants of Mecca and Medina, a tradition that was expanded and maintained under the rule of successive sultans.[41] The government in Istanbul also often wrote to provincial authorities, such as the governor of Jeddah and Medina, to ensure that these guests of the sultan were provided with assistance.[42]

But while migration to the Holy Cities had a long history—dating, as many Ottoman sources would put it, to "times of old"—it was not always sanctioned by religious authorities. The founders of the Hanafi and Maliki legal schools, Abu Hanifa an-Nu'man and Malik ibn Anas, are said to have viewed the practice to be "mekruh" (inadvisable or suspect). This was due to concerns that prolonged residence in proximity to holy space would inevitably sully its sanctity and diminish the believer's respect toward the Kaaba. These apprehensions were no doubt related to concerns that unrestricted migration would hamper pilgrims' ability to fulfill their duty and that it would change the nature of the cities.[43] From a governmental standpoint, there were also serious concerns about housing shortages and the high cost of living in the Hijaz. The year-round residence of nonnatives added to the burdens of provisioning the province with adequate supplies of grain and ensuring there was enough potable water.[44] In the nineteenth century, these challenges were compounded by periodic outbreaks of cholera and plague. At the end of each hajj season, Ottoman authorities made announcements that pilgrims should return home and worked to remove (or effectively deport) and repatriate those who could not afford the journey. But there was no mechanism in place to regulate the duration of mücaveret.

Not surprisingly, the same factors that led to the rise of mass pilgrimage also contributed to greater interest among Central Asians in moving to the Holy Cities. For the pious, this was in part a consequence of reinvigorated scholarly networks extending from and across Central Asia, the Caucasus, Crimea, India, and the Hijaz. Nineteenth-century ulema like Shihabbadin Marjani (1818–89) and Hamidullah Almushev (1855–1929), for example, mention students and scholars from the Russian Empire at various Tatar and Daghestani madrasas and tekkes they visited.[45] According to Baymirza Hayit, prior to the Saudi conquest of the Hijaz in the 1920s, there were more than a hundred houses in Mecca for the accommodation of pilgrims from Turkestan.[46] Likewise, the travelogues and photographic albums of European orientalists are full of images and pseudo-ethnographic descriptions of and references to Central Asians. In Ottoman governmental sources, mentions of mücavirin frequently pop up in directives to grant support to people like the Naqshbandi shaykh Mirza Hamid Efendi, who had lived in Medina with several of his Sufi disciples for more than fifteen years prior to petitioning the central government for financial assistance,[47] or Hacı Muhammed Efendi, who asked the Ministry of the Interior for charity (*sadaka*) to cover his rent. Writing in 1895, he described himself as an invalid from Bukhara who had been living in Mecca with his family for more than twenty years.[48] Neither indigent paupers nor wealthy elites or famous ulema, these residents often depended on some form of patronage to offset the high cost of living in the Haremeyn.

Even as the Porte classified many of the non-Ottoman Muslims traveling to Mecca and Medina as foreigners, a strong sense of honoring the sultan-caliph's duties toward the pious continued. This was especially true for mücavirin from places like Bukhara. Although it would be an exaggeration to say that the majority of pilgrims traveling in the steamship era possessed substantial religious or cultural capital, figures from among the Bukharan ulema maintained considerable prestige, which they drew on in petitions for state support. When an individual wrote, "Your servant, a native of Bukhara and adept of the Naqshbandi way, wishes to live in the Haremeyn for a life of piety and prayer," he or she was activating a set of concepts and associations that were successful strategies for currying favor. "Bukhara the Noble," which Ottomans often conflated with much of Russian-ruled Central Asia, was a kind of shorthand for individuals of honor who were worthy of the sultan's respect and benefaction. They were people like Hacı Aşur and his sons: full-time pious people who were essential to legitimating the sultan's power as caliph. The basis of legitimacy had to be backed by effective rule (i.e., institutions that ensured order, justice, supportable taxes) and deeds that were "performed on a regular basis to remind subjects continually of the foundations of normative legitimacy." In a state where the sultan's legitimacy was sacred authority, "it would only naturally be shored up by deeds of a religious nature."[49]

Whereas the focus in much of the literature is on orchestrated spectacles of Ottoman power—such as those described by Mirim Khan in his visit to the Hamidiye Mosque for Friday prayer—these quotidian forms of patronage and support constituted a significant form of "factual legitimacy" that created, maintained, and reinforced the spiritual bond between the ruler and the umma.[50] As such, government subsidies to mücavirin should be thought of as part of an expansive repertoire of Ottoman patronage, which included higher profile projects such as a Hijaz railway. Launched in 1900, this famous railroad project would eventually connect Istanbul via Damascus to Arabia. In addition to transporting pilgrims, the sultan envisioned it as a way to more fully integrate the Hijaz into the empire's political, military, and economic structure. By the time the line reached Medina, in September of 1908, the central government had also embarked on other technopolitical projects, such as investing in waterworks to address perennial water shortages and erecting telegraph lines to improve communications to the capital and mark out Ottoman sovereignty on the ground.[51] The less visible work of subsidizing diverse Muslim communities through the provision of salaried positions, stipends, food subsidies, and lodging continued.

Ottoman support of mücavirin was not simply an example of the instrumentalization of the caliphate. Rather, it marked the fulfillment of duties toward the umma that preceded the articulation of pan-Islamic politics and discourse during the reign of Sultan Abdülhamid II. The abundance of examples from the early and mid-nineteenth century remind us that the caliphate was not only or primarily a religious or political tool but an integral dimension of Ottoman politics throughout the life of the empire—including the period of centralizing reforms of the nineteenth century. Men of "noble sciences" like Molla Hoca Baba Özbek could ask for support to move to Medina to study public works and for imperial decrees to be sent to the Şeyhülharem and to the director of the Prophet's mausoleum for arranging accommodations—and expect favorable responses.[52] Bukharans were aware of their reputations for piety and scholarship and had clear expectations of the Ottoman state. In the case of Molla Hoca, who was described as meriting respect, the Porte drafted a decree to the specified officials in which "of the Uzbek people" (*Özbek ahalisinden*) was crossed out and replaced with "Bukharan," suggesting that provenance from this city carried more prestige.[53] Around the same time, the grand vizierate sent decrees to Ottoman authorities in Egypt and Jeddah, directing them to assist another shaykh, Muhammed Emin Reşad Efendi, said to be a famous prayer reciter. The governors were instructed to accord him "the full respect and esteem he deserved."[54]

In exchange for this benevolence, shaykhs and dervishes sometimes promised to pray for the well-being of the sultan. In an 1848 petition, for example, Şerif Efendi wrote that he would pray for the "augmentation, life and power" of Sultan Abdülmecid in return for support during his move from Istanbul to Medina. He did not neglect to mention the precedent of appointing those in need with a salary and monthly wheat allotments. After confirming that Şerif Efendi was a member of the Naqshbandi order, an important shaykh, and a well-regarded prayer reciter, and finding him worthy of imperial favor and benevolence (*lûtf, atıfet*), the minister of finance enumerated that arrangements should be made "as in similar cases." Both the petitioner and the vizier were acting on established tradition. In the case of Şerif Efendi, the Ottoman official writing the memorandum specified that he should be given a salary as soon as he arrived and that the accounting should be taken care of later. The salary would come from a fund the Ministry of Pious Endowments had earmarked for supporting mücavirin.[55]

Consonant with the changes in petitioning practices among pilgrims at large, many would-be mücavirin began to describe themselves as "powerless," "in need," "destitute," and "poor" (*bikuvvet, muhtac, garip, fakir*). At times, they stated that they were guests of the sultan (for example, Şeyh Ahmed) and, as was customary in the petitioning canon, positioned themselves as the sultan's slaves or subjects. On the government side, change was in the air much earlier and, by the mid-nineteenth century, the Porte issued an imperial decree stating that new salary appointments for unbudgeted positions had been forbidden. Thus, it was the misfortune of the Bukharan dervish

Muhammed Şerif Bey—who had written a petition that began with Persian poetry and prayers for the sultan's health and success—that he was not immediately appointed with a salary, as he had so ardently hoped for. Although the government deemed him deserving of imperial aid, he would have to wait for a position to become available.[56] It is not clear how long he waited. Likewise, in 1861, a Bukharan dervish who asked for a position at a madrasa and a "sufficient quantity of wheat" so that he could live in Mecca and a Bukharan couple who requested lodging to facilitate their residence were told they would have to wait until positions were vacated.[57]

But even in the face of fiscal austerity, patronage continued. Central Asians already living in Istanbul or en route to the Hijaz were provided with governmental assistance to carry out their dreams of living in the Haremeyn. Some specified that they hoped to stay for one to two months; others left the length of their intended stay open-ended. Although their names and places of origin differed, the petitioners' intentions and plans were more or less the same, as was the government's response. This was to write to authorities in Mecca and Medina with instructions to facilitate the residence of people of noble or pure intentions and who were of poor or modest means. The petitioners were overwhelmingly adepts of the Naqshbandi order, self-described ulema and knowledge seekers, or prayer leaders and Quran reciters. In addition to couples and families, older women past childbearing age could and did apply for government appointments. In 1888, the Interior Ministry arranged a salary from "the treasury of the prophet" (*hazine-yi nebeviye*) and a wheat subsidy for a certain Ayşe Hanım, resident in the Eyüp Kashgari Lodge.[58] Ayşe Hanım was described as a woman of "pure intentions" descended from the lineage of Uwais ibn Unais al-Qarani, a Muslim martyr from Yemen who lived during the lifetime of the Prophet.

In 1900, the Ministry of the Interior instructed the navy to make arrangements for the free passage of two Bukharans, Samir and Ömer Ali, who wanted to settle in Mecca.[59] The next year, a Naqshbandi prayer leader named Buharalı Hacı Şerif Efendi asked the government to support his residence in Medina. Şerif Efendi had lived "for some years" in Kabataş, a waterfront neighborhood on the European side of Istanbul, and had already been on the hajj. Before packing up his belongings and moving, he asked the central government to appoint him with a salary (*maaş tahsisi*) and wheat allotment so that he would not suffer hardship when he arrived in Arabia. The Porte made arrangements for him to receive a monthly salary of 150 kuruş and a ration of wheat—even though there was no position open at the time.[60] A number of similar cases, including authorization to increase the salaries of existing mücavir and make appointments to their children, suggest that the Porte was, once again, inconsistent. In 1903, for example, the Hamidian government authorized an increase of two hundred kuruş (from five hundred to seven hundred) to the salary of a Kashgari hajji named Aşur, who had initially settled in Medina in 1901. It also approved the appointment of a monthly stipend of one hundred kuruş to each of his three children.[61]

Many of these individuals ended up staying in the Holy Cities for years. But people who openly expressed a wish to become Ottomans and permanently migrate to Mecca and Medina were not given permission to do so; the central government made clear this was not an option and steered them to other parts of the empire. In petitions dating to 1903–4, two small groups of Russian subjects from Turkestan wrote to the grand vizier, explaining that they were en route to perform the pilgrimage and wanted to become Ottomans and settle in the Hijaz. The first petition was from an Andijani named Muhammed Ömer, writing on behalf of himself, his wife and daughter, and two friends from Marghilan and Bukhara. In the second petition, written on the same day, a Bukharan named Hacı Rehim wrote on behalf of himself, his wife, and his two-year-old son. He wanted to quit his Russian subjecthood and become an Ottoman. On the back of both, there were notes from offices within the Interior Ministry and Citizenship Affairs Bureaus, which stated that the petitioners had come with families, and they had asked to be registered as Muslim refugees, *muhacirin*.[62] In fact, neither of the petitioners had; they only stated that they were going to the Hijaz and wanted to become Ottoman subjects. In the correspondence about their request, the Ministries of the Interior and Foreign Affairs repeated that the petitioners had asked to be registered as migrants and that their cases were being forwarded to the Muslim Refugee Commission. One note specified that "there was no precedent for the settlement of muhacir in the Hijaz" and that after the hajj, the families could become naturalized—on the condition that they settle somewhere else.[63]

Effectively, the Porte was trying to limit the type (and scope) of migration to the Hijaz and to distinguish among muhacir (refugees) and mücavir (pious residents of the Holy Cities). Despite these efforts, ultimately, both were forms of Muslim migration. What were people like Hacı Aşur if not state-supported migrants? The little bit we know about him tells us that he was not a pilgrim and that—despite not being a religious figure worth noting in the correspondence attached to his appeal—he was able to settle in Medina along with his family. He was not simply a foreign Muslim living for a fixed time in Arabia—somehow outside of Ottoman life—but a member of an enduring community that was "intrinsically dual in nature, local to Mecca [or Medina and Jeddah] on the one hand, while linked to their original home communities on the other."[64]

By allowing these Sunni Central Asian Muslims to reside in the Hijaz, the Ottoman government was, in its own words, putting people into place or space (*yerleştir-*) and enabling them to make the Hijaz their country (*tavattun*). And it was doing this at the same time that it tried to classify them as ecnebi. As an Ottoman statesman writing in 1903 put it, "Even if according to the law of nations, these people [non-Ottoman Sunni Muslims resident in the Hijaz] should be counted as foreign subjects," it should not be forgotten that they considered the empire their home, and their "hearts beat with excitement of this country."[65] In voicing his opposition to restricting the legal rights of mücavirin, this statesman was aware of the danger of enforcing legal difference among Muslims in the Holy Cities, and he warned that the central government's policies—taken up in the name of the caliphate—would do damage to the Ottomans. His sentiments captured those of many Ottomans who resisted the central government's categories of Ottoman and foreigner.

Insider-Outsiders

The position of Bukharan and other Central Asian communities in the Hijaz finds echoes in other diasporic communities, such as the Hadrami diaspora in the Indian Ocean world. As Engseng Ho argues in his magisterial work on mobility, pilgrimage, and genealogy, these Yemeni descendants of the Prophet became "local cosmopolitans" as they traveled and settled in different parts of the Indian Ocean world. They were at once a society of persons linked to a distant place on the edge of the Arabian peninsula, and insider-outsiders whose status was determined through what Ho terms a "relatively stable structure of perception" that "valorizes the local and diminishes or even demonizes the foreign."⁶⁶ Naturalization, in the sense of becoming a citizen of a place, was not just a political process and was worked out on the ground through genealogies of *sayyids* (descendants of the Prophet Muhammad), self-narration, burial, pilgrimage, and, of course, marriage. Marital unions with local women, sometimes to multiple women in multiple ports, created a wide-ranging kinship network stretching across a vast ocean. Children and their mothers, often living with the families of the women, were crucial to the mechanism of making members of the diaspora into locals. For Central Asians, webs of connection extended from the oases of Transoxiana, the Ferghana Valley, and Chinese Turkestan into the Indian subcontinent, Arabian Peninsula, and other Ottoman lands and can likely be traced back to the early expansion of the Naqshbandi order in the fifteenth century.⁶⁷

Although this form of migration was a defining feature of Meccan and Medinan society, it is seldom studied in the context of Ottoman imperial subjecthood. Then, as now, the mücavir was more than a relic of an older time; he or she was a liminal subject—somewhere between being a resolute local and a nonnative migrant. Increasingly, the mücavir was a problem for states trying to define membership in a political community (whether Ottoman, Hashemite, or Saudi), while also governing universal Islamic space. The prevalence of these liminal subjects was not an anomaly but an indicator of the challenges of instituting a secular nationality or subjecthood boundary in a Muslim empire where different metrics of belonging continued to inform what it meant to be not only an Ottoman but also a foreigner. While it might be tempting to think of these pious migrants as unique—or to conceive of Central Asians as exceptions within these larger Muslim diasporic communities—their stories testify to the spectrum of gray spaces that emerged in the era of nationality reform. As Neha Vora argues in the context of Dubai, where members of the Indian diaspora became exceptional or "impossible citizens," groups that we might see as exceptional are in many ways "quintessential citizens." This is by virtue of modes of belonging that have traditionally fallen outside narrow definitions of citizenship and porosity between boundaries that extend beyond the legal.⁶⁸

In a sea of exceptions, there was no normative experience for foreign Muslims, not only during the Ottoman era but also well after the dynasty collapsed. Mücavirin remained part of distinct Meccan and Medinan communities and did not immediately become Saudis after the establishment of the kingdom in 1932. According to the Saudi citizenship law, "Ottoman Citizens born in Saudi Arabian land or residents inside the Kingdom from 1332 Hijra—1914 A.D.[—]until 22/3/1345 [30 September 1926] Hijra and who did not acquire a foreign citizenship prior to this date" were able to become Saudis. The same was true for non-Ottoman citizens. Foreign Muslims who were not able to become Ottomans prior to the collapse of the empire and those who had obtained foreign citizenship in the dying days of the extraterritorial world of empires were in a precarious position. Members of long-standing diasporas were not guaranteed citizenship in the cities that had been their only real homelands.[69]

Taking a longer view of this phenomenon reminds us that contemporary issues linked to new forms of globalization had a very long pedigree. The Uzbek and Uyghur diasporas in today's Mecca, Medina, and Jeddah are part of the afterlife of this period of transimperial mobility and travel. Still carrying appellations like "To'ra" and "Khan" that evoke their connections to Central Asia, or geographic names that signal ties to places like Bukhara and have become Arabicized along the lines of "al-Bukhari," their surnames hint at a liminal status that began to develop in the late Ottoman era. Similar to diasporic Indian communities in the Gulf, they point to the continued problems faced by local cosmopolitans who never become fully indigenized. Their position speaks to both the rootedness of this form of residence and its precarity. Citizenship and its attendant privileges are primarily the preserve of Arabs, and people whose families have ties to the region as far back as the Ottoman era remain perennial insider-outsiders whose residence and status is insecure.

Religious travel to Ottoman lands could lead to two types of long-term residence, both distinguished from pilgrimage. The first was a type of migration and long-term residence in cities like Istanbul, the second a form of pious residence in the Holy Cities. Many Muslim foreign nationals who settled in Istanbul or the Hijaz—like foreign protégés, protected persons, and other transimperial subjects—found ways to straddle these legal categories and to circumvent restrictions that modernizing empires began to institute in the nineteenth century. But many did not. I have argued that this was because they were not compelled to. Thus, while cases of people living as residents without naturalizing—and not having any major problems—might seem unimportant, even banal, these stories are essential for our understanding of legal nationality and subjecthood in the late Ottoman Empire. Glimpses into the lives of ecnebi who had no problems marrying and buying land, or who could petition a sovereign who was not technically their own, are just as important for understanding the evolution of imperial subjecthood and citizenship as the more riveting stories of people who successfully took advantage of situations of overlapping or divided sovereignty in imperial borderlands and frontiers. Again and again, their stories point to the challenges of making certain types of imperial space and locally constructed views of communal belonging conform to new, top-down conceptions of territory and sovereignty.

The stories of de facto Ottomans also show that foreign Muslim subjects did not become Ottomans *only* because of their religious identity. Prior to the abrogation of the Capitulations, people like Hacı Sahib were content, after all, to *not* become Ottoman nationals. There is no doubt, however, that being part of the "ehl-i sünnet" ("people of the Prophet's Sunna—i.e., Sunni Muslims) facilitated the process when they decided to convert their nationality and that religion was not completely divorced from naturalization.[70] But rather than "formally [breaking] the connection between religion and citizenship,"[71] the First World War began the process of severing the main source of anxiety surrounding foreign Muslims: their access to the Capitulations. Whereas non-Muslims—Ottoman and non-Ottoman—were increasingly regarded as threats to the empire, the caution surrounding Sunni Muslim foreign nationals began to lift when they could no longer claim foreign protection. At least in the case of Bukharans and other Central Asians, the threat was not entirely in the person of the foreign Muslim but the foreign state that offered them protection.[72] When people like Hacı Sahib and Murad Efendi became naturalized, the process of telsik was a formalization of their membership in the empire. At the same time, their stories show that despite the rhetoric of Tanzimat-era decrees and nationality reform, Ottoman subjecthood was not decoupled from religion.[73] As histories of non-Muslims have shown, the biggest challenges to the political and social integration of non-Muslim groups such as Sephardi Jews as full-fledged members of the polity was the shift from civic Ottomanism toward Islamic Ottomanism in the Hamidian and Young Turk periods. For example, it was only by aligning their interests with the Islamic Ottoman state that Sephardi Jews were able to solidify their position as a loyal non-Muslim but distinctively Ottoman *millet* (ethno-religious community).[74]

Finally, tracing the interconnections between pilgrimage and migration is crucial for making sense of why European consuls sought ardently to extend their protections to Muslims in the Hijaz and why the Porte became increasingly cautious about the status and rights of mücavirin to landholding. Whereas pilgrims came and went, these guests of God stayed indefinitely and blended into local communities in ways that the Porte had limited power to regulate. Through simultaneous attempts to limit their numbers *and* to furnish them with the patronage they merited as pious men of religion, the Porte once again laid bare its ambivalence on the question of just how foreign these foreign Muslims were.

{ CONCLUSION }

A RETURN TO SULTANTEPE

AS THE OTTOMANS ENTERED the Great War that would bring about the empire's collapse, statesmen were still revisiting seemingly intractable questions about nationality and protection. Despite decades of legal opinions and negotiations, the confusion surrounding the status and rights of Central Asians had not diminished, and the Foreign Ministry had yet to enunciate a positive statement on what it meant for mahmi to be protected by the caliphate but excluded from Ottoman nationality and the nascent citizenry. In January of 1916, just months before the Arab Revolt that would open a new front in the war and lead to the ultimate loss of the Hijaz, the Ottoman governor (*muhafiz*) of Medina, Basri Pasha, wrote to the Interior Ministry about the vexed position of long-term residents in the city. He explained that although mücavirin had long since cut off ties with their homelands, established families, and become business and property owners, they had not been able to obtain Ottoman identity papers. Basri Pasha implied that this was due to the government's failure to develop localized naturalization procedures. In fact, he had been writing to Istanbul about this precarious situation since at least 1913, describing how Central Asians who wanted to become Ottomans were hamstrung by Russian and Ottoman bureaucratic intransigence. Because of fears that Russian authorities would not recognize the naturalization of Central Asians, the government in Istanbul had stopped allowing them to become Ottomans, effectively conceding sovereignty to consular agents. He suggested that the state apply a model in use for Tunisians (former Ottomans who became subjects of a French protectorate and who tried frequently to pass as Algerians to benefit from French nationality). He advocated requiring those who wanted to naturalize to sign oaths renouncing all future claims of foreign protection and to acknowledge that failure to abide by these oaths would result in confiscation of property and immediate exile. Basri Pasha also admonished his colleagues in Istanbul to show some flexibility: Medina's pious residents, he suggested, were inherently different from other foreigners and had long since made the City of the Prophet their homeland (*vatan*).[1]

That same winter, Hijaz governor Galib Pasha corresponded with Istanbul about the status of mücavirin in the other Holy City, Mecca. In yet another familiar script, he wrote that long-term residents were continuing to involve foreign consuls in their commercial and administrative affairs. He opined that all foreigners living in the city for three to five years should, by law, be considered Ottomans (*Osmanlı add edilmesi*).[2] While the two authorities had different views of the problem—Basri Pasha asserting that mücavirin were Ottomans in all but name and Galib Pasha voicing concerns about foreign consuls and the Capitulations—both were essentially proposing ways to facilitate the naturalization of "foreign Muslims" and to bring them, legally, into the Ottoman fold. They were rehashing the same questions that had occupied their predecessors during the reigns of Sultan Abdülmecid and Abdülhamid II, as well as the Young Turk government. The fault lines in the Ottoman nationality project were still there, the question of foreign Muslims just one crack among many.

In Istanbul, the Office of Legal Counsel was also revisiting the protection question. This time, it was prompted by a recent attempt by Austria-Hungary to represent Kashgaris. Perhaps the outbreak of the war had led this Ottoman ally to consider cultivating protégés in Istanbul with ties to China. "From the very beginning," the Office of Legal Counsel stated, "the imperial government's established position has been that Muslim subjects of independent foreign governments are, while in Ottoman lands, under the protection of the Islamic caliphate." After summing up the 1890 landmark legal opinion on Afghans, the office noted a 1913–14 ruling on Moroccans. Unlike Algerians, who were recognized as French nationals, Moroccans were added to the list of people from "independent Muslim states" who were protected by the caliphate. After an inconclusive discussion on the affairs and status of non-Muslim Chinese subjects (who could not be "protected" by the caliphate), legal jurists recommended a stopgap measure to deal with the Kashgaris in question. "For now," they advised the Interior Ministry "to settle . . . these types of Asian Muslims" in Sufi lodges (*tekaya ve zevaya*) that were designated for such purposes. Describing them as "poor people . . . in need of assistance," the Ministry drew on tropes about poverty that had long informed both petitioning and patronage and that, in effect, minimized the Kashgaris' agency in turning to European powers for support.[3] It was striking that the Office of Legal Counsel—not a religious ministry or office—had again proposed an answer to a problem of international law and sovereignty through recourse to Islamic institutions. The Ottoman central government was still improvising, and Bukharans and Kashgaris—as well as Tunisians, Moroccans, and Afghans—were still seeking foreign protection from European powers that would represent their interests. Like empires in disparate contexts and times, the Ottomans were trying to "enfold these [people] into the state's protection."[4] The alternative was to allow them to obtain foreign protection or nationality, opening the door to more intervention and creating a precedent for Austro-Hungarian involvement in the affairs of Chinese Muslims.

Although the ministry did not have a specific term for "these kinds of Muslims," they were people whom this book has identified as the sultan's spiritual subjects: Muslims from informally colonized lands who were categorized as foreigners, denied the right of a viable legal nationality, and claimed as subjects of the Ottoman caliphate. As migrants, they were often prevented from converting to Ottoman nationality (*tebdil-i tabiiyet*) as a result of fears that they would later revert or that their Ottoman subjecthood would not be recognized by European powers. Now, in the context of the empire's latest attempt to abrogate the Capitulations, there remained no real obstacles to their naturalization. After being sent to Sultantepe or the Bukhara Dergahı, or one of the Kashgari lodges in Eyüp, they would either wait out the war and return home or become naturalized as Ottomans. Like Hacı Sahib and Murad and their families, "these Muslims" would fill out preprinted naturalization forms and become Ottoman subjects—even if this was not their first choice—and, later, Turkish citizens. Their legal liminality was resolved only when there was no longer a threat of Russian or British protection. In just a few short years, in 1918, the Interior Ministry would decide to treat people from Bukhara like locals and to accord them the rights and privileges of Ottoman subjects.[5]

Without attention to the extraterritorial dynamics that created their liminality after 1869, it might be tempting to assume that the relatively smooth naturalization of Central Asians was a testament to pan-Islamism and the increasing salience of Turkic identities. But to do so would be a mistake. Like *identity*—a term that often "tends to mean too much (when understood in a strong sense), too little (when understood in a weak sense), or nothing at all (because of its sheer ambiguity)"—this book has challenged the value of pan-Islamism or pan-Turkism as analytical categories to explain the range of interactions between Central Asians and the late Ottoman state. It has argued that their "use and abuse . . . affects not only the language of social analysis but also—inseparably—its substance."[6] As we have seen, despite the rhetoric of pan-Islamic unity, in practice, the Hamidian and Young Turk governments accepted Russian rule in Central Asia and classified Turkic peoples in the empire based on how they had been subjugated. Through novel engagements with international law, both regimes denied certain groups a viable legal nationality specifically because they were *not* formally colonized by European powers. Whereas the Porte ultimately acquiesced in and recognized European jurisdiction over Indians, Jawis, Algerians, and other colonial subjects (with the exception of the Hijaz, which it maintained was exempt from the Capitulations), it insisted that people from protectorates were under its exclusive jurisdiction. Even though some Central Asians were formally colonized, the frequent conflation of Bukhara and Russian Turkestan, and Russia's insistent claims of protecting people who were not tsarist subjects, muddled these distinctions. While there is no denying that the Ottoman state promoted the caliphate to augment and legitimize its authority, it was willing to use the tools of European international law to differentiate among members of the umma—and to do so based on deeply problematic legal fictions about "semi-sovereignty" and "independence" that justified informal colonialism. The House of Osman had not only accepted the logic of European imperialism; it had also borrowed colonial methods to ensure its own survival, whether in borderlands and new hinterlands or in growing communities of migrants from abroad.[7]

Beyond Ottomans, foreigners, and protégés, there were variegated types of membership in the late Ottoman Empire, which we lose sight of in attempts to fit the Ottoman story into a mold that derives from a very peculiar and narrow Western model and conceptual vocabulary. In making the case for the emergence of spiritual subjecthood—a form of belonging formed as much by praxis and pilgrimage networks as by government responses to extraterritoriality—this study has offered a new way to think about belonging in an empire that was ruled by a sultan/caliph, and it has invited further engagement with the role of the hajj in late Ottoman history. Alongside the merchants in port cities and trade entrepots who became protected persons; the Jewish "model *millet*" of Istanbul and Salonica working to solidify its position in a changing empire; Christian, Muslim, and Jewish elites in Palestine participating in post-Tanzimat provincial councils; and Circassian or Chechen refugees setting up farms and homesteads in remote corners of Anatolia and Greater Syria, with tools and funds they were given with their Ottoman identity papers—we can now envision Bukharan and Kashgari hajjis setting up prayer-bead businesses in Istanbul or Medina, hedging their bets about nationality and passing as Ottomans.[8] While my focus has not been explicitly on the making of imperial citizens—a process that involves a different kind of discussion about political participation and rights—this story broadens our understanding of the genealogy of Ottoman subjecthood and Turkish citizenship, nonetheless, by highlighting the ways that "these kinds of Muslims" shifted the meaning of both nationality and foreignness. Unlike people who were already subjects of the sultan (though not necessarily "Ottoman" in the sense of an imperial or patriotic identity), Central Asians came into the empire as foreigners. For them, the process of becoming Ottoman was a legal one that involved acquiring Ottoman nationality. In a sense, many of the Bukharans, Kashgaris, and Andijanis were already members of local communities in Ottoman lands, long before they formalized their legal status as subjects—thus offering insight into the spectrum of subjecthood across the empire prior to the Great War.

Including Central Asians in the history of nationality reform not only adds to the picture; it changes it by pointing to the salience of understudied religious communities and networks in the late Ottoman Empire. By beginning to disaggregate encounters among Ottomans and Muslims from abroad—and taking them out of the "pan-" framework—we see an empire where religion constrained and limited the field of governmental reforms, produced understudied imperial burdens, and created heightened connections to Muslims from abroad. Keeping sight of religious sensibilities in a history of the hajj—even though it is one of the more challenging parts of writing about experiences of ordinary people coming into contact with the state—helps us understand how and why these heightened connections occurred. Even if spiritual subjects were an anomaly—which, given the connections between former Ottoman subjects in the Balkans and Ottomans, and comparisons of Afghans and Bukharans to Tunisians and, later, Moroccans, is unlikely—they tell us something important about religion in the late Ottoman state.[9] Whatever we choose to call it—nationality, subjecthood, or citizenship—the making of Ottomans was not a secular process. Hajjis, Muslim migrants, and pious residents were among the various constituents the Porte considered in calculations about the sovereignty of the empire and the "glory of the caliphate."

These were the considerations of a Muslim power. To recognize this does not imply that the government was solely "motivated by religious texts or visions" or that it could not simultaneously pursue strategies based on "liberal civilizationalism and a desire . . . to be part of the Eurocentric world order."[10] Instead, it means engaging with the idea that a Muslim empire (like hajjis themselves) could have multiple agendas and visions—some of which clashed, competed, and constrained its field of action—and calling into question what it means to be a Muslim empire or what makes something Islamic rather than pan-Islamic, and why the distinction matters. Grappling with how Islam informed governmental policies or praxis requires historians to question assumptions about the religious and secular as two distinct spheres and to recognize that the tendency to contrast the two and to systematically connect them with binaries such as the "sacred" and "profane" is constitutive of Western history and historiography, and that such binaries do not map neatly onto the Ottoman experience.[11] The alternative is to contribute to the ongoing reification of the idea that the Ottoman Empire was instrumentalizing religion to augment its authority and to compete with other imperial powers. There is something lost in thinking of religion in these terms and as an object that states could manipulate, co-opt, and utilize. Working toward deconstructing "spiritual" authority also offers a path toward a fuller picture of the constellation of meanings embedded in *ecnebi* at the end of empire, when the state was defining Ottoman Christians as outsiders, targeting them for deportation and denaturalization at the same time that it was allowing foreign Muslims to formalize their membership in the polity.[12]

The echoes of spiritual subjecthood continued to reverberate long after the empire collapsed and, indeed, well after the 1923 Treaty of Lausanne recognized the territorial sovereignty of the Turkish nation-state and ended the extraterritorial order that had haunted the Ottomans. After a brief attempt to separate the caliph's spiritual and temporal power and to arrogate his political authority to the Turkish National Assembly in Ankara, in 1924 Mustafa Kemal abolished the caliphate altogether. The following year, he ordered the closure of Turkey's Sufi orders and lodges. In the early years of the republic, nationalist ideologues would begin to write alternative accounts of historical Turkic relations, as Mustafa Kemal and his supporters posited spurious ruptures from the Ottoman past.[13] Yet in the arena of citizenship, the Ottoman past figured prominently. As Lerna Ekmekçioğlu has argued in the context of Armenians' efforts to reconstitute their community after the genocide, this former Ottoman *millet* (ethnoreligious community) assumed a form of citizenship that borrowed from the Ottoman system to rule "People of the Book" (*dhimmi*). In what she terms "secular dhimmitude," the relationship between a Muslim-majority nation-state and its Christian citizens was governed by an Islamic legal category that, in theory, had no place in the laicist order.[14] As a tool of both political marginalization and inclusion, the logic of secular dhimmitude was in some ways similar to the exclusion and inclusion of foreign Muslims from the Islamic Ottoman Empire. Now, the republic, which effectively treated Armenians as "step-citizens," welcomed Muslims who had earlier been legal liminal actors into the citizenry—and in ways it never would non-Muslims.

Whereas inter- and transimperial histories often start by invoking global processes and ruptures, or stories about empires or people who made it into the archive because they were in some sense exceptional, this book intentionally began in the courtyard of a small Sufi lodge in Istanbul amid scenes of day-to-day life. In part, this was to illustrate that hajj was not just something happening in a distant province at a set time of year but a ritual woven into the structure and life of Ottoman cities. It was also meant to root the history of Ottoman–Central Asian connections in a site we can imagine, with a magnolia tree that evokes the passing of seasons, and the stories of people who constituted networks we often speak of in the abstract. In lieu of broad brushstrokes, my goal has been to draw a more fine-grained picture of the people, places, contradictions, and experiences that informed pilgrimage and migration in Ottoman, inter-Asian, and global history. As I reached the conclusion of this book, reading the 1915 Office of Legal Counsel decision to place "these kinds of Muslims" in such sites seemed to me almost apocryphal. But it reflected the reality that as Central Asians and Ottoman statesmen both navigated complex trajectories and terrains, it seemed that they all ended up back at places like Sultantepe.

If we were to peer into the courtyard during the Great War, we would see a decline in pilgrims traveling to and from Mecca and Medina. In their place would be migrants looking for employment, joining the military, and figuring out their next steps. It is likely that a significant number of the people recorded in the registers had at some point taken actions to draw in Russian and British authorities, effectively being part of the protection question that occupied Ottoman statesmen. Among the hajjis at the lodge—and they were overwhelmingly hajjis—we would thus find people who had sought outside protection (some with more luck than others) and had been offered caliphal protection instead. As the Ottomans fought the British and Russians in a growing global conflagration, many of those with Russian passports or British protection would finally elect to naturalize. The Muslim pilgrimage had brought them to the empire, and the politics of hajj patronage and imperial protection had made them into a new kind of Ottoman.

Many of these Ottomans would later become Turks, joined by migrants who traveled along the old hajj routes and were integrated into communities across former Ottoman lands that first took root in the early modern period. Those who arrived in the old Ottoman capital would find functioning Sufi communities in the Buhara Dergahı in Sultanahmet and the Özbekler Tekkesi in Üsküdar, even though both were supposed to have ceased operating as mystical brotherhoods. In concluding this book, I offer two final peeks into how Sultantepe continued to live on in Republican Turkey. The first glimpse is from a letter tucked into one of the guest registers. Dated 12 December 1936, "My shaykh Necmeddin Efendi," it begins. "First, let me start with a special greeting and kiss your two hands." In a series of questions about the health and well-being of the shaykh and the people at the tekke, the writer sent his greetings and kisses to an Osman Bey, Hacı Celil Efendi, and Hacı İbrahim Ağa. He mentions that although he stopped by on several occasions, he was not able to find the shaykh, and he asks him to keep him in his prayers. After dating and signing the letter, the author—a certain Türkistanlı Abdulmalik, who identifies himself as a gendarme from Meğriköy (today's Bakırköy in Istanbul)—adds a note at the very end: "Our countrymen [*hemşerilerimiz*] were going to petition to go to Anatolia as *muhacir* [refugees]. Please let me know what happened in this matter."[15]

FIGURE 13. Sultantepe Özbekler Tekkesi guest register, entry from 1958. Photograph by author.

The second glimpse is on the penultimate page of the last tekke register I was able to find. At the bottom of the page, Necmeddin Efendi noted: "Hacı Seyyid Ali has died. Fifteen years ago, he came to the dergah. On Friday 1-4-1958 he passed away at the Numune Hospital, and was buried in the dergah's graveyard. The money for the deceased's funeral was taken from the 400 lira found on his person, and spent on his funeral. His identity photograph is attached to this register." Next to Hacı Seyyid Ali's photograph, the shaykh signed his name, "the *hadim* (servant) of the dergah, Necmeddin."[16] In doing so, he testified not only to the hajji's death but also to the ways that the lodge had continued to care for members of its community and circumvented the legal structures of a new polity by continuing to operate as a Sufi lodge. Hacı Seyyid Ali would be laid to rest in the same cemetery as the hajjis who took their last journeys while in Istanbul, back in the days when the Ottomans were the custodians of the pilgrimage.

ACKNOWLEDGMENTS

Throughout the last decade I have thought a lot about Mirim Khan's admonition that there can be no hajj without hardship and felt certain the same was true about writing a book. Although many of his fellow travelers left much to be desired, my companions on this journey have been nothing short of wonderful. It is with great pleasure that I offer them my gratitude.

My first debt is to a community of extraordinary scholars who have shaped my thinking about law, religion, empire, networks, and transregional history. Robert McChesney, Jane Burbank, Zachary Lockman, Leslie Peirce, Mehdi Khorrami, Khaled Fahmy, Ariel Salzmann, Fred Cooper, Larry Wolff, and the late Tony Judt played an important role in my development as a historian. From my days as an undergraduate at NYU through the inception and completion of this project, Robert McChesney has been a steadfast source of support and a model of integrity. If this book approaches in some small measure the value of one of his studies on Central Asia, it is due in large part to his mentoring. Working with Jane Burbank, whose intellectual rigor and generosity are legendary for good reason, has been a joy and a privilege. As an interlocutor and friend, she has challenged my thinking at crucial junctures and made my scholarship so much richer in the process. Adeeb Khalid has been an unwavering mentor—reading, critiquing, and encouraging me to try to shift conversations about Central Asian history in new directions. His work has been a model of scholarship, his humor and friendship a source of relief in moments of absurdity. Cemil Aydın's visionary approach to global Islamic history has given me so much to think about. I thank him for sharing his exuberance and insights in conversations from Seoul to Durham to New York.

I was very lucky to join a vibrant history department at The City College of New York, which felt like home from the first day. This is due in large part to a student body that continually reminds me of why I chose this profession and of the importance of public education. It is also due to my brilliant colleagues. I thank my chair, Anne Kornhauser, and dean, Erec Koch, for their support and encouragement during the completion of this book. Craig Daigle, Clifford Rosenberg, Seiji Shirane, and Eric Weitz read parts of the manuscript and helped me frame and clarify its arguments. I thank them and Mikhal Dekel, Barbara Naddeo, Adrienne Petty, and Barbara Syrrakos for their camaraderie and encouragement. Andreas Killen offered insightful feedback, read many more versions of chapters than I can adequately thank him for, and has been a terrific mentor and friend. Moe Liu-d'Albero has enriched my time at City and helped me navigate many administrative challenges. Anny Bakalian welcomed me into the extended CUNY family with gusto and offered much-needed support after the loss of my father. I also extend my deepest thanks to Beth Baron, who sponsored the workshop "The 'Subjects' of Ottoman International Law" at the CUNY Graduate Center and organized a manuscript workshop that greatly improved this book. Her commitment to junior faculty, social history, and Middle East Studies is truly inspiring.

It was my good fortune to meet Michael Christopher Low at a conference in Leiden and to later realize a project with him and Aimee Genell on international law. My understanding of Ottoman and global history has expanded exponentially as a result of our joint ventures, and my friendship with each of them is a treasured gift. Both have read and carefully commented on the manuscript with great erudition, for which I am immensely grateful. That they gave so much of their time while preparing their own groundbreaking books for publication makes them even more wonderful. Emily Greble, who came into my life at the Remarque Institute and has been a force of nature ever since, deserves special mention. The stories I wanted to tell have always made sense to her, and I thank her for helping me share them, as well as for a deeply rewarding friendship. My beloved friend Susan Gunasti was instrumental in helping me articulate the salience of religion in Ottoman history. I am also thankful for Christine Philliou, Dominique Reill, and Seçil Yılmaz, whose formidable intellects are matched by tremendous grace and humor. Guy Burak and Timur Hammond—along with Beth Baron and Emily Greble—were incredibly generous in reading the entire manuscript, and I thank them for enriching it with the vast breadth of their knowledge.

Between New York and Istanbul, many friends and colleagues provided comments, erudite insights, challenges to my thinking—and joy. My warmest thanks to Faiz Ahmed, Önder Eren Akgül, Mustafa Aksakal, Leyla Amzi-Erdoğdular, Alex Boodrookas, Allison Brown, Jeffrey Culang, Sam Dolbee, Lerna Ekmekçioğlu, Tolga Esmer, Stacy Fahrenthold, Elizabeth Frierson, Chris Gratien, Zoe Griffith, Jane Hathaway, Iris Warren Henry, Masha Kirasirova, Baz Lecocq, Matt MacLean, Jessica Marglin, James Meyer, Marijana Misevic, Metin Noorata, Yekaterina Oziashvili, Uğur Peçe, James Pickett, Jim Ryan, Kent Schull, Rabia Şirin, Eric Tagliacozzo, Malissa Taylor, Nükhet Varlık, Joshua White, Carole Woodall, and Murat Yıldız. *Katta rahmat* to Eric Schluessel for fielding my many questions about Central Asia with such generosity of spirit.

In homes away from home, Guzal Aripdjanova, Joshua Kucera, Kaan Nazlı, and Yankı and Şule Yazgan offered inestimable hospitality. There is no way for me to properly thank Belkıs Özbek, who graciously welcomed me into her world and taught me so much about embracing the present. Ayhan Han, Başak Tuğ, and Umut Türem helped make Istanbul warmer, and Hilola Nazirova fostered the sense that Tashkent was closer. My gratitude goes to Ulrike Freitag, for welcoming me to Zentrum Moderner Orient, and to Nikolaos Chrissidis and Gelina Harlaftis, for reminding me of the Mediterranean's centrality, in the ideal setting of Crete.

In Tashkent, everyone at the Navoi Library, Central State Archive, and Biruni Institute was exceptionally helpful, particularly Bakhtiyar Babadjanov and Shovosil Ziyodov. I also thank the staff of the Başbakanlık Archives in Istanbul, especially, Fuat Recep, Ayten Ardel, and Ertuğrul Çakır for facilitating my research and making it such a joyful experience. I will be forever grateful to Mustafa Budak for vouching for me when I needed it most and to Ethem Özbekkangay, who provided access to the Sultantepe archives and trusted me with sources on pilgrims that give life to this study. Jo'ra Boy Bo'teko'z,

Hakan Karateke, Selim Kuru, and Wheeler Thackston were remarkable Ottoman and Chaghatay teachers. My thanks also go to Timur Kocaoğlu and Grace Martin Smith, for their help when I first embarked on this project, and to Turgay Erol and Murat Kargılı, for allowing me to use images from their gorgeous book on the hajj in postcards.

Crucial financial support for the research and writing of this book was provided by the National Endowment for the Humanities, the Social Science Research Council (SSRC) Transregional Fellows Program, PSC-CUNY Research Award Program, CUNY Faculty Publication Program, and the CUNY Book Completion Award. Seteney Shami, Engseng Ho, Cemil Aydın, Mimi Hanaoka, and Masha Kirasirova made my most recent SSRC fellowship especially rewarding. At the Remarque Institute, I thank Katherine Fleming for support of the final stages of writing. Samantha Paul was kind beyond words and helped me find the elusive peace I needed. The SSRC, International Research and Exchange Board, American Research Institute in Turkey (ARIT), and Fulbright-Hays also funded early stages of research in Turkey and Uzbekistan. Many thanks to Nancy Leinwand at ARIT and Holly Danzeisen at the SSRC for their efforts to support this project. I would like to express my appreciation to the Schoff Fund at the University Seminars at Columbia University for help in publication. Material in this work was presented to the University Seminar in Ottoman and Turkish Studies.

I also presented parts of this book at workshops at Harvard University, Vanderbilt University, Smith College, and the CUNY Graduate Center. I thank the organizers and participants for their valuable feedback, particularly Lauren Benton, Lisa Ford, Julia Phillips Cohen, Samira Sheikh, Anand Vivek Taneja, Moses Ochonu, David Gutman, Ilham Khuri-Makdisi, and Vladimir Hamed-Troyansky. Will Hanley and Will Smiley sharpened my analysis of all things related to nationality and subjecthood and have been fantastic friends. I thank James Baldwin for co-organizing a panel on petitioning that informs Chapter 4. Sections of Chapters 2 and 3 were published in *Modern Asian Studies* and *IJMES*. My thanks to the reviewers of these articles as well as the anonymous readers of the manuscript for their constructive and rich feedback. I'd also like to express my gratitude to Tim Harper and Sunil Amrith for inviting me to publish my first article on inter-Asian connections. Many years later, writing my first book on this topic has been a wonderful experience, thanks to the inimitable Kate Wahl, Leah Pennywark, Jessica Ling, Joe Abbott, and the outstanding team at Stanford University Press. Kate's faith in this project has meant the world to me. She gave me the courage to write the book I wanted to write, and I thank her for supporting it throughout a long gestation period.

I also thank my family, particularly my sisters, Saadet, Şerafet, and Serpil. I want to express my deepest regard and appreciation to my beloved brother and first mentor, Ahmet, who painstakingly read many versions of this book and helped me see it through to the end. *Velhasıl kelam*, my final expression of gratitude, is reserved for my parents. Long before I became a historian, these two intensely complicated and beautiful people helped me understand global history in ways they probably never imagined. They gave me the wherewithal to research and write historical accounts that grew from seeds they planted during my childhood. I have done my best to honor them through my work and I dedicate this book to them. It is my deepest wish that my father, whom I imagine in an orchard in Kashgar, can see how much he lives on in all that I do. My hope is that one day I will visit the landscape of his most vivid stories and find people who are once again free—both to enjoy the sweet fruits of their native land and to travel to the spiritual center of their faith.

NOTES

Abbreviations

BAŞBAKANLIK OSMANLI ARŞİVİ (BOA)

A.AMD	Sadaret Amedi Kalemi
A.MKT	Sadaret Evrakı Mektubi Kalemi
A.MKT.MHM	Sadaret Mektubi Mühimme Evrakı
A.MKT.NZD	Sadaret Mektubi Kalemi Nezaret ve Devair Evrakı
A.MKT.UM	Sadaret Mektubi Kalemi Umum Vilayat Evrakı
BEO	Bab-ı Ali Evrak Odası
C.HR	Cevdet Hariciye
C.ML	Cevdet Maliye
DH.EUM	Dahiliye Nezareti Emniyet-i Umumiye
DH.EUM.ECB	Dahiliye Emniyet-i Umumiye Ecanib Kalemi
DH.EUM.THR	Dahiliye Emniyet-i Umumiye Müdiriyeti Tahrirat Kalemi
DH.H	Dahiliye Nezareti Hukuk Kalemi Evrakı
DH.HMŞ	Dahiliye Nezareti Hukuk Müşavirliği
DH.İD	Dahiliye Nezareti İdare Evrakı
DH.İ.UM.EK	Dahiliye Nezareti İdare-i Umumiye Kalemi Ekleri

DH.MB.HPS	Dahiliye Nezareti Mebani-i Emiriye Hapishaneler Müdiriyeti Evrakı
DH.MKT	Dahiliye Nezareti Mektubi Kalemi
DH.MUİ	Dahiliye Nezareti Muhaberat-ı Umumiye İdaresi Evrakı
DH.SN.THR	Dahiliye Nezareti Sicill-i Nüfus Tahrirat Kalemi
DH.UMVM	Dahiliye Nezareti Umur-ı Mahalliye-i Vilayat Müdiriyeti Evrakı
HAT	Hatt-ı Hümayun
HR.H	Hariciye Nezareti Hukuk Kısım Evrakı
HR.HMŞ.İŞO	Hariciye Nezareti Hukuk Müşavirliği İstişare Odası Evrakı
HR.MKT	Hariciye Nezareti Mektubi Kalemi
HR.SYS	Hariciye Nezareti Siyasi
HR.TO	Hariciye Nezareti Tercüme Odası Evrakı
İ.DH	İrade Dahiliye
İ.HR	İrade Hariciye
İ.HUS	İrade Hususi
İ.ML	İrade Maliye
İ.MVL	İrade Meclis-i Vala
İ.TAL	İrade Taltif
MV	Meclis-i Vükela Mazbataları
ŞD	Şura-yı Devlet Evrakı
Y.A.HUS	Yıldız Sadaret Hususi Maruzat Evrakı
Y.A.RES	Yıldız Sadaret Resmi Maruzat Evrakı
Y.EE	Yıldız Esas Evrakı
Y.MTV	Yıldız Mütenevvi Maruzat Evrakı
Y.PRK.A	Yıldız Perakende Sadaret Maruzatı
Y.PRK.ASK	Yıldız Perakende Askeri Maruzat
Y.PRK.AZJ	Yıldız Perakende Arzuhal ve Jurnaller
Y.PRK.ŞD	Yıldız Perakende Şura-yı Devlet
Y.PRK.UM	Yıldız Perakende Evrak-ı Umumi
ZB	Zabtiye Nezareti

JOURNAL ABBREVIATIONS

AHR	*American Historical Review*
CSSAAME	*Comparative Studies of South Asia, Africa and the Middle East*

CSSH	*Comparative Studies in Society and History*
IJMES	*International Journal of Middle East Studies*
JIS	*Journal of Islamic Studies*
JOTSA	*Journal of the Ottoman and Turkish Studies Association*
MES	*Middle Eastern Studies*

CALENDAR (HİCRİ MONTHS)

M	Muharrem
S	Safer
Ra	Rebiülevvel
R	Rebiülahir
Ca	Cemaziyelevvel
C	Cemaziyelahir
B	Receb
Ş	Şaban
N	Ramazan
L	Şevval
Za	Zilkade
Z	Zilhicce

Preface: On Twists and Turns

1. Lerna Ekmekçioğlu analyzes the treatment of minorities in early Republican Turkey—particularly in the context of European imperial powers' infringements on Ottoman sovereignty at the end of empire and during the interwar minority protections regime—and shows how fears of reproducing European interventions led Turkey's new leaders to both forcibly include non-Muslim Turkish citizens *and* to exclude them from "Turkness." See Ekmekçioğlu, "Republic of Paradox."

Introduction: The Terrain of Transimperial Pilgrimage

1. Mustafa Kara's work on religion in the late Ottoman Empire highlights how pervasive Sufism and its institutional structures were in Ottoman social and cultural life. See Kara, *Din Hayat Sanat Açısından Tekkeler ve Zaviyeler*. On the mosques, tekkes, and other Islamic institutions of Üsküdar, see Haskan, *Yüzyıllar Boyunca Üsküdar*.

2. On the Naqshbandiyya in Ottoman history see LeGall, *A Culture of Sufism*; Algar, "Tarîqat and Tarîq"; and Abu-Manneh, "The Naqshbandiyya-Mujaddidiyya."

3. The sources on the lodge are primarily from a private collection I was allowed to access in 2007, which I refer to throughout as the Sultantepe Özbekler Tekkesi Arşivi (SÖTA). The collection is not archived or catalogued, and I refer to sources by the date of the document or the date of the register. This letter is addressed from the Eyüp Dergahı to Sultantepe postnişin, dated 10 Eylül 1315 (22 Sept. 1899). In addition to miscellaneous documents such as this letter, the SÖTA includes three guest registers. The registers are labeled as "Nüfus ve Kayıt Defteri" (identity and registration register), "Künye Defteri" (register of names), and "Resmi Misafirin Defteri" (official guest register) and they cover the years 1899–1906, 1907–23, and 1919–25, respectively. There are inconsistencies in the register entries in each.

4. SÖTA Register 1, "Üsküdar Sultantepesi'nde Kain Özbekler Dergahı'nın Nüfus ve Kayıt Defteri, fi 1 Zilkade 1316/fi 1 Mart 1315" [The Identity and Registration Register of the Uzbek Dergah located in Üsküdar, Sultantepe, 13 March 1899 through 9 January 1906]. Henceforth, "SÖTA Register 1." Entry no. 12.

5. I have not been able to find consistent statistical data on Central Asians traveling via Istanbul in the BOA. Kane estimates that twenty-five thousand Russian Muslims were traveling through Black Sea ports by the early twentieth century. See Kane, "Odessa," 2. It is not clear if this includes all Muslims from Russian-ruled territories. According to Reichmuth, "the number of pilgrims from all of Russia reached 184,000 in 1911, the number from Turkestan alone 50,000 in 1912, quoted as an increase by a factor of two within ten years." The figures he provides are based on Russian railway authorities and newspapers and seem very high. See Reichmuth, "Semantic Modeling," 216.

6. On nineteenth-century Muslim migrations and refugees, see Blumi, *Ottoman Refugees, 1878–1939*; Frantantuono, "Migration Administration"; Hamed-Troyansky, "Refugees and Empires"; and Gün, "Flight and Refuge." James H. Meyer also investigates return migration between the Russian and Ottoman Empires in "Immigration, Return."

7. On the treaty see Smiley, "The Burdens of Subjecthood"; and Davison, "'Russian Skill.'"

8. BOA, Y.PRK.ŞD 3/34, 1320 Z 29 (29 March 1903).

9. For classic studies on Russian conquest and rule see Becker, *Russia's Protectorates*; and Pierce, *Russian Central Asia*. More recent works include Sahadeo, *Russian Colonial Society*; and Morrison, *Russian Rule in Samarkand*. On Chinese Turkestan see Kim, *Holy War in China*; and Brophy, *Uyghur Nation*.

10. Brophy, *Uyghur Nation*, 7. Brophy quotes Muhammad Imin Bughra, a leader in Republican-era politics in Xinjiang, as saying that Qing and Republican-era rule was a period of "'two-and-a-half governments'—Russia and Britain counting for one each, and the Qing only half—a pithy description of what scholars refer to as semicolonialism" (7). Brophy draws out the significance of extraterritoriality in Xinjiang and explains that it "increasingly resembled the spheres of influence spreading throughout coastal China and Manchuria, dotted by treaty ports where foreigners enjoyed special

privileges" (7). While I often refer to the Qing and Republican period as "Chinese," this follows the Ottoman archival sources; Xinjiang was under Qing rule (a Manchu dynasty) from the late 1750s to 1911–12, followed by the Republic of China (through 1949). My use of "Chinese Turkestan" also follows Ottoman designations and distinguishes Kashgar and its environs from Russian Turkestan. On the Qing and post-Qing periods, see Millward, *Eurasian Crossroads*.

11. Ahmed, *Afghanistan Rising*.

12. For an example of this common usage see BOA DH.İD 61/77, 13 R 1330 (1 April 1912). "Her sene mevsim-i hacda Rusya ve Buhara gibi mahall-i baideden Dersaadet'e gelerek ..."

13. For example, through the 1950s, the Buhara Dergahı hosted émigrés from the Soviet Union and China, who lived in and/or communed at the lodge. The lodge's last shaykh, Abdurrahman Efendi (d. 1953), was involved in the activities of an organization that met there called Türkistan Gençler Birliği. See Yeşilot et al., *İstanbul'daki Türkistan Tekkeleri*.

14. On the treaty and the expansion of international law—which emerged as a Eurocentric framework for the practice of international relations by diplomats, based on treaty and customary law and, increasingly, the Capitulations—see Özsu, "Ottoman Empire"; Palabıyık, "Emergence of the Idea"; Genell, "Autonomous Provinces"; Smiley, *From Slaves to Prisoners*; and Rodogno, *Against Massacre*. Samera Esmeir elucidates how "international" law became a new branch of law regulating interstate relations. See Esmeir, "On Becoming Less."

15. Özsu, "The Ottoman Empire," 129; and Ahmad, "Ottoman Perceptions."

16. On the usage of *sahih*, see BOA, HR.HMŞ.İŞO 176/29, 4 L 1308 (13 May 1891).

17. I want to credit Ariel Salzmann for her use of the term "spiritual citizenship" in an early work on Ottoman citizenship and political participation. Her argument that pan-Islam "offered Muslims a type of spiritual 'citizenship' within an imaginary 'umma' superimposed over the modern political map" was important in shaping my thinking at the outset of this project. See Salzmann, "Citizens in Search," 51.

18. Although I use the term *subjecthood* and focus on nationality in this book, much of the literature uses "imperial citizenship" and "citizenship" to describe similar forms of imperial belonging. This is true of Eric Lohr's excellent history of Russian citizenship from the mid-nineteenth century through the 1930s. Writing in the context of naturalization, migration, and border policies aimed at Russian and Soviet citizens, he defines the citizenship boundary as "the line between members and nonmembers, on the rules and practices that define the boundary, and on the various ways citizenship was acquired, lost, ascribed, or removed." Lohr, *Russian Citizenship*, 3. For a study that explores foreigners' roles in the construction of nationality and citizenship in early nineteenth-century Central America, see Dym, "Citizens of Which Republic?"

19. On the protracted problem of European protégés see Hanley, *Identifying with Nationality*; Lewis, *Divided Rule*; and Sonyel, "The Protégé System." A recent and in-

sightful work on the reach of extraterritoriality that informs my analysis is Stein, *Extraterritorial Dreams*. On the Capitulations see Özsu, "Ottoman Empire"; Ahmad, "Ottoman Perceptions"; Van den Boogert, *The Capitulations*; and Spagnolo, "Portents of Empire."

20. Fahmy, "Jurisdictional Borderlands," 315.

21. On the Jeddah consular system see Freitag, "Helpless Representatives?" On British consular courts in Iraq see Stephens, "An Uncertain Inheritance"; and Çetinsaya, "The Ottoman View."

22. For an exploration of similar developments focusing on British subjects, see Low, "Unfurling the Flag."

23. Mary Dewhurst Lewis's work on French North Africa is indispensable for understanding the complexity of overlapping and divided sovereignty and the kinds of legal practices it gave rise to among people from informally colonized lands such as Tunisia (which was similar to Afghanistan and Bukhara in the context of international law). See Lewis, *Divided Rule*. Other important studies that reveal rich insights into legal pluralism include Marglin, "The Two Lives of Masʿud Amoyal"; Stein, *Extraterritorial Dreams*; and Clancy-Smith, *Mediterraneans*. On the Indian context see Beverly, *Hyderabad*. James Meyer shows how Muslims held on to Russian nationality through various ruses while also passing as Ottomans. See Meyer, *Turks across Empires*. For comparative insight on these practices in Xinjiang see Brophy, *Uyghur Nation*.

24. Will Hanley's innovative approach to nationality is particularly useful for thinking about how people understood legal personhood and for grasping how it differed from citizenship. See Hanley, *Identifying with Nationality*. For groundbreaking works on legal pluralism see Benton, *Law and Colonial Cultures*; and Benton and Ross, *Legal Pluralism and Empires*. For an important study in the Central Asian context see Sartori and Shahar, "Legal Pluralism."

25. Benton discusses this within the context of how conquered peoples in the Americas engaged with the Spanish legal order. See Benton, "Historical Perspectives," 61.

26. Early studies by historians of China and Japan help us to understand these issues in global perspective. See, e.g., Stern, *The Japanese Interpretation*; Scully, *Bargaining with the State*; Scully, "Taking the Low Road"; and Dudden, *Japan's Colonization of Korea*. More recent literature that sheds important comparative light on the Ottoman context includes Cassel, *Grounds of Judgement*; and McKeown, *Melancholy Order*.

27. For seminal studies of how the Hamidian government promoted pan-Islamism to counter European encroachments on its sovereignty and legitimize its Islamic authority, see Deringil, *The Well-Protected Domains*; Karpat, *The Politicization of Islam*; and Özcan, *Pan-Islamism*. On the different forms of pan-Islamism, see Khalid, "Pan-Islamism in Practice." For critiques of pan-Islam to explain Ottoman foreign policy, see Reynolds, "Buffers, Not Brethren"; and Dyer, "Pan-Islamic Propagandists?" For an early but important article on pan-Islamic ideology and its constraints (and salience) in Southeast

Asia, see Reid, "Nineteenth Century Pan-Islam." Newer scholarship on this topic that significantly revises our understanding of the role of religious ideology—and that shifts from the perspective of colonial empires and their anxieties—includes Can and Low, "The 'Subjects'"; Ahmed, *Afghanistan Rising*; and Aydın, *The Idea of the Muslim World*.

28. BOA, DH.MUİ 93/43, 6 Ca 1328 (15 June 1910); and BOA, DH.İD 61/77, 13 R 1330 (1 April 1912).

29. On the Ottoman caliphate see the important recent studies by Hassan, *Longing for the Lost Caliphate*; and Yılmaz, *Caliphate Redefined*. Additional works that discuss the caliphate's significance in Ottoman history include Turan, *Hilafetin Tarihsel Gelişimi*; Karpat, *The Politicization of Islam*; and Deringil, *The Well-Protected Domains*. For a recent study that engages with this institution more critically, see Aydın, *The Idea of the Muslim World*.

30. Yılmaz, *Caliphate Redefined*, 279.

31. See Gelvin and Green, *Global Muslims*; and Green "Spacetime."

32. Huber, *Channelling Mobilities*.

33. Michael Reynolds refers to this twinning of pan-Turkism and pan-Islamism as "the Panturanic thesis," which he critiques as "one of Ottoman historiography's most commonly reproduced theses but not one of its better-researched ones." He provides an important critique of the notion of brotherhood between Ottomans and Russian Muslims. See, Reynolds, "Buffers, Not Brethren," 137. Two early and influential studies of these ideologies are Landau, *The Politics of Pan-Islam* and *Pan-Turkism*.

34. For an extended discussion of Ottoman–Central Asian political relations in the longue durée see Can, "Trans-Imperial Trajectories."

35. Meyer, *Turks across Empires*, 2. On the ideologues of pan-Turkism see also Shissler, *Between Two Empires*.

36. Yeşilot, Çelik, and Varol, *İstanbul'daki Türkistan Tekkeleri*, 31, 16.

37. Cohen, *Becoming Ottomans*, 3.

38. According to Aydın, this was an idea of a unified global Muslim community, which emerged both in opposition to and in concert with narratives of Western civilization and progress based on racialized views of humanity. In their challenges to European civilizational superiority, prominent Islamic modernists and pan-Islamic ideologues reified this ordering of the world without questioning the inherently problematic dichotomy at its core. See Aydın, *The Idea of the Muslim World*, 3.

39. Important recent studies on Ottoman imperial subjecthood and citizenship include Cohen, *Becoming Ottomans*; Campos, *Ottoman Brothers*; Campos, "Imperial Citizenship"; and Kern, *Imperial Citizen*. For imperial citizenship in comparative and interimperial frameworks see Khoury and Glebov, "Citizenship, Subjecthood, and Difference in the Late Ottoman and Russian Empires."

40. Roff, "Sanitation and Security," 143.

41. Daniel Brower was among the first historians to argue that Tsarist Russia became a patron of Central Asian pilgrims as a consequence of attempts to regulate the

hajj in Russian Turkestan. More recently, leading scholars of European empires and hajj have significantly revised our understanding of the complex motives and goals of Russian and British pilgrimage regulation. In countering the historiographical focus on epidemiological concerns and surveillance and of conflictual relationships between empires and their Muslim populations, Eileen Kane and John Slight have argued for considering the Russian and British Empires as patrons and sponsors of the hajj. Their works compare Russian and British strategies to those of previous Muslim empires, including the Ottoman. See Brower, *Turkestan*; Kane, *Russian Hajj*; and Slight, *The British Empire*. Other important studies in this growing field of scholarly inquiry include Tagliacozzo, *The Longest Journey*; Brower, "The Hajj from Algeria"; Ryad, *The Hajj and Europe*; and Porter and Saif, *The Hajj*. While not directly related to pilgrimage, Robert Crews's study explores imperial Russia's engagement with Muslim populations. See Crews, *For Prophet and Tsar*.

42. Christine Philliou and Alan Mikhail provide an overview of historiographical comparisons to other empires. See Mikhail and Philliou, "The Ottoman Empire and the Imperial Turn." Similarly, Dina Khoury and Dane Kennedy productively compare the Ottoman and British Empires in the long nineteenth century in a special issue of *CSSAAME*.

43. For an influential discussion of problems in approaching religion outside of tradition, particularly Islamic discursive traditions, see Asad, *Idea of an Anthropology*. On the question of what makes something Islamic, see Ahmed, *What Is Islam?*

44. Tsing, "The Global Situation," 330.

45. On the limits of area studies in the Middle East context, see Lockman, *Contending Visions*. For a positive appraisal of area studies expertise and its value for critical scholarship and global history, see Kennedy, "Globalizing Knowledge."

46. Valentina Izmirlieva makes an analogous—and instructive—argument about the range of experiences among Orthodox pilgrims to Jerusalem in this era. See Izmirlieva, "Christian Hajjis."

47. BOA, HR.HMŞ.İŞO 207/6, 4 Za 1331 (5 Oct. 1913).

48. Low, "The Mechanics of Mecca," esp. 4–5, 9.

49. Low, "Unfurling the Flag." Deringil also draws attention to how the wealth and power of foreign Muslims in the Hijaz started to cause concern in Istanbul. His contention, however, that foreign Muslims were seen as a potential fifth column is based on a narrow reading of policy making at the highest levels and an assumption that "Ottoman" and "foreigner" were meaningful categories in the Hijaz, where belonging was determined in a variety of ways that did not necessarily align with the view from Yıldız Palace. See Deringil, *The Well-Protected Domains*, 58.

50. On how empires ruled multiconfessional and -ethnic populations through a variety of strategies ranging from accommodation to the manipulation of difference, see Burbank and Cooper, *Empires in World History*. Burbank explores this idea further,

specifically within the context of imperial citizenship in polities based on differentiated right, and challenges the idea that citizenship existed only in nation-states. See Burbank, "An Imperial Rights Regime." For an exploration of rule through difference in the Ottoman context see Barkey, *Empire of Difference*. Kuehn's study of Ottoman rule in Yemen, and what he terms the "politics of difference," also productively explores differentiated rule in the empires' borderlands, including signs of colonial characteristics. See Kuehn, *Empire, Islam, and Politics*.

51. Aydın uses this term to describe how the caliphate was articulated as a defensive instrument of diplomacy and foreign policy. He writes that the Ottomans claimed "spiritual sovereignty over Muslims globally and leverag[ed] this influence in political wrangling with the British and other European empires. Seeking a competitive edge by any means available, empires variously used the idea of global Muslim solidarity to weaken their rivals, justify alliances with them, and bolster propaganda campaigns." My use of the term is closer to his description of spiritual sovereignty as "partly a mirror image of European empires' claims on behalf of the rights of Ottoman Christians. If Christian monarchs could assert rights over the caliph's Christian subjects, the caliph could assert his spiritual authority over Muslim subjects of other monarchs." See Aydın, *The Idea of the Muslim World*, introduction and chap. 4. It is important to note that the nature of Ottoman claims of caliphal protection were largely limited to their own territories: in the system of international law, the sultan-caliph had no basis on which to make claims of extraterritorial authority over either his own legal nationals or Muslims who were protected by the caliphate.

52. Allen and Hamnett, *A Shrinking World?* David Harvey, who originated the concept, defines it as "processes that so revolutionize the objective qualities of space and time that we are forced to alter, sometimes in quite radical ways, how we represent the world to ourselves." See Harvey, *The Condition of Postmodernity*, 249. On space-time compression in the context of hajj see Green, "The Hajj as Its Own Undoing."

53. This study's approach to Sufism presents it as the pilgrims and shaykhs did: as one (important) facet of their identities. The book is not aimed at reconstructing a "real" or "authentic" Sufi type, whether in the form of a pilgrim, a dervish, or a lodge. Alexander Knysh takes on some of the pitfalls of searching for "authenticity" in his *Sufism: A New History*.

54. Harvey, *The Condition of Postmodernity*, 350.

55. For a provocative discussion of the usefulness of the term "nonelites," see Kotsonis, "Ordinary People."

56. On liminal subjects in other settings see Carlston, *Double Agents*; Haour, *Outsiders and Strangers*; and Arsan, *Interlopers of Empire*.

57. Turner, "The Center Out There."

58. Malcolm X, *Autobiography of Malcolm X*, 340–41.

59. In his discussion of Malcolm X, Michael Wolfe writes, "Pilgrims bring to Mecca what they find there. Malcolm X brought a lifelong hunger for racial equality." Wolfe, *One Thousand Roads*, 488.

Chapter 1. Rewriting the Road to Mecca

1. This is a Chaghatay manuscript in mixed prose and verse, preserved at the Biruni Institute for Oriental Studies in Tashkent, Uzbekistan, and catalogued as "Hajjnoma-i Turkiy," MS Turki IVANUz no. 12057; it is attributed to Muhammad Oxund [Akhund] Toshkandiy. The text is undated, but the author mentions being in Mecca in Dhu al-Hijjah of 1320 (March of 1903). The work is written in the *nastaliq* hand and contains 147 folios. The manuscript is not consistently or clearly numbered; my pagination begins from the first folio, which starts with the recitation of God's name and the lines "Ki bismillāhir-raḥmānir-raḥīm deb Xudoni yod etib yo karim deb, qiloydirmen safar qilsa inoyat / rafiqim bo'lsa tavfiqi hidoyat." Each folio has two pages, and each page (generally) has eleven lines. Folio 1, side B begins: "Minib otashg'a chiqtim su boshida." See Ziyodov, "The Hajjnâmas."

2. "Hajjnoma-i Turkiy" [hereafter HT], folios 56–59.

3. The author refers to himself as Mirim Khan in folio 18a [manuscript 12057] and writes, "Kamine hojji Mirim Khan duosın ijobat qil." In lithograph 4243 this is corrected to "Solih'ning duosın." According to Shovosil Ziyodov, the author's full name was either Imom-i Mullo Mirim Khan b. Mullo 'Ali Muhammad O'g'li, or Imom-i Domullo Mirim Khan b. Oxund Mullo Savranboy. Ziyodov speculates that ms. 12057 is a copy of one of the published lithographs, with Mirim Khan's name replacing the original author's. See Ziyodov, "The Hajjnâmas," 228. Given, however, that the lithographs were published between 1907 and 1915, and that they are redacted, it would seem that ms. 12057 preceded them. There may be another manuscript that has not yet been catalogued. Lithograph no. 4243 (fifty-nine pages) was published by Mirzo Ahmad bin Mirzo Karim in 1915 in Tashkent; lithograph no. 4242 (fifty-nine pages) was published by Qori Shokir bin Domulla Zokir (undated); and lithograph no. 4241 (seventy-two pages) was published by O'tib-rasul bin Muhammad in 1907. All three are preserved at the Biruni Institute. I have not been able to compare all lithographs with the manuscript discussed here, but as noted, lithograph no. 4243 differs considerably from ms. 12057 and was clearly edited for style, grammar, and length. Some extended critiques, for example about Kashgaris, were not reprinted. There are also other changes such as the name of an Ottoman inn (from Davud Han to Halil Han) that suggest it was either updated or censored.

4. On reading practices of manuscripts see Thum, *Sacred Routes*.

5. Green, "The Rail Hajjis," 101. On this genre see Metcalf, "The Pilgrimage Remembered."

6. HT, folios 4, 24.

7. HT, folio 96: "Hamma maqsud izlab keladurlar; hamma mayub izlab keladurlar; Tillarda maqsudin jumla barobar, hamma shoh, gado, maskin barobar; Bu yerda boy istig'no qilolmas, duo eylab o'zin ortuq ko'rolmas; Tavfdin xoli yo'q shoh [u] gadolar, hamma o'z xolig'a xub mubtalolar."

8. As Dick Davis writes in his introduction, the poem is organized around the theme of the hoopoe trying to admonish and convince the different birds to go on the journey, many of whom have objections and concerns. See Attar, *Conference of the Birds*, 17.

9. This term is both used and discussed in literature on the rise of mass pilgrimage and its convergence with major epidemics of cholera. It is also common in Ottoman sources as "fukera-yı hüccac." For critical approaches to its usage see Arnold, *Colonizing the Body*; and Singha, "Passport."

10. Bashir, *Sufi Bodies*, 2.

11. For a discussion of the routes in the early modern era see McChesney, "The Central Asian Hajj-Pilgrimage"; Pearson, *Pilgrimage to Mecca*; and Zarcone, *Sufi Pilgrims*.

12. Kane, "Odessa," 2. For an extended discussion of Russian hajj routes and infrastructure, see Kane, *Russian Hajj*, chap. 2 and 3. John Slight also provides an excellent overview of steamship-era hajj routes, including the routes through India. See Slight, *The British Empire*, chap. 1.

13. Pilgrims from Chinese Turkestan frequently complained to Ottoman authorities about problems obtaining visas from Russian authorities en route to Ottoman lands. For one example see BOA, Y.PRK.AZJ 51/71, 29 Z 1323 (24 Feb. 1906).

14. Kane, *Russian Hajj*, 111.

15. HT, folio 13. The process of "helalleşmek" is to mutually give or forgive all that has been or may have been unjustly taken or done (usually performed on deathbeds, before battles, or before long separations).

16. Necipoğlu, "Life of an Imperial Monument," 199.

17. Freely and Sumner-Boyd, *Strolling through Istanbul*, 53.

18. Necipoğlu, "Life of an Imperial Monument," 200–201.

19. Deringil, "Legitimacy Structures," 346.

20. Quoted in Brophy, *Uyghur Nation*, 87.

21. HT, folio 14. This was corrected in the lithograph version I consulted. Corruption of the Hagia Sophia's name was common; in a shorter unpublished manuscript written by a near contemporary, the author calls it "the mosque of a man named Ayaz Sufi." See "Dar bayon-i roh-i hajj," folio 5.

22. Nina Ergin has pioneered work on the aural dimensions of piety in the early modern Ottoman context. See Ergin, "Soundscape of Sixteenth-Century Istanbul."

23. Ahmed, *What Is Islam?*, 41–42.

24. Bashir, *Sufi Bodies*, 43–44.

25. Green, "The Hajj as Its Own Undoing."

26. For a classic study on this topic, see Hobsbawm and Ranger, *The Invention of Tradition*. For studies that explore how the invention of tradition informed Ottoman and Russian imperial rule, see Deringil, *The Well-Protected Domains* and Wortman, *Scenarios of Power*.

27. Deringil, *The Well-Protected Domains*, 23.

28. HT, folio 20.

29. Necipoğlu, *Architecture, Ceremonial and Power*, 59.

30. On the debt administration see Birdal, *Political Economy*.

31. On the revived caliphate and its connection to power in the Hamidian period see Deringil, "Legitimacy Structures"; Deringil, "The Invention of Tradition"; Georgeon, *Sultan Abdülhamid*; and Fortna, "Reign of Abdülhamid II."

32. Green, "The Rail Hajjis," 101.

33. Quatert, *The Ottoman Empire, 1700–1922*, 92.

34. Hammond discusses the history of Eyüp in his study of Muslim urban identity and place-making in Istanbul. See Hammond, "Mediums of Belief," 4–5.

35. HT. See folio 22 for his description of Eyüp Sultan.

36. Thum, *Sacred Routes*.

37. On the significance of *mi'rāj* see Gruber and Colby, *Prophet's Ascension*. On Sufism see Green, *Sufism*; and Knysh, *Sufism: A New History*.

38. Tanman, "Hırka-i Şerif Camii."

39. HT, esp. folios 31–33.

40. Green, "The Hajj as Its Own Undoing," 193.

41. HT, folio 21, p. 41.

42. Quoted in Kane, *Russian Hajj*, 151–52.

43. Kane, 47.

44. HT, folios 6–9.

45. Kane, *Russian Hajj*, 48. On pan-Islamic paranoia see Morrison, "Sufism."

46. Daniel Brower discusses attempts to ban foreign passports to the Ottoman Empire, and the problems in enforcing them. See Brower, *Turkestan*, chap. 4.

47. On rule through difference in the Russian context see Werth, *The Tsar's Foreign Faiths*.

48. Dukchi Ishan's unpublished treatise discusses bans on travel to Mecca. See IVAN RUz MS 1725, "'Ibrat al-Ghafilin" [Admonition to the Heedless].

49. See Komatsu, "The Andijan Uprising Reconsidered," 46.

50. For a discussion of the impact of colonial rule on communities in Taskent, see Sahadeo, *Russian Colonial Society*.

51. The governorate-generalship was established in 1867 and comprised lands conquered from Khiva, Bukhara, and Khoqand. All three rulers were left on their thrones but ruling greatly reduced territories. The territory of [Russian] Turkestan expanded continuously until 1889, by which time it also included the lands of the Turkmens. A reduced Khoqand was initially a protectorate, but it was abolished and its lands incorporated into Turkestan in 1878. The rump states of Bukhara and Khiva remained protectorates until 1917. For background on the conquest and administration of these states see Becker, *Russia's Protectorates*; and Pierce, *Russian Central Asia*, as well as newer studies cited in note 9 of my introduction.

52. On the newspaper's establishment and Kaufman's decree see Khalid, *Politics of Muslim Cultural Reform*, chap. 3.

53. On Ostroumov see Khalid, *Politics of Muslim Cultural Reform*, esp. 87–89. Ac-

cording to Kane, the newspaper had a "print run of five hundred to six hundred copies." See Kane, *Russian Hajj*, 204n70.

54. *TVG*, 17 Feb. 1897. Technically, Bukhara had an emir, not a khan. The difference in title was because the ruler was not a Chinggisid.

55. *TVG*, 5 Feb. 1897, 1. "Mazkur toun kasali Hindiston'dan o'tub Rusya mamlakatinda paydo bo'lmasin deb va Rusya hukumatdorlari Rusya mamlakatiga tobi Musulmon fuqarolarini ishbu yilda Makka-i Mukarrama'ga hajj qilmoq ichun . . . bormasinlar deb hukm qilibdir." Chuma kasali was likely a reference to cholera, outbreaks of which were prevalent in this period in the Hijaz (and India); see Sarıyıldız, "Hicaz'da Salgın Hastalıklar ve Osmanlı Devleti'nin Aldığı Bazı Önlemler."

56. Low, "The Mechanics of Mecca," 31, chap. 3.

57. *TVG*, 8 March 1897, 6.

58. *TVG*, 29 March 1897, 5.

59. *TVG*, 8 August 1897.

60. *TVG*, 20 August 1897.

61. *TVG*, 15 March 1897, 5; 25 August 1897, 6.

62. For a discussion of these shifts and examples of advertisements in the *TVG*, see Kane, *Russian Hajj*, chap. 3.

63. Green, "The Rail Hajjis," 101.

64. HT, folios 56–58. The ihram is a white garment that male pilgrims wear as they enter the state of ritual purity required to perform the hajj; it also symbolizes the funeral shroud that all Muslims wear when buried.

65. HT, folio 59: "Ko'ruban Makka shahrin shod bo'lduk, g'am u qayg'u kitib ozod bo'lduk; Mashaqqatsiz kishi topqoymu maqsud, mashaqqatsiz kishiga bo'lmag'ay sud; Mashaqqat boshqa olg'an bo'ldi majnun, chu g'avvos bo'lmay tobmas durr-i maknun."

66. HT, folio 5. The couplet reads, "Taloship Qirg'iz, Qipchoq Qashqar / ajab beor benomus zang'ar." *Zang'ar*, is not in any Uzbek or Turkic dictionary I have consulted. My thanks to Jo'ra Boy Bo'tako'z, a native of Andijan born in the 1920s, who provided this translation.

67. HT, folio 47.

68. HT, folio 47. This entire section is omitted from the lithograph version of the text. This may be because the publisher hoped to sell the book in Chinese Turkestan. *Sunna* refers to the Prophet Muhammad's words and acts, which were recorded in collections of hadith and are accepted (together with the Quran) as a source of Islamic law by Sunni Muslims.

69. HT, folio 96.

70. HT, folio 96.

71. HT, folio 59.

72. Ludden, "Presidential Address," 1058.

73. Ho, *The Graves of Tarim*, 120.

74. Turner, "Betwixt and Between."

Chapter 2. Sufi Lodges as Sites of Transimperial Connection

1. Various petitions from people originating from Chinese Turkestan describe the problems they experienced in Russia and ask for representatives or guides to be appointed on their behalf. See, e.g., a letter from Kashgaris dated 7 Ağustos 1322 in BOA, DH.MKT 1110/67, 11 B 1324 (31 August 1906).

2. Undated letter draft from Şeyh [İbrahim?] Edhem Efendi (1829–1904), which seems to be to the Ministry of Pious Endowments, since it mentions the paucity of the tekke's existing endowed funds and the significant financial strains it faced.

3. Ahmed bin Tohta was a fifteen-year-old from Kashgar. SÖTA Register 1, entry no. 397. Gureba-yı Müslimin was an endowed hospital for the Muslim poor built by Bezmiâlem Valide Sultan, the mother of Sultan Abdülmecid. See Shefer, "Charity and Hospitality."

4. This was a form of identity and travel document, similar to an internal passport. On its history, see Turna, 19. *Yüzyıldan 20. Yüzyıla Osmanlı Topraklarında Seyahat, Göç ve Asayiş Belgeleri*.

5. *Dhikr* (Ottoman, *zikir*), which literally means remembering or reminding, represents the ways of reminding oneself of God. In Sufi devotional practice, dhikr may be an act of individual devotion or a collective devotion with specific formulas and prayers defined by the *tariqa* (Sufi order or brotherhood).

6. This vignette is based on entries in SÖTA Register 1, in fall through winter 1905–6 (numbers 372 through 424); and a 5 Şaban 1323 (15 Oct. 1905) petition addressed to an unspecified shaykh. Entry 423 is for Hacı Azım, age 48, and Entry 424 is for his son, Bekir, age 8. Both are listed as from Kashgar, and headed to the Hijaz. The petition was on behalf of a group of men from Chinese Turkestan and was probably written by Mehmed Salih Efendi, who was the postnişin from 1904 until his death in 1915. He succeeded İbrahim Edhem Efendi, who presided over the lodge from c. 1855 to 1904. During part of this period, he shared the post with his brother, Mehmed Sadık (1846–1915). According to Münir Atalar, the imperial caravan steamship transported pilgrims and the annual gift, or "purse" (surre), to Mecca. It included payments to Bedouin tribes for safe conduct, payments to the sharif of Mecca, and monies for people who served in various Ottoman-funded religious institutions in Mecca and Medina. Until 1864, the surre traveled overland to Damascus. From 1864 to 1908 it departed Istanbul by sea, via steamship. After 1908, it traveled by rail. The practice of the imperial caravan ended with WWI and Ottoman loss of control over the Hijaz. See Atalar, *Osmanlı Devletinde Surre-i Hümayûn*.

7. Smith, "Özbek Tekkes of Istanbul."

8. In his work on Chittagong, Willem van Schendel explores how people turned a place into a meaningful place in what he terms "spatial moments" ocurring between 1600 and 2010. I am particularly influenced by his approach to dimensions of socio-spatial relations and differentiation between space and place. See van Schendel, "Spatial Moments," 98–99.

9. On the history of the Eyüp Kaşgari Tekkesi see Gürler, "Eyüp'te bir Kalenderhane"; Zarcone, "Kaşgari Tekkesi"; and Smith, "Kaşgari Dergâh in Istanbul." For a

comprehensive overview that addresses the manifold discrepancies in the literature on the history of this and the other Greater Istanbul lodges, see Yeşilot, Çelik, and Varol, *İstanbul'daki Türkistan Tekkeleri*, 223–53.

10. Ottoman sources and works in the secondary literature sometimes refer to this and the Eyüp Kaşgari Tekkesi as the "Eyüp Tekkesi" or as the "Özbekler Tekkesi," leading to confusion about their histories. On the Kalenderhane see Zarcone, "Kalenderhane Tekkesi"; and Yeşilot, Çelik, and Varol, *İstanbul'daki Türkistan Tekkeleri*, 179–219.

11. Discussed in Zarcone, "Kalenderhane Tekkesi," 398–400.

12. On the description as an Uzbek Naqshbandi lodge ("Nakşibendiye-i Özbekiye tekkesidir"), see BOA C.EV 12061, 22 Z 1229 (5 Dec. 1814). For the populations it served, see BOA, MVL485/109, 5 C 1282 (26 Oct. 1865).

13. See Özcan, "Özbekler Tekkesi Postnişini," 204–8. This assertion, however, is dubious, since the British would be well aware that the Ottomans under Abdülhamid II had no coherent diplomatic goals regarding the colonized and semiautonomous states of Central Asia or any interest in alarming Russia by infringing on tsarist interests in the region. Moreover, by the time the pilgrimage had started to lead to intensified connections between the Ottomans and Central Asian pilgrims (not political or diplomatic officials from Central Asia), the panoply of Russian, Chinese, and British colonies, protectorates, and imperial territories were not able to conduct foreign policy. Diplomatic missions had already tapered off by the late 1870s. On this history see Can, "Trans-Imperial Trajectories," chap. 1.

14. Tanman, "Buhara Tekkesi," 325; Tanman, "Özbekler Tekkesi," 199–200.

15. Ayvansarayi, *Hadikatü'l-Cevami*, 240. Smith summarizes the story in "Özbek Tekkes of Istanbul."

16. Smith, "Özbek Tekkes of Istanbul." See also Yeşilot, Çelik, and Varol, *İstanbul'daki Türkistan Tekkeleri*, 257–62.

17. SÖTA, document dated 24 Haziran 1331 (7 July 1915): "Buhara ve Hive hanlıkları ahalisiyle Türkistan-ı Rus ve Çini Müslümanlarından hacc-ı şerife azimet ve berayı ziyaret-i darü'l-hilafet-i aliye ve merkez-i saltanat-ı seniyeye gelen gureba ve fukaranın iskân ve iaşesine mahsus ve küll-i yevm küşade bir müessese-i hayriyedir."

18. For example, the Turkestani tekke in Tarsus stipulated in its endowment deed that guests could stay a maximum of three days. See Kunter, "Tarsustaki Türkistan Zaviyelerinin Vakfiyeleri." This seems to have been the norm and is confirmed by Shefer, "Charity and Hospitality."

19. See Adıvar, *Türkün Ateşle İmtihanı*, 62–80; and Adıvar, *House with Wisteria*.

20. Driven in large part by Atâ Efendi's role in transferring weapons through the tekke and the shelter it provided İsmet İnönü (1884–1973; commander of the Turkish Western Army in the War for Independence and the second president of the Turkish Republic) and the novelist Halide Edib [Adıvar] (1884–1964), Sultantepe was the only Sufi lodge that Atatürk did not officially shut down in 1925, although it was not supposed to continue operating as a Sufi tekke. On the lodge in the resistance see Altun, "Kuvayı

Milliyecilerin Gizli Sığınağı ve Ardındaki Bilinmeyenler: Özbekler Tekkesi"; Çelik, *Milli Mücadelede Din Adamları*; and Karakoç, "Milli Mücadele'de Üsküdar," 151–59.

21. "Burası artık tekke değil, bari müzeye dönüşsün," *Milliyet*, 27 Dec. 2006.

22. For example, Smith writes that the shaykhs at the Kashgari lodge in Eyüp "served as ambassadors of sorts to the Ottoman government for various Central Asian powers." Smith, "Kaşgari Dergâh in Istanbul," 215. The theme of acting as an unofficial consulate also runs through the discussion of Istanbul's Central Asian lodges in Yeşilot, Çelik, and Varol, *İstanbul'daki Türkistan Tekkeleri*.

23. Keshavarzian, *Bazaar and State*, 40.

24. In his work on this topic, Thierry Zarcone analyzes the relations between the Turks of the East and West from what he describes as the angle of "dervishism." He writes, for example, that he is interested in focusing on dervishes' "spiritual preoccupations, the vector of the political and the social, and the relationship between pan-Turkism and pan-Islamism." He criticizes Smith and Bektaş for ignoring the vaster historical and sociological perspective of Central Asian Sufism, and he describes these Sufi lodges as intermediary sites for pilgrims that sought to guard their specificity as mystical centers, so as not to become *simple* hostels for pilgrims. See Zarcone, "Histoire et croyances," 139.

25. Zarcone draws on a late Ottoman Sufi journal, for example, to suggest that these pilgrims were (and were perceived as) dervishes who begged for money in the streets of Istanbul. See Zarcone, *Sufi Pilgrims*.

26. BOA, DH.MTV 40-1/24, 6 B 1329 (3 July 1911).

27. BOA, DH.MB.HPS. 149/21, 9 R 1332 (7 March 1914).

28. BOA, DH.MUİ 53-1/24, 11 Jan. 1910.

29. Statistical data compiled from records in SÖTA Register 1.

30. SÖTA Register 1, entry no. 142.

31. SÖTA Register 2, Künye Defteri, 27 Kanunuevvel 1322–18 Teşrinievvel 1339 (9 Jan. 1907–18 Oct. 1923). The cover of this register reads "Üsküdar Sultantepesi'nde Özbekler Dergahı'nda mükim dervişanın künye defteridir." It is signed by Mehmed Necmeddin Efendi. Because the register covers a broad period that includes the First World War, the figures discussed here should be regarded as very preliminary and pending further research that takes into account the effects of Ottoman and Russian involvement in the war.

32. SÖTA Register 1, entries 173–78, 180.

33. Based on data in SÖTA Register 1.

34. Based on data in SÖTA Register 2. From 1899 to 1906, there were 242 people registered from "China," while in the period 1907 through 1923 there were only 110. The numbers from the Ferghana Valley reported less change: 169 and 166 respectively. Owing to both overlap and the likelihood that some of the registers were lost, these figures are not conclusive in terms of the total numbers of pilgrims in any given year.

35. Both sources cited from Zarcone, *Sufi Pilgrims*, 18–20, 39. Quoted from *Muhibban* 2, no. 1 (1911): 110. The expression Zarcone erroneously translates is "çakı, bıçak bileyerek, tabak çanak kenetleyerek beş on para kazanmağa çalışan."

36. SÖTA, document dated 24 Haziran 1331. This source describes the lodge's mission. I confirmed the point about working in 2007 in conversations with Grace Martin Smith and Belkis Özbek (Özbekkangay), daughter of Atâ Efendi.
37. SÖTA Register 1, entries 150 and 151.
38. SÖTA Register 1, entry 156.
39. The position he occupied at the school is not clear. On his various official positions see Yeşilot, Çelik, and Varol, *İstanbul'daki Türkistan Tekkeleri*, 295–96.
40. The twenty-five-year-old hajji Muhiddin, for example, worked at a coffeehouse in Mahmutpaşa for a little more than two months before going to Mecca in the fall of 1911. See SÖTA Register 2, entry no. 130.
41. Private conversation in August of 2009 with Belkıs Özbek, who grew up at Sultantepe and remembers some of the workers from her childhood.
42. Clifford, "Travelling Cultures," 96–116. A record of another guest, Hacı İsmail, indicates that this traveler traced and retraced an arc from Istanbul to Adana and Konya before leaving for Tefkurdağ. Thirty-five years old and from Khoqand, Hacı İsmail was unbearded (*köse*) and a dwarf (*cüce*). After arriving at the tekke on 17 February 1912, he left on 18 March 1912 for the Molla Tekke, returning ten days later and leaving shortly thereafter on 5 April for Adana. He then proceeded to make another trip to Adana, then to Konya and Bagdad—overland—in 1913. In between trips he continually returned to the dergah. SÖTA Register 2, entry no. 173.
43. *Seyyah vermek* usually means to decree a period of travel for a member of a Sufi order. In the context of these registers, we find that guests are usually given a "seyyah" only after engaging in some sort of unacceptable behavior such as drinking, gambling, violence, or inappropriate sexual relations. Hence, I generally translate the term as being expelled, although it could also be translated as being "sent away."
44. SÖTA Register 2, entry no. 229. The shaykh's notes are: "Kahvede iskambil oynadığından dergahdan tard edilmiştir. Islah-ı hal eylemekle fi 1 Kanunuevvel 330 dergaha tekrar kabul edilmiştir. 1 Kanunuevvel 331 askere alınmıştır. 7 Kanunusani 331 terhis olunarak gelmiştir. 7 Haziran 332 münasebetsiz ahvalinden dolayı dergahdan ihrac edilmiştir."
45. SÖTA Register 1, entry. no. 42.
46. SÖTA Register 1, entry no. 50. The date of the family's departure is hard to make out; it looks like 1337 but is likely 1317. It seems odd that the postnişin would expel a 101-year-old man.
47. SÖTA, Eyüp Dergah to Sultantepe postnişin, 10 Eylül 1315 (22 Sept. 1899).
48. SÖTA Register 1, entries 36, 37, and 38.
49. SÖTA Register 1, entry no. 45.
50. SÖTA Register 2, entry no. 62.
51. SÖTA Register 2, entry no. 293.
52. SÖTA Register 2, entries 199 and 201.

53. SÖTA Register 1, entry no. 361.
54. SÖTA Register 1, entry no. 114.
55. SÖTA Register 2, entry no. 130.
56. My research in the İstanbul Müftülüğü Arşivi makes clear that central governmental oversight was limited, even in cases involving allegations that shaykhs were involved in deviant behaviors. See Can, "Connecting People," 26–27.
57. Silverstein, "Sufism and Governmentality," 176. For a rich discussion of reforms aimed at "suspect individuals," see Yılmaz, *Serseri, Anarşist ve Fesadın Peşinde*.
58. Silverstein, "Sufism and Governmentality," 184.
59. Gündüz, *Osmanlılarda Devlet-Tekke Münasebetleri*, 155.
60. SÖTA Register 1, entry no. 16.
61. SÖTA Register 1, entries 31 and 32.
62. The hospital was established by Bezmialem Valide Sultan, the mother of Sultan Abdülmecid (r. 1839–61), and opened in April of 1845. It had 201 beds, twelve wards, a pharmacy, a head doctor, and a doctor's assistant, alongside rooms designated for a pharmacist, surgeon, and director. It also had a kitchen, hamam, and laundry facilities. The endowment deed stipulated that patients be fed nutritious meals, with meat when possible, and that onions—even if the market rate was a gold piece per bulb—should always be purchased for the kitchens. Eye and surgery wards were added in 1892–93, and ear, nose, and throat specialization was added in 1905. In 1909, a laboratory was built, in 1912 a library, in 1914 X-ray facilities, in 1915 orthopedics and pathological anatomy, and in 1918 urology. See Bayram, "Sağlık Hizmetlerimiz," 37.
63. BOA Zabtiye Nezareti, 11 April 1909.
64. SÖTA Register 1, entry no. 283.
65. SÖTA Register 1, entry no. 39.
66. SÖTA Register 1, entry no. 49.
67. SÖTA Register 1, entry no. 90. (There are two entries, both listed as 90; this is the second one in the register.)
68. SÖTA Register 1, entry no. 95.
69. Özbek, *Osmanlı İmparatorluğu'nda Sosyal Devlet*, 175.
70. Özbek, 175. Also see Gülden Sarıyıldız's article on the Ottoman guesthouse for poor pilgrims, "II. Abdülhamid'in Fakir Hacılar İçin Mekke'de İnşa Ettirdiği Misafirhane."
71. Özbek, "Imperial Gifts," 204.
72. Özbek, "Philanthropic Activity," 69.
73. See Brower, *Turkestan*, chap. 4.
74. Behar, *A Neighborhood in Ottoman Istanbul*, introduction.
75. Norihiro Naganawa makes a similar argument about tekkes and the system of pilgrimage guides in the Hijaz in Naganawa, "The Hajj Making Geopolitics," 190.

Chapter 3. Extraterritoriality and the Question of Protection

1. BOA, DH.EUM.THR 53/28, 20 Ş. 1328 (2 Nov. 1910). The conflation of Bukhara and Russian Turkestan was very common. See, for example, BOA, DH.MB.HPS 149/21 (1332), where both the petitioners and the state use the two synonymously. "Acizleri Buhara'nın Mergilan kasabası ahalisinden olup." The hospital had turned over his money and clothes to the Üsküdar Police, since he had no heirs.

2. SÖTA Register 2, Künye Defteri, entry no. 3.

3. Hanley, *Identifying with Nationality*, 135.

4. Mary Dewhurst Lewis uses the phrase "borrowed nationalities" to describe how French authorities in Tunisia viewed non-European protégés such as Algerians. See Lewis, *Divided Rule*, 61.

5. Throughout this chapter I use the term *nationality* to mean a type of affiliation with a state that enabled claims to rights, without modern connotations of loyalty or political citizenship. This is in line with Will Smiley's usage, also in the context of negotiations over Russo-Ottoman sovereignty. As Smiley succinctly puts it, "all Russian subjects, when abroad, were Russian 'nationals'—sharing membership of the same state, regardless of their status within that state." See Smiley, "The Burdens of Subjecthood," 91n87.

6. See Lewis, "The Geographies of Power," 809.

7. BOA, HR.HMŞ.İŞO 177/34, 11 July 1892.

8. BOA, HR.H 571/27, 2 July 1892; and BOA, HR.HMŞ.İŞO 177/34, 11 July 1892.

9. For selected studies on the problem of semisovereignty see Genell, "Autonomous Provinces"; and Pickett, "Written into Submission."

10. Stein, *Extraterritorial Dreams*, 7.

11. For literature on extraterritoriality and the Capitulations see my introduction, particularly note 19.

12. For one of many examples, see BOA, HR.H 572/13, 20 Feb. 1896. The case involves a naturalized Ottoman who wanted to go to Bukhara to sell property and was offered a Russian passport.

13. BOA, HR.HMŞİŞO 221/11, 5 Nov. 1919, summarizes five decades of Ottoman and citizenship- and nationality-related problems and provides the 1869 law in full. For an English translation of the law, see Flournoy and Hudson, *Collection of Nationality Law*.

14. Hanley, "What Ottoman Nationality Was and Was Not."

15. Prior to the Tanzimat, *ecnebi* was primarily used as a term to describe people from Christian lands. See also, Can, "The Protection Question."

16. BOA, DH.SN.THR 54/45, 3 August 1914. On the government's decision not to implement the Tanzimat reforms in Yemen and other "exceptional provinces," see Kuehn, *Empire, Islam, and Politics of Difference*.

17. On the Russian consulate in Jeddah, see Freitag, "Helpless Representatives?"; Kane, *Russian Hajj*. It should be noted that throughout this period, there were also numerous cases of Russian consular authorities who impeded the ability of Central Asians to settle estates in Bukhara and Turkestan. In 1895, a Medina resident of twenty-two years stated that he was not given a visa to go to Bukhara to sell property. See BOA, HR.H 571/75, 26 Feb. 1895. In 1897, for example, another Bukharan resident in Istanbul complained to the Porte that he was not able to receive his share of his deceased cousin's estate and asked for Ottoman authorities to intervene on his behalf. See BOA, HR.H 162/12, 19 July 1897. The Russian consulate in Istanbul also made it difficult for people who had quit their Russian subjecthood and become naturalized to travel to Russian-ruled territories. See BOA, HR.HMŞ.İŞO 138/3, 13 May 1905.

18. Sarah Abrevaya Stein describes competition over Jewish protégés in Salonica during the Balkan Wars in these terms. Calling them "seductive subjects," for whom "the pursuit of [foreign, in this case Portuguese] papers did not necessarily entail the attenuation of loyalty in [an]other direction." See Stein, *Extraterritorial Dreams*, 26, 35.

19. Lohr, *Russian Citizenship*, 32–33. Alexander Morrison writes that even if Russian colonial administrators like Mikhail Afrikanovich Terent'ev (a general staff officer and former administrator who later wrote a major history on the Russian conquest of Central Asia), asserted that inhabitants of Turkestani cities were "considered to be as much Russian citizens as those of Moscow," his claim was false. Subjects of Russian Turkestan, Morrison writes, "were not accorded equal rights with the population of European Russia." Morrison, "Metropole," 338.

20. BOA, HR.H 571/27, 2 July 1892; and BOA, HR.HMŞ.İŞO 177/34, 11 July 1892.

21. On the standard of civilization and the Ottoman Empire's position, see Aydın, *The Politics of Anti-Westernism in Asia*; and Anghie, *Imperialism, Sovereignty, and the Making of International Law*. For a comparative study of sovereignty and extraterritoriality in the "semicivilized" states of Japan, the Ottoman Empire, and China, see Kayaoğlu, *Legal Imperialism*.

22. Lewis, *Divided Sovereignty*.

23. BOA, HR.TO 369/98, 1 March 1886.

24. On conscription see Beşikçi, *Ottoman Mobilization*; and Kern, *Imperial Citizen*.

25. BOA, HR.TO 369/98, 1 March 1886. On British Indians and consular courts in Iraq see Stephens, "An Uncertain Inheritance"; and Çetinsaya, "The Ottoman View." On conscription see Beşikçi, *Ottoman Mobilization*; and Kern, *Imperial Citizen*.

26. Aimee M. Genell has detailed many of the inner workings and the provenance of the Office of Legal Counsel. She explains that two brothers of German origin, Alfred and Carl, worked as legal advisers but that neither signed his first name. She finds more evidence linking Carl to the Office and links Alfred as the German representative to the Ottoman Public Debt Administration. See Genell, "The Well-Defended Domains." There is also a concise description of the Office in the *Başbankanlık Osmanlı Arşivi Rehberi*, 381–82.

27. On the two decisions see BOA, HR.TO 365/86, 27 Jan. 1881; and BOA, HR.TO 369/98, 1 March 1886. For a file that summarizes Office of Legal Counsel and Council of Ministers decisions and restates the position that Afghans were protected by the Islamic caliphate ["zaten himaye-yi hilafet-i islamiyede bulunan Afganların bundan böyle de himaye-yi mezkureden müstefid olmalarına devam etmeleri"], see HR.HMŞ. İŞO 195/43, 1 Ra 1327 (23 March 1909).

28. The reference to tribes here should be understood in the context of Russian subjecthood/extraterritoriality, where prominent tribal and clan leaders were sometimes given subjecthood rights in negotiations for colonial expansion.

29. BOA, HR.TO 369/98, 1 March 1886.

30. Hanley, *Identifying with Nationality*, 210.

31. See, for example, Deringil, *The Well-Protected Domains*, 57–58.

32. In some instances, this could also work in the opposite way, such that Bukharans were still treated like Russian subjects. For example, in a 1913 case, an Ottoman imperial employee was prohibited from selling land to two Bukharans. The Interior Ministry reasoned that although the men who wanted to purchase the land were Bukharan and not Russian subjects (even if the Ottoman government had not accepted Russia's protection of Bukhara), because of Russia's continual interventions in various affairs, they should be prohibited from purchasing land. The Interior Ministry also invoked the fact that Bukhara was not a signatory to the protocol on land sales. See BOA, DH.H 64/71, 22 N 1331 (25 August 1913). In the case of Afghanistan, the British had made clear that the Afghan emir did not have the power to conduct foreign policy by sending the Porte a copy of the agreement signed with the emir. See, e.g., BOA, HR.TO 264/51, 8 Sept. 1890.

33. Eileen Kane and John Slight explore the manifold motivations for extending patronage to Russian and British subjects in Ottoman lands and document how Muslims mobilized their status as foreign nationals to avail themselves of consular services and extraterritorial privileges and protections. See Kane, *Russian Hajj*, esp. chaps. 1 and 2; Slight, *The British Empire and the Hajj*, esp. chapters 2 and 3.

34. Benton, "Shadows of Sovereignty."

35. Ahmed, "Contested Subjects," 342.

36. BOA, HR.SYS 1304/2, June 1895.

37. Ahmed, "Contested Subjects," 342–43; see also Ahmed, *Afghanistan Rising*.

38. M. Christopher Low also traces the subversion of the logic of the Capitulations in his study of extraterritoriality and foreign, particularly Indian and Jawi, Muslims in the Hijaz. See Low, "Unfurling the Flag." See also his forthcoming book, *Imperial Mecca*.

39. This is an adaptation by James Meyer of Stephen Kotkin's idea of "speaking Bolshevik," in Kotkin's *Magnetic Mountain*, to show how Russia and Russian Muslims articulated social, economic, and political conflicts. See Meyer, "Speaking Sharia."

40. BOA, DH.MKT 2736/37, 19 M 1327 (10 Feb. 1909); BOA, DH.MKT 2691/30, 30 Za 1326 (24 Dec. 1908). Also, in 1908 the Foreign Ministry stated that Kashgaris

were under the protection of the "hilafet-i mukaddese-i islamiye" (holy Islamic caliphate) but did not engage at all with tsarist arguments about shari'a. BOA, HR.HMŞ. İŞO 194/68, 6 Z 1326 (30 Dec. 1908); BOA, DH.MKT 2691/30, 30 Za 1326 (24 Dec. 1908).

41. BOA, DH.MKT 2691/30, 30 Za 1326 (24 Dec. 1908); BOA, DH.MKT 2736/37, 19 M 1327 (10 Feb. 1909).

42. On the common tropes and scripts destitute pilgrims used to appeal for aid, see Low, " 'The Infidel Piloting the True Believer'"; Singha, "Punished by Surveillance"; Slight, *The British Empire*.

43. BOA, HR.HMŞ.İŞO 194/68, 6 Z 1326 (30 Dec. 1908); BOA, DH.MKT 2736/37, 19 M 1327 (10 Feb. 1909).

44. Kane posits that in cases involving inheritance, the Porte was concerned with maintaining a lucrative source of revenue. While this income did offset state expenditures on pilgrims, I have seen no evidence in Ottoman records related to these cases that suggests that the Porte's primary concern was financial. Rather, Ottoman sources suggest the driving concern in inheritance disputes was related to sovereignty. In many instances, it is not clear if the estates were channeled to the Ottoman imperial treasury, or if they were seized by tekke shaykhs or provincial authorities (or the sharifs of Mecca). On contested estates see Kane, *Russian Hajj*, 40, 62–63, 75–77.

45. Marglin, "The Two Lives of Mas'ud Amoyal," 665.

46. Brophy, *Uyghur Nation*, 74–79.

47. Ahmed, "Contested Subjects," 336.

48. For an excellent overview of the threat posed by the British in terms of the expansion of extraterritorial rights and plans to install a rival caliphate, see Low, "The Mechanics of Mecca." A growing area of research explores how Ottoman engagement with international law informed governance of autonomous and "exceptional" provinces. Aimee Genell, in particular, traces Ottoman understandings of autonomy and sovereignty and the impact of Mehmed Ali's khedivate. See Genell, "Autonomous Provinces." For an analysis of these issues and their connection to subjecthood, see Can and Low, "Introduction." On sovereignty in imperial borderlands see Blumi, *Rethinking the Late Ottoman Empire*; and Minawi, *Ottoman Scramble*.

49. BOA, A.MKT.UM 511/80, 25 R 1278 (30 Sept. 1861).

50. To preempt European intervention, the law stipulated that future disputes or legal matters involving property would be subject to Ottoman legal jurisdiction alone. It also required states to sign separate protocols in order for their subjects to benefit from the law. Though selectively enforced, this stipulation could be used to prevent subjects of protected states from acquiring real estate, since their home countries could not independently sign such international agreements. See BOA, BEO 4338/325334, 17 Jan. 1915. The protocol is also referenced in an earlier source, BOA, Y.PRK.UM 5/57, 21 S 1300 (1 Jan. 1883).

51. M. Christopher Low elaborates that the council used the autonomous status of the holy cities "to deflect and circumvent the internationally binding requirements of the Capitulations and prevent the application of foreign protection beyond Jeddah." See Low, "The Mechanics of Mecca," 136–37. In discussing landholding in the Hijaz, Deringil draws on a source in the BOA, Y.A.RES 15/38 file, which states, "If we remain indifferent to the accumulation of property by devious means in the hands of foreign Muslims, with the passage of time we may find that much of the Holy Lands have been acquired by the subjects of foreign powers. Then, the foreigners, as is their wont, after lying in waiting for some time, will suddenly be upon us at the slightest opportunity and excuse and will proceed to make the most preposterous claims." This quote accurately reflects the Şura-yı Devlet's position but does not fully represent debates within the government. Deringil, *The Well-Protected Domains*, 60.

52. It is common to come across phrases in these sources that acknowledge that Central Asians had "until recently" (at various points between the 1880s and 1910s) been treated as Ottomans. An 1887 Council of Ministers (Meclis-i Vükela) decision, for example, begins by stating that "even though Central Asians residing in the empire have until recently been treated as Ottomans . . . ," BOA, MV 17/38, 30 Ca 1304 (24 Feb. 1887).

53. BOA, Y.A.RES 15/38, 17 Ca 1299 (4 April 1882). Cezmi Eraslan cites similar numbers in *Abdülhamid ve İslam Birliği*, 31.

54. BOA, Y.A.RES 15/38, 17 Ca 1299 (6 April 1882): "Şimdi orada bulunan tebaa-yı ecnebiyeye dahi şumuli tabii ise de bunlar hayli vaktden beri oralarda tavattun ile yerlü hükmüne girmiş ve belki kendüleri dahi tebaa-yı ecnebiye iddiasından vazgeçmiş oldukları halde uhdelerinde bulunan emlak satdırılması şan-i celil-i hilafet-i seniyeye cüsban olamayacağı mülahazasına nazaran . . ." (translated in note 51 above).

55. BOA, HR.TO 517/37, 27 C 1293 (6 June 1876); and BOA, Y.PRK.AZJ 1/72, 26 C 1294 (8 July 1877).

56. On this case, see BOA, HR.H 158/15 (1 April 1880). It is not clear whether the mücavir in question, Muhammed Ali İman Efendi, was an Ottoman subject. There is no mention of his status in the petition or in the diplomatic correspondence that ensued.

57. BOA, Y.A.RES 15/38, 24 S 1299; and BOA, Y.PRK.ASK 13/16, 10 S 1299 (1 Jan. 1882).

58. Brophy, *Uyghur Nation*, 13.

59. BOA, DH.MKT 543/13, 11 R 1320 (18 July 1902). The question of Mir Bedreddin's (Badr al-Din) identity is thorny. He may have been the son of the chief qadi (qazi al-quzat) of Bukhara, Mulla Mir Sadr al-Din Kuttalani, but according to Robert McChesney, there is no evidence that he ever went to the Hijaz. McChesney (personal communication) contends that he may have had a surrogate acting in his name. On the chief qadi and his son see Allworth et al., *Personal History*, 97n50. Reichmuth also writes about this line and their involvement in Bukharan Haremeyn endowments. See Reichmuth, "Semantic Modeling," chap. 4.

60. The Bukharan pilgrimage leader provided the guarantee (*kefalet*). This was an official appointed by the sharif of Mecca and a member of the most important guilds in the Hijaz.

61. Reichmuth, "Semantic Modeling, 214.

62. Deringil, *The Well-Protected Domains*, 57.

63. On the uncertainties of colonial law and legal pluralism see Merry, "Colonial Law"; and Stephens, "An Uncertain Inheritance." Stephens traces how legal uncertainty frustrated both colonial authorities and litigants in British consular courts in Iraq but concludes that "uncertainty and certainty were mutually constitutive" (771) and ultimately expanded the reach of imperial law.

64. According to Lohr, a defining feature of Russian citizenship through 1914 was an "attract and hold" approach that sought to counter "a persistent shortage of people and a sense that immigration and naturalization helped expand the economic power of the empire, while emigration and denaturalization were to be avoided for the same reason." Lohr, *Russian Citizenship*, 5, and chap. 4. Meyer makes a similar argument in his "Immigration, Return."

65. The cases examined here support Smiley's argument that interimperial mobility regulations "hardened the empires' human and geographic boundaries" and could result in foreign subjecthood becoming a liability. Smiley, "The Burdens of Subjecthood," 73.

66. BOA, DH.SN.THR 54/45, 5 Ca 1331 (12 April 1913).

67. Deringil, *Conversion and Apostasy*, 187.

68. BOA, DH.SN.THR 54/45, copy of letter from Medine Muhafız ve Kumandanlığı 15 Ca [1]331 (22 April 1913).

69. BOA, DH.SN.THR 54/45 nos. 14 and 16, correspondence between Foreign Ministry and Medine Muhafız. Officials in Medina and the province at large advocated repeatedly on behalf of the needs of long-term residents, raising questions about relationships among the Central Asian community, the guild of pilgrimage guides, and the sharif. This might suggest a type of patron-protégé relationship with mutual economic benefit.

70. BOA, DH.SN.THR 54/45, 11 N 1332 (3 August 1914). See documents from Hicaz Vilayet to Dahiliye, 2 Şubat [1]329; Hariciye to Dahiliye, 16 L 1331; Hariciye to Dahiliye, 16 L 1331.

71. BOA, DH.SN.THR 54/45, 11 N 1332 (3 August 1914).

72. On Ottoman frustrations with international law and diplomacy in the last years of empire, see Aksakal, "Not 'By Those Old Books.'"

73. BOA, Y.PRK.ŞD 3/34, 29 Z 1320 (29 March 1903).

Chapter 4. Petitioning the Sultan

1. BOA, DH.MKT 1027/35, 6 L 1323 (4 Dec. 1905).

2. BOA, DH.MKT 1217/67, 24 L 1325 (30 Nov. 1907), Dahiliye Mektubi Kalemi to

the Sadrazam, 5 Şubat 1323. On Black Sea quarantine stations see Ayar, *Osmanlı Devletinde Kolera*, 28–29; Yaşayanlar, "Hicaz Yolunda Kolera," 178–203.

3. BOA, DH.İD 61/77. Petition dated 7 Nisan 327 (20 April 1911).
4. On legal posturing see Benton, "Historical Perspectives," 63.
5. See Baldwin, "Petitioning the Sultan." For other major works on petitioning in the Ottoman Empire, see Peirce, *Morality Tales*; Ben-Bassat, *Petitioning the Sultan*; Sarıyıldız, *Sokak Yazıcıları*.
6. In his study of these practices in Egypt John Chalcraft approaches petitioning as a site of encounter and negotiation between subjects and the Khedive. See Chalcraft, "Engaging the State," 304.
7. For examples see BOA, İ.MVL 203/6455, 12 Ca 1267 (15 March 1851); BOA, A.MKT.NZD 77/42, 16 B 1269 (25 April 1853).
8. Nurten Kılıç-Schubel, "Rethinking the Ties between Central Asia and the Ottoman Empire," 259–72, 262.
9. On Central Asian petitioning practices see Sartori, *Explorations*. On Central Asian petitioning in legally plural orders see Sartori and Shahar, "Legal Pluralism."
10. BOA, C.ML 8120, 2 Ş 1255 (8 Sept. 1842).
11. BOA, A.MKT 7/27, 25 R 1259 (25 May 1843).
12. See BOA, İ.MVL 203/6455, 12 Ca 1267 (15 March 1851).
13. BOA, İ.MVL 203/6455, letter in file dated 3 R 1267 (5 Feb. 1851).
14. BOA, İ.MVL 203/6455, Meclis-i Vala decision dated 25 R. 1267 (27 Feb. 1851). See also A.MKT.NZD 30/75, 25 S 1267 (30 Dec. 1850), which is a letter to the Ministry of Finance (Maliye Nezareti) that summarizes the petition and the decision of the grand vizier and Meclis-i Vala to appoint the shaykh and his family with a salary.
15. BOA, DH.İD 61/77. Petition dated 23 Ağustos 1328 (5 Sept. 1912).
16. BOA, DH.İD 61/77. Petition dated 19 Ağustos 1328 (1 Sept. 1912).
17. BOA, DH.İD 61/77. See the response attached to the petition dated 23 Ağustos 1328.
18. See Maksudyan, "Orphans, Cities, and the State," 494–95.
19. See Düzbakar, "Osmanlı Devleti'nin Dilencilere Bakışı"; and Özbek, *Osmanlı İmparatorluğu'nda Sosyal Devlet*, esp. chap. 3. Özbek explains that with the proclamation of the 1890 regulation on begging, unemployed and homeless beggars were to be imprisoned from one to three months, then sent to their locale of origin, where they would be kept under police surveillance. Although begging became increasingly associated with threats to public order and morality, its policing was not stringently executed, as evidenced by numerous stories in the Ottoman press bemoaning the tolerance toward mendicants exhibited by the Ministry of Police.
20. A good starting point for an overview of the history and functions of these institutions is the *Türkiye Diyanet Vakfı İslâm Ansiklopedisi*.

21. Özbek, *Osmanlı İmparatorluğu'nda Sosyal Devlet*, 84–90. These regulations are summarized and full references provided (88–90).

22. Maksudyan, "Orphans, Cities, and the State," 495.

23. On Ottoman bankruptcy and the establishment of the PDA see Akarlı, "Problems of External Pressures." Özbek also discusses the challenges faced by the state in the aftermath of the Russo-Ottoman War; see Özbek, "Osmanlı İmparatorluğu'nda Dilenciler."

24. Singha, "Passport"; Low, "Empire and the Hajj," 269–90.

25. Studies of Ottoman colonialism and nesting orientalism have explored how the Ottoman state adopted and adapted the European civilizing mission to rule tribal populations, participate in the colonial land-grab in Africa, consider new methods of colonial rule in borderlands like Yemen, and engage with the international legal order to maintain its sovereignty. See, for example, Deringil, " 'They Live'"; Makdisi, "Ottoman Orientalism"; Kuehn, *Empire, Islam, and Politics*; and Minawi, *Ottoman Scramble*.

26. On Russia's investment in the Black Sea routes and hajj infrastructure, see Kane, *Russian Hajj*, especially chapters 3 and 4.

27. BOA, İ.HUS 160/24, 21 L 1325 (27 Nov. 1907).

28. BOA, A.MKT.MHM 557/2, 23 L 1325 (29 Nov. 1904).

29. BOA, A.MKT.MHM 557/2. Grand Vizier to the Ministry of the Interior, 14 Teşrinisani 1323 (27 Nov. 1907).

30. BOA, DH.MKT 1217/67, 24 L 1325 (30 Nov. 1907). In a telegraph dated 25 Teşrinisani 1323 (8 Dec. 1907), the sender complained that he ventured to send a second telegraph because the matter was time sensitive and pilgrims were complaining about being held.

31. BOA, A.MKT.MHM 590/15, 17 M 1325 (2 March 1907).

32. BOA, Y.PRK.A 14/61, 12 L 1325 (18 Nov. 1907).

33. BOA, Y.PRK.A 14/61, 101.

34. Özbek, "The Politics of Welfare," 248.

35. Özbek, "The Politics of Welfare," 248.

36. BOA, MV 137/117, 1 Ra 1328 (13 March 1910).

37. BOA, DH.İD 61/77, petition in file, dated 13 Nisan 1327 (26 April 1911).

38. BOA, DH.İD 61/77, doc. no. 2, 26 Ş 1327 (31 August 1910), Head of the Istanbul Municipality to the Ministry of the Interior. Although the şehremini referred specifically to Muslims from Russia and Bukhara, the correspondence also pertained to pilgrims from Chinese Turkestan.

39. BOA, DH.İD 61/77, doc. no. 29, Dahiliye to Sadrazam, 21 Teşrinievvel 1327 (4 Dec. 1911). The correspondence from the Interior Ministry states that there were still reported cases of cholera in Istanbul and that it was widespread in parts of Anatolia (see doc. no. 30, Şehremini to Dahiliye Nezareti).

40. BOA, DH.İD 61/77, doc. no. 3, dated 20 Ağustos 1320 (2 Sept. 1910).

41. BOA, DH.İD 61/77, doc. no. 109, Ministry of Public Safety to the Interior Ministry, 18 Nisan 1327 (2 May 1911). There are also examples in the file of police registers of pilgrims, as well as indications that the burden for dealing with them was shifting from the Porte to the police in managing their mobility.

42. BOA, DH.İD 61/77, doc. no. 8, petition from Hacı İdris to the caliph. Dated Nisan 1327 (April 1911).

43. BOA, DH.İD 61/77, doc. no. 9, petition from Hacı Halime, Hacı Kadir, and Hacı Fazıl to the caliph. Dated 5 Nisan 1327 (18 April 1911).

44. BOA, DH.İD 61/77, doc. no. 10, Şehremaneti to Dahiliye Nezareti, 7 Nisan 1327 (20 April 1911).

45. BOA, DH.İD 61/77, Bab-ı Ali: Dahiliye Nezareti to Sadrazam, memo, 3 Ca 1328/29 Nisan [1]327 (12 May 1911).

46. BOA, DH.İD 61/77, Dahiliye Nezareti, Muhaberat-ı Umumiye Dairesi to Sadrazam, 2 Mayıs 1326 (15 May 1910).

47. BOA, DH.İD 61/77, doc. no. 16, Dahiliye to Sadrazam, 27 Nisan 1327 (10 May 1911).

48. In 1905, for example, one official at the Porte wrote that many of these beggars were blind, handicapped, and sick and that they had been firmly warned by authorities not to engage in activities that bothered the public. See BOA, A.MKT.MHM 707/35, 7 N 1323 (14 Nov. 1905).

49. BOA, DH.İD 61/77, doc. no. 53, 15 Eylül [1]328 (26 Sept. 1912).

50. Deringil, *Conversion and Apostasy*, 216. Also see BOA, A.MKT.MHM 581/4–20, 7 August 1901 for concern about how poor pilgrims appear.

51. BOA, DH.İD 61/77, Dahiliye Nezareti Muhaberat-ı Umumiye Dairesi'nden Şehremaneti Vekalet-i behiyesine [ve] Emniyet-i Umumiye Müdiriyet-i behiyesine, fi 26 Nisan 326 (9 May 1910).

52. BOA, DH.İD 61/77, Dahiliye Nezareti Evrak Müdiriyeti to Sadrazam. The text reads, "ve oralarda eksik olmayan ecnebi züvvara karşı merkez-i hilafet-i islamiye[de] ... Çin Müslümanlarının nasıl i'zaz edildiğini lisan-ı hali ile izah ediyorlar."

53. BOA, DH.MUİ 93/43, Dahiliye to Sadrazam, memo, 6 Ca 1328 (16 May 1910).

54. BOA, DH.İD 61/77, 13 R 1330 (1 April 1912).

55. BOA, DH.İD 61/77. There are a number of documents within the file related to this fire.

56. BOA, DH.İD 61/77, Dahiliye Nezareti to Sadrazam, drafted 13 Teşrinisani 1327 (18 Nov. 1911).

57. BOA, DH.İD 61/77. Bab-ı Ali Daire-i Sadaret to Dahiliye Nezareti, 3 Teşrinisani 1327 (8 Nov. 1911).

58. In 1894, the Ottomans posted a public statement in Jeddah: "Notice is hereby given to all Mussulman [*sic*] pilgrims, whether they be Ottoman or foreign subjects, who

have come here from all parts of the world to perform the sacred duties of the pilgrimage, that it is His Imperial Majesty the Sultan's good and gracious pleasure and earnest desire that they be protected from all sorts of oppression or vexation, that they are to be looked upon as His Majesty's welcome guests and are therefore to be treated with proper respect and that it be considered a sacred obligation to afford them all facilities in their affairs." It also stated, "Pilgrims are to be free in the performance of the sacred duties of the Haj, and should the necessity arise everyone will find the doors of government open at all times." The context was ongoing corruption in which the sharif of Mecca played a major role. See "Attempts to Protect Malays and Other Pilgrims from Commercial Exploitation, 1893–95," in Rush, *Records of the Hajj*, vol. 4, *The Ottoman Period (1888–1915)*, 195–201.

59. BOA, DH.İD 61/77, doc. no. 14, Bab-ı Ali Dahiliye Nezareti, undated. The text reads, "Hac mevsimi müteakib limanımıza gelen vapurlardan çıkmağa isteyen bu gibi fukara burada beş on gün kaldıktan sonra memleketlerine avdet için mikdar-ı kâfi nakide malikiyetini ısbat eylediği takdirde şehire çıkarılmalıdır. Böyle yapılırsa ertesi sene bunların arkası kesilir. Hükûmet de bunların mesuliyet-i maneviyyelerinden kurtulur efendim."

60. BOA, DH.İD 61/77, doc. no. 37. Date of draft is 6 Teşrinisani [1]328 (19 Nov. 1912). This "reminder" was one that many other statesmen and foreign observers also advocated with regard to their own imperial subjects. For example, Tagliacozzo writes, "Snouck [Hurgronje] argued that Indies subjects should be reminded before they left home that the Hajj was compulsory only for adults who could perform it without burdening their families, a warning that he hoped might stem at least a small amount of the enthusiasm for this journey that was so important—yet also so dangerous—to many." See Tagliacozzo, "Snouck Hurgronje," 141–42.

61. BOA, DH.İD 61/77, Minister of Pious Endowments (Evkaf Nazırı) to the Grand Vizier, 25 N 1330 (7 Sept. 1912).

62. According to Reichmuth, Tsarist Russia closed the Istanbul route in 1914, in an announcement by the governor of Baku in August. See Reichmuth, "Semantic Modeling," 116.

Chapter 5. From Pilgrims to Migrants and De Facto Ottomans

1. On Jerusalem see Zarcone, *Sufi Pilgrims*. For the Tarsus lodge see Kunter, "Tarsustaki Türkistan Zaviyelerinin Vakfiyeleri," 31–50. There is no comprehensive study on the empire's Central Asian lodges beyond İstanbul, but there is a rich archival record in the BOA on their construction and administration in cities that include but are not limited to Bursa, Medina, Jeddah, and Baghdad. It is also possible to trace the appointment of shaykhs to these tekkes through records of the İstanbul Müftülüğü Arşivi, particularly Tekke ve Zaviye Defterleri, Genel no. 1777.

2. Frantantuono, "Migration Administration"; Hamed-Troyansky, "Refugees and Empires."

3. My analysis of foreignness departs from that of Rishad Choudhury, who contends that labels such as "Hindi" designated these persons as "outsiders" in the eyes of the state. He writes, for example, "Now, there is little question that the words [*Hindi, Hindu*] were meant to imply 'foreignness' of a kind within Ottoman realms. Judging from Ottoman records, it is certainly evident that 'Hindi' designated 'outsiders' of sorts in the eyes of the state." But given how common it was to refer to groups by such ethnic or geographical terms (e.g., *Afgan, Çerkes*, etc.), it is doubtful that the use of *Hindi* alone implied anything connected to being an outsider or foreigner in the sense of *ecnebi*. See Choudhury, "The Hajj Between Empires," unpublished manuscript.

4. As I mentioned in my preface, this was an anticolonial revolt in the Ferghana Valley, led by a Sufi Naqshbandi shaykh named Dukchi Ishan. In its wake, 546 people, including Dukchi Ishan, were captured, 415 of whom were sent to a field court-martial. The shaykh and five of his associates were publicly hanged on 12 June 1898 in front of the local population, which was forced to attend the execution. Dukchi Ishan was buried in an unmarked plot to prevent his grave from becoming a shrine. The Mingtepe settlement where his lodge was located was razed and replaced by a new Russian settlement. See Komatsu, "The Andijan Uprising Reconsidered," 46.

5. As James Meyer explains in the context of Russian-Ottoman migrations, "for many Russian Muslims immigrating to the Ottoman Empire, Russia remained an option to be retained, like their passports, for future consideration and possibilities." See Meyer, "Immigration, Return," 21.

6. On procedures to quit Russian subjecthood, see Lohr, *Russian Citizenship*.

7. Beşikçi, *Ottoman Mobilization*, 59–62.

8. Bouquet, "Non-Muslim Citizens."

9. BOA, DH.İD 61-1/51, 7 R 1333 (22 Feb. 1915).

10. On Murad Şah see BOA, DH.EUM.ECB 5/39, 11 July 1916. On the form see BOA, DH.İ.UM.EK 5/141_1, 24 S 1333 (11 Jan. 1915).

11. Behar, *A Neighborhood in Ottoman Istanbul*, 161–67.

12. SÖTA, undated letter to Şeyh Sadık Efendi and another statement dated March 1904. In both documents, two lodgers from Khoqand and Marghilan signed formulaic letters attesting to the statement that they would henceforth make no claims to foreign citizenship. The first (undated) reads: "Acizleri Hokand ahalisinden olub bu kere Devlet-i Aliye tabiiyetine dahil olmak üzere misafir bulunduğum Üsküdar'da Özbekler dergahı şeyhi Sadık Efendi'den olbabda lazım gelen ilmühaberi ahz eylemiş olduğumdan fimaba'd katiyyen tabiiyet-i ecnebiye iddiasında bulunmayacağımı mübeyyin işbu senedim mumaileyh şeyh efendiye i'ta kılındı." The second example, dated 25 Şubat [1]319 (9 March 1904), states that "Bad-ı sened oldur ki, Acizleri Merginan ahalisinden olub Devlet-i Aliye tabiiyetine dahil olmak üzere şeyh efendiden lazımgelen ilmühaberi ahz eylemiş olduğumdan fimaba'd tabiiyet-i ecnebiye iddiasında bulunmayacağıma mübeyyin işbu senedim mumaileyh şeyh efendiye i'ta kılındı." I say

other Sufi lodges as well because I have come across many documents related to people who were naturalized but were never recorded in official sources. For example, in a 1914 telsik case involving an Indian man, the Interior Ministry realizes he had obtained Ottoman identity papers twenty years prior in Jerusalem. See DH.SN.THR 50/52, 11 Ca 1332 (7 April 1914).

13. BOA, DH.HMŞ 31/131, 22 Ş 1333 (5 July 1915).
14. See Chapter 3 for references to the law and protocol.
15. The language used to discuss "problem" subjects often changes according to confession of the subject in question. In this period the government frequently used *muzır* in reference to apostates and subjects of the empire like Armenians. See Deringil, *Conversion and Apostasy*; and Gutman, *Politics of Armenian Migration*.
16. BOA, DH.İD 61-1/58, 14 Ra 1333 (30 Jan. 1915). He was described as "şayan-ı itimad" and "eshab-ı hüsnühal."
17. Hanley, *Identifying with Nationality*, 275.
18. Meyer, "Immigration, Return," 16.
19. SÖTA Register 2. We can assume that none of these volunteers were Ottoman subjects, since the shaykh specified when men had Ottoman nationality or identity papers and also when they were "taken into" the military. See in this register entries no. 305: Hacı Kuşluk, "askere alınmıştır"; and no. 325: Hacı Kârı Mahmud, "Osmanlıdır" (but memleket listed as Marghilan, and he is sixty-six).
20. The record has his arrival as 12 Şubat 1328 (25 Feb. 1913), and his departure for Medina on 15 Mart 1328 (28 March 1912). This may indicate a prior trip to Medina that was added later, or the date was entered incorrectly, perhaps 1328 instead of 1329. Sultantepe Künye Defteri, SÖTA Register 2, entry 207. This is in keeping with what Mona Hassan describes as efforts that reached "a fever-pitch" between 1911 and 1913, when non-Ottoman Muslims raised funds for the Ottomans and "actively espoused the Ottoman cause in the press and literature, organized hundreds of meetings as well as boycotts, sent medical missions, and even arranged for the dispatch of military volunteers." See Hassan, *Longing for the Lost Caliphate*, 10.
21. SÖTA Register 2, entry no. 123.
22. SÖTA Register 2, entry no. 238.
23. BOA, MV 109/107, 1 C 1322 (13 August 1904).
24. It was possible for a Bukharan subject to serve in a Medinan military battalion without becoming naturalized or renouncing claims to Russian nationality. See BOA, ZB 4/38, 21 Za 1288 (1 Feb. 1872).
25. BOA, HR.SYS 1304/2, Urgent communication from Imperial Embassy of Russia to Ottoman Ministry of Foreign Affairs, entry no. 686, 15/28 May 1913.
26. For a file that provides an overview on nationality and marriage, see BOA, ŞD 2256/23, 2 B 1306 (4 March 1889).
27. Kern, *Imperial Citizen*.

28. Clancy-Smith, *Mediterraneans*, 200.

29. Low, "The Mechanics of Mecca," 32–33.

30. BOA, ŞD 2256/23, Bab-ı Ali Hariciye İstişare Odası [10 Jan. 1889].

31. BOA, DH.MKT 1035/23, 26 L 1323 (24 Dec. 1905).

32. Ho, *The Graves of Tarim*.

33. Reichmuth, "Semantic Modeling," 217.

34. The pasha described them as "Maghrebis, Egyptians, Indians, Turks, and Damascenes" who wanted to be neighbors of the Prophet and to live in lands where Islam had won honor and radiated its light to the world's old lands. Rıfat Paşa, *Miratü'l-Haremeyn*, 357.

35. Zarcone, *Sufi Pilgrims*, 2–3. While the presence of expansive and wealthy mercantile diasporas in the Hijaz and Greater Syria—as well as Shiites in Iraqi shrine cities—makes clear that mücavirin were not exclusively pious men and women, the political economy and scope of that type of migration awaits further research.

36. See Ochsenwald, "Ottoman Arabia," 30.

37. BOA, Y.PRK.ASK 13/16, 10 Ş 1299 (27 June 1883). I thank Michael Christopher Low for clarification on the usage of *Javanese* versus *Jawi*—that Ottoman documents count Jawis as all Southeast Asians from Malaya, Singapore, and Indonesia (i.e., Java, Sumatra, even sometimes including Chinese and Filipinos) and that as a category *Jawi* included Javanese that were Dutch subjects, as well as Malays that were British subjects.

38. BOA, Y.PRK.UM 5/63, 19 Ra 1300 (28 Jan. 1883). This estimate is on the conservative side. According to Low, there were at least fifteen thousand Indians in the Hijaz and at least twenty-five thousand between the three groups. See Low, "Unfurling the Flag," 318.

39. Hanioğlu, *A Brief History*, 11–12.

40. BOA, DH.MKT 378/45, 28 Za 1312 (23 May 1895).

41. Rıfat Paşa, *Miratü'l-Haremeyn*, 594–98.

42. See, e.g., BOA, A.MKT.UM 443/78, 30 Ca 1277 (14 Dec. 1860), instructing the Ottoman governor to help Muhammed Yunus Efendi of Khoqand, who was described as a man of limited means.

43. Bozkurt, "Mücâvir," 445–46.

44. On grain provisioning see Mikhail, *Nature and Empire*; on potable water see Low, "Ottoman Infrastructures."

45. "Hamidulla Al'mushev: Hadj-name" and "Rihlat al-Marjani" (Puteshestvie Mardzhani) in Nurimanov and Mukhetdinov, *Khadzh Rossiiskikh Musul'man*, 11–22.

46. Quoted in Zarcone, *Sufi Pilgrims*, 4.

47. BOA, A.MKT.UM 406/74, 3 Za 1276 (23 May 1860).

48. BOA, DH.MKT 378/45, 28 Za 1312 (23 May 1895).

49. Karateke, "Opium for the Subjects?" 112–13.

50. In trying to answer the question of why the Ottoman dynasty managed to stay

in power for so long, Hakan Karateke investigates the normative and "factual" dimensions of Islamic legitimacy: "Factual legitimacy . . . implies a practical policy to arouse positive feelings of comfort and security amongst the people. It begins with endeavors to ensure welfare, justice, order (which have been for the people even more important than justice), to propagate religiosity and traditionalism, to instill the image of a victorious Sultan, prosperous state and generous ruler." See Karateke and Reinkowski, "Introduction," 6; and Karateke, "Opium for the Masses?"

51. A growing area of scholarship on technopolitics, particularly desalination projects and building of telegraph lines, shows how the state sought to establish its power on the ground. See, e.g., Low, "Ottoman Infrastructures"; Minawi, "Beyond Rhetoric"; Minawi, *Ottoman Scramble*; and Özyüksel, *The Hejaz Railway*. For an earlier and authoritative work on the railway system see Ochsenwald, *The Hijaz Railroad*.

52. Sources in the SÖTA show that one of the shaykhs at Sultantepe was involved in Ottoman construction of public works in the Hijaz in this period. The petitioner might have been connected to the shaykh; otherwise, it seems odd that a Bukharan would travel all the way to Mecca to study public works. BOA, A.MKT.UM 221/5, 6 Ca 1272 (28 Feb. 1856). Molla Hoca began his petition by stating that he was from the Uzbek people (Özbek ahalisinden) and that he had arrived in Istanbul from the "land of [the] Uzbek[s]" (canib-i Özbek'den Dersaadet'e vusul). I note this here because this was rather unusual.

53. This might also have been connected to a system of quotas for mücavirin that was based on provenance or ethnicity. This hypothesis was brought to my attention by Guy Burak and requires further research in the Ottoman Surre-i Hümayûn registers.

54. BOA, A.MKT.UM 126/47, 10 Ca 1269 (19 Feb. 1856).

55. BOA, A.MKT.MHM 4/95, 25 Ca 1264 (29 April 1848).

56. BOA, A.MKT.NZD 77/42, 13 B 1269 (22 April 1853).

57. BOA, A.MKT.UM 500/16, 13 Ra 1278 (18 Sept. 1861); A.MKT.UM 465/68, 5 L 1277 (16 April 1861).

58. BOA, DH.MKT 1558/19, 19 S 1306 (25 Oct. 1888).

59. BOA, DH.MKT 2441/70, 29 Ş 1318 (22 Dec. 1900).

60. BOA, A.MKT.MHM 4/95, 25 Ca 1264 (29 April 1848).

61. BOA, İ.ML 1321/59, 24 Nisan 1319 (7 May 1903).

62. While both petitioners explicitly state that they are headed to the Hijaz with their families and want to abandon their Russian nationality (terk-i tabiiyet) and become Ottoman subjects, the notes on the back of each stress that the petitioners have Russian nationality and have requested to be muhacirin—a term that does not appear in either request. The government's reclassification may suggest sensitivity to settling families in the Hijaz. See BOA, MKT.MHM 524/14, 28 L 1321 (17 Jan. 1904).

63. BOA, A.MKT.MHM 524/14, 28 L 1321 (17 Jan. 1904). For example, when twenty-three Bukharan families (seventy-six individuals) migrated to the empire in 1895, they were referred to as muhacirin and settled in Deyr-i Zor, a province in Greater Syria border-

ing Aleppo, Syria, Diyarbakir, Mosul, and Baghdad. The government allocated twenty-five thousand kuruş for their settlement, which would cover homesteads, seed for sowing, and livestock. It also made additional allotments for food supplies (*iaşe*) until the families could produce their own agricultural yields. The money was specifically appropriated from funds for muhacirin (*muhacirin tahsisat-ı umumiyesinden*). Three years later, however, when another twenty-three families were being settled in Zor, it became clear that only three households from 1895 had remained: twenty had sold their farming equipment (*ziraat edvatı*) and relocated to Damascus. See also A.MKT.MHM 504/1, 27 C 1316 (12 Nov. 1898).

64. Aydın and Ho, "Mecca InterAsia," n.p.

65. BOA, Y.PRK.ŞD 3/34, 29 Z 1320 (29 March 1903).

66. Ho, *The Graves of Tarim*, 68, and chap. 3, "A Resolute Localism."

67. Thierry Zarcone traces some of these connections in his study of the Uzbek Naqshbandi lodge in Jerusalem. See Zarcone, *Sufi Pilgrims*. Mansour Bukhary has recently published a volume with biographical information on Central Asian mücavirin in Mecca and Medina, which can be used to reconstruct a fuller picture of migration to the Holy Cities. See Bukhary, *'Ulama'ma wara'al-nahr*.

68. Neha Vora's anthropological approach sheds important light on citizenship beyond the binaries of legal and illegal membership in a nation; see Vora, *Impossible Citizens*, 1–35.

69. For the full text of the Saudi Nationality Law see www.moi.gov.sa/wps/wcm/connect/121c03004d4bb7c98e2cdfbed7ca8368/EN_saudi_nationality_system.pdf?MOD=AJPERES.

70. Historians interested in the Ottoman foundations of citizenship in the post-Ottoman Middle East have referenced the Law on Ottoman Nationality to argue that citizenship was not "at all tied to religion," and that after 1869 it was acquired through "the provisions of jus sanguinis, jus soli or by naturalization." See, for example, Lauren Banko, "Imperial Questions." While this view is based on the language of the law, in practice, Ottoman archival records suggest that religion was still an important factor in naturalization, as well as land sales. The question of Sunni identities comes up in several documents, including the opinion by a member of the Şura-yı Devlet I quoted in my introduction (Y.PRK.ŞD 3/34).

71. Deringil, *Conversion and Apostasy*, 195–96.

72. In mixed batches of naturalization paperwork in Interior Ministry and Citizenship Affairs Bureau dossiers, circa 1915, requests from (Sunni) Muslims were often quickly approved, whereas non-Muslims were rejected. On the same day in February of 1915, for example, the Interior Ministry approved the naturalization of a Muslim Russian subject from Samarqand and refused the petition of a non-Muslim Russian subject named Aron. No explanation was provided for either decision (BOA, DH.İD 61-2/2, 10 Feb. 1915. This is a topic in need of further study, but it seems to suggest that Sunni religious identities played a role in naturalization.

73. Selim Deringil argues that it was comparatively more difficult for non-Muslims to be accepted as Ottomans and that they were often privately stigmatized as foreigners (*yabancı*) and infidels (*gavur*). See Deringil, *Conversion and Apostasy*, 157.

74. Cohen, *Becoming Ottomans*, 79.

Conclusion: A Return to Sultantepe

1. BOA, DH.EUM.ECB 4/24, 11 Ca 1334 (16 March 1916), document dated 15 Ra 1334 (22 Jan. 1916). For related earlier correspondence, see BOA, DH.SN.THR 54/45, Medine Muhafız ve Kumandanlığı, 15 Ca [1]331 (22 April 1913).

2. BOA, DH.EUM.ECB 4/24, deciphered copy of letter from Hicaz Valisi ve Kumandanı Galib, dated 4/12 Şubat [1]331.

3. BOA, HR.SYS 1304/2, Bab-ı Ali Hariciye Nezareti İstişare Odası, 22 July 1915. By 1916, some within the Interior Ministry denied that they had ever recognized Russia's conquest of Turkestan and claimed that the people of Turkestan, like Afghans, were protected by the caliphate. See BOA DH.EUM.ECB 5/40 12 N 1334 (13 July 1916).

4. Perl-Rosenthal, *Citizen Sailors*, 273.

5. BOA DH.UMVM 125/11, 2 S 1337 (7 Nov. 1918).

6. Brubaker and Cooper, "Beyond 'Identity,'" 1, 2.

7. For studies of Ottoman colonialism see Chapter 4n25.

8. On Ottoman imperial citizenship see note 39 of my introduction.

9. On the enduring connections between former Ottoman subjects in the Balkans to the empire, and the significance of spiritual connections to the caliphate, see Amzi-Erdoğdular, "Afterlife of Empire."

10. Cemil Aydın makes a similar argument. See Aydın, "Globalizing the Intellectual History," 162–66.

11. My analysis here is informed by Talal Asad's work on Islam and secularism. See, for example, his classic essay, *The Idea of an Anthropology of Islam*.

12. In his work on Armenian migration and return migration, David Gutman shows how, despite the "spirit" of Tanzimat reforms, there was a lack of standardization in government policy, including naturalization and denaturalization, across confessions and ethnic groups—including Ottoman Christians. See Gutman, *Politics of Armenian Migration*.

13. For an overview of this period see Zürcher, *The Young Turk Legacy*.

14. For a full discussion of "secular dhimmitude" see Ekmekçioğlu, *Recovering Armenia*, esp. chap. 4. For her earlier work on the idea of "step-citizens" see "Republic of Paradox."

15. SÖTA, Türkistanlı Abdulmalik to Şeyh Necmeddin Efendi, 25 Dec. 1936.

16. SÖTA Register 2, Künye Defteri. Necmeddin Efendi used the Uzbek *o'lgen* to say he died rather than the Turkish *öldü*.

BIBLIOGRAPHY

Archives

TURKEY

Başbakanlık Osmanli Arşivi (BOA), Istanbul, Turkey.
İstanbul Müftülüğü Arşivi, Istanbul, Turkey. Meclis-i Meşâyih Defterleri; Tekke ve Zaviye Defterleri, Genel no. 1777. Tesvid tarihi 17 Cemaziyelahir 1327, Tebyiz Tarihi 22 Cemaziyelahir 1327.
Sultantepe Özbekler Tekkesi Archive [private], Istanbul, Turkey.

UZBEKISTAN

Alisher Navoiy Nomidagi O'zbekiston Milliy Kutubxonasi (Alisher Navoi State Library).
O'zbekistan Respublikasi Fanlar Akademiyasi Abu Rayhon Biruniy Nomidagi Sharqshunoslik Instituti (The Republic of Uzbekistan Academy of Sciences, Collection of the Biruni Institute of Oriental Studies).
O'zbekistan Respublikasi Markaziy Davlat Arxivi (Central State Archive of the Republic of Uzbekistan).

Unpublished Primary Sources

BIRUNI INSTITUTE OF ORIENTAL STUDIES

IVAN RUz MS 1725. "Ibrat al-Ghafilin" [Admonition to the Heedless]. Undated manuscript authored by Muhammad Ali Sabyr.
IVANUz MS 9379/3. "Dar bayon-i roh-i hajj" [Opisanie Puti Hadj]. Manuscript

authored by Mirza Olim Maxdum ibn Domullo Mirza Rahim Toshkandiy, 7 Rajab 1305/20 March 1888.

IVANUz MS 12057 (Turki). "Hajjnoma-i Turkiy" (HT). Undated manuscript authored by Muhammad Oxund Toshkandiy.

IVANUz no. 4243 (lithograph). Hajjnoma-i Turkiy, lithograph edition, edited by Mirzo Ahmad bin Mirzo Karim, 59 pages. Tashkent: Tipografiia Hasana Arifjanova, 1915.

ALISHER NAVOI STATE LIBRARY

Turkiston Viloyatining Gazeti (TVG). Tashkent, 1870–1917.

Published Primary Sources

Ekici, Cevat, and Kemal Gurulkan, eds. *Belgelerle Osmanlı-Türkistan İlişkileri (XVI–XX Yüzyıllar)*. Ankara: T. C. Başbakanlık Devlet Arşivleri Genel Müdürlüğü, 2004.

Koltuk, Nuran, ed. *Osmanlı Belgelerinde Doğu Türkistan*. İstanbul: Türk Dünyası Belediyeler Birliği Yayınları, 2016.

Mustafayev, Shahin, and Mustafa Serin, eds. *History of Central Asia in Ottoman Documents: Spiritual and Religious Ties*. 3 vols. Translated by Ali Efendiyev. Samarkand: International Institute for Central Asian Studies, 2011.

Nurimanov, I. A., ed. *Khadzh Rossiiskikh Musulman: Sbornik putevykh zametok o Khadzhe*. Nizhnii Novgorod: Izd. "Medina," 2008.

Rush, Alan, ed. *Records of the Hajj: A Documentary History of the Pilgrimage to Mecca*. 10 vols. London: Archive Editions, 1993.

Published Secondary Sources

Abu-Manneh, Butrus. "The Naqshbandiyya-Mujaddidiyya in the Ottoman Lands in the Early 19th Century." *Die Welt des Islams* 22, no. 1/4 (1982): 1–36.

Adıvar, Halide Edib. *House with Wisteria: Memoirs of Halide Edib*. Charlottesville, VA: Leopolis, 2003.

———. *Türk'ün Ateşle İmtihanı: İstiklal Savaşı Hatıraları*. İstanbul: Can Yayınları, 2007.

Ahmad, Feroz. "Ottoman Perceptions of the Capitulations, 1800–1914." *JIS* 11, no. 1 (Jan. 2000): 1–20.

Ahmed, Faiz. *Afghanistan Rising: Islamic Law and Statecraft between the Ottoman and British Empires*. Cambridge, MA: Harvard University Press, 2017.

———. "Contested Subjects: Ottoman and British Jurisdictional Quarrels *in re* Afghans and Indian Muslims." *JOTSA* 3, no. 2 (Nov. 2016): 325–46.

Ahmed, Shahab. *What Is Islam?* Princeton, NJ: Princeton University Press, 2016.

Akarlı, Engin Deniz. "The Problems of External Pressures, Power Struggles, and Budgetary Deficits in Ottoman Politics under Abdulhamid II (1876–1909): Origins and Solutions." PhD diss., Princeton University, 1976.

Aksakal, Mustafa. "Not 'By Those Old Books of International Law, but Only by War': Ottoman Intellectuals on the Eve of the Great War." *Diplomacy and Statecraft* 15, no. 3 (2004): 507–44.

———. *The Ottoman Road to War in 1914: The Ottoman Empire and the First World War.* Cambridge: Cambridge University Press, 2008.

Algar, Hamid. "Tarîqat and Tarîq: Central Asian Naqshbandîs on the Roads to the Haramayn." In Papas, Welsford, and Zarcone, *Central Asian Pilgrims*, 21–136.

Allen, John, and Chris Hamnett, eds. *A Shrinking World? Global Unevenness and Inequality.* Oxford: Oxford University Press, 1995.

Allworth, Edward, Ṣadr Ẓiyāʻ, Sharīf Jān Makhdūm, R. Shukurov, and M. Shukurov, eds. *The Personal History of a Bukharan Intellectual: The Diary of Muhammad-Sharif-i Sadr-Ziya.* Leiden: Brill, 2004.

Altun, Mehmet. "Kuvayı Milliyecilerin Gizli Sığınağı ve Ardındaki Bilinmeyenler: Özbekler Tekkesi." *Toplumsal Tarih*, no. 112 (Nisan 2003): 18–23.

Amzi-Erdoğdular, Leyla. "Afterlife of Empire: Muslim-Ottoman Relations in Habsburg Bosnia Herzegovina, 1878–1914." PhD diss., Columbia University, 2013.

———. "Alternative Muslim Modernities: Bosnian Intellectuals in the Ottoman and Habsburg Empires." *CSSH* 59, no. 4 (2017): 912–43.

Anghie, Anthony. *Imperialism, Sovereignty, and the Making of International Law.* Cambridge: Cambridge University Press, 2002.

Arnold, David. *Colonizing the Body: State Medicine and Epidemic Disease in Nineteenth-Century India.* Berkeley: University of California Press, 1993.

Arsan, Andrew. *Interlopers of Empire: The Lebanese Diaspora in Colonial French West Africa.* New York: Oxford University Press, 2014.

Asad, Talal. *Genealogies of Religion: Discipline and Reasons of Power in Christianity and Islam.* Baltimore: Johns Hopkins University Press, 2009.

———. *The Idea of an Anthropology of Islam.* Occasional Papers Series, Center for Contemporary Arab Studies, Georgetown University, 1986.

Atalar, Münir. *Osmanlı Devletinde Surre-i Hümayûn ve Surre Alayları.* Ankara: Diyanet İşleri Bakanlığı Yayınları, 1991.

Attar, Farid ud-Din. *The Conference of the Birds.* Translated by Afkham Darbandi. Harmondsworth: Penguin, 1984.

Ayar, Mesut. *Osmanlı Devletinde Kolera: İstanbul Örneği (1892–1895).* İstanbul: Kitabevi Yayınları, 2007.

Aydın, Cemil. "After the 'Muslim World': Beyond Strategic Essentialism." The Immanent Frame: Secularism, Religion, and the Public Sphere. Oct. 17, 2017.

https://tif.ssrc.org/2017/10/17/after-the-muslim-world-beyond-strategic-essentialism.

———. "Globalizing the Intellectual History of the Idea of the 'Muslim World.'" In *Global Intellectual History*, edited by Samuel Moyn and Andrew Sartori, 159–86. New York: Columbia University Press, 2013.

———. *The Idea of the Muslim World: A Global Intellectual History*. Cambridge, MA: Harvard University Press, 2017.

———. *The Politics of Anti-Westernism in Asia: Visions of World Order in Pan-Islamic and Pan-Asian Thought*. New York: Columbia University Press, 2007.

Aydın, Cemil, and Engseng Ho. "Mecca InterAsia." Unpublished concept paper. Social Science Research Council. InterAsian Connections V: Seoul Workshop. Seoul, Korea, April 2016.

Ayvansarayi, İsmail. *Hadikatü'l-Cevami*. Vol. 2. İstanbul: Amire Matbaası, 1281/1864–65.

Baldwin, James E. "Petitioning the Sultan in Ottoman Egypt." *Bulletin of SOAS* 75, no. 3 (2012): 499–524.

Banko, Lauren. "Imperial Questions and Social Identities." *Revue des mondes musulmans et de la Méditerrané* 137 (May 2015): 95–114.

Barak, On. *On Time: Technology and Temporality in Modern Egypt*. Berkeley: University of California Press, 2013.

Barkey, Karen. "Aspects of Legal Pluralism in the Ottoman Empire." In Benton and Ross, *Legal Pluralism and Empires*, 83–109.

———. *Empire of Difference: The Ottomans in Comparative Perspective*. Cambridge: Cambridge University Press, 2009.

Bashir, Shahzad. *Sufi Bodies: Religion and Society in Medieval Islam*. New York: Columbia University Press, 2011.

Bayram, Sadi. "Sağlık Hizmetlerimiz ve Vakıf Gureba Hastahanesi'ne Ait Bir Defter." *Vakıflar Dergisi, sayı* 14 (1982): 101–18.

Becker, Seymour. *Russia's Protectorates in Central Asia: Bukhara and Khiva, 1865–1914*. Cambridge, MA: Harvard University Press, 1968.

Behar, Cem. *A Neighborhood in Ottoman Istanbul: Fruit Vendors and Civil Servants in the Kasap İlyas Mahalle*. Albany: State University of New York Press, 2003.

Ben-Bassat, Yuval. *Petitioning the Sultan: Protests and Justice in Late Ottoman Palestine*. London: I. B. Tauris, 2014.

Benton, Lauren. "Historical Perspectives on Legal Pluralism." *Hague Journal on the Rule of Law* 3, no. 1 (Jan. 2011): 57–69.

———. *Law and Colonial Cultures: Legal Regimes in World History, 1400–1900*. Cambridge: Cambridge University Press, 2002.

———. "Shadows of Sovereignty: Legal Encounters and the Politics of Protection in the Atlantic World." In *Encounters Old and New in World History: Essays*

Inspired by Jerry H. Bentley, edited by Alan Karras and Laura Mitchell, 136–51. Honolulu: University of Hawai'i Press, 2017.

Benton, Lauren, Adam Clulow, and Bain Attwood, eds. *Protection and Empire: A Global History*. Cambridge: Cambridge University Press, 2017.

Benton, Lauren, and Richard Ross, eds. *Legal Pluralism and Empires, 1500–1850*. New York: New York University Press, 2013.

Beşikçi, Mehmet. *The Ottoman Mobilization of Manpower in the First World War: Between Voluntarism and Resistance*. Leiden: Brill, 2012.

Beverly, Eric. *Hyderabad, British India, and the World: Muslim Networks and Minor Sovereignty*. Cambridge: Cambridge University Press, 2015.

Birdal, Murat. *The Political Economy of Ottoman Public Debt: Insolvency and European Financial Control in the Late Nineteenth Century*. London: I. B. Tauris, 2010.

Blumi, Isa. *Ottoman Refugees, 1878–1939: Migration in a Post-Imperial World*. London: Bloomsbury Academic, 2013.

———. *Rethinking the Late Ottoman Empire: A Comparative Social and Political History of Albania and Yemen, 1878-1918*. New York: Gorgias, 2010.

Bouquet, Olivier. "Non-Muslim Citizens as Foreigners Within: How *Ecnebi* Became *Yabancı* from the Ottoman Empire to the Turkish Republic." *Middle Eastern Studies* 53, no. 3 (2017): 486–99.

Bozkurt, Nebi. "Mücâvir." In *İslâm Ansiklopedisi*. Vol. 31. İstanbul: Türkiye Diyanet Vakfı, 2006.

Brophy, David. *Uyghur Nation: Reform and Revolution on the Russia-China Frontier*. Cambridge, MA: Harvard University Press, 2016.

Brower, Benjamin C. "The Hajj from Algeria." In Porter and Saif, *The Hajj: Collected Essays*, 108–14.

Brower, Daniel. "Russian Roads to Mecca: Religious Tolerance and Muslim Pilgrimage in the Russian Empire." *Slavic Review* 55, no. 3 (1996): 567–84.

———. *Turkestan and the Fate of the Russian Empire*. London: Routledge, 2012.

Brubaker, Rogers, and Frederick Cooper. "Beyond 'Identity.'" *Theory and Society* 29, no. 1 (Feb. 2000): 1–47.

Bukhary, Mansour. *'Ulama'ma wara'al-nahr Al-Muhajirin lil-Haramayn*. Madina: Dar al-Mirath al-Nabawi lil-Dirasat wa al-Tahriq wa Khidmat al-Turath, 2d31 1434.

Burbank, Jane. "An Imperial Rights Regime: Law and Citizenship in the Russian Empire." *Kritika* 7, no. 3 (Summer 2006): 397–431.

Burbank, Jane, and Frederick Cooper. *Empires in World History: Power and the Politics of Difference*. Princeton, NJ: Princeton University Press, 2011.

Campbell, Elena. *The Muslim Question and Russian Imperial Governance*. Bloomington: Indiana University Press, 2015.

———. "The 'Pilgrim Question': Regulating the Hajj in Late Imperial Russia." *Canadian Slavonic Papers* 56, no. 3/4 (Sep.–Dec. 2014): 239–68.

Campos, Michelle U. "Imperial Citizenship at the End of Empire: The Ottomans in Comparative Perspective." *CSSAAME* 37, no. 3 (2017): 588–607.

———. *Ottoman Brothers: Muslims, Christians, and Jews in Early Twentieth-Century Palestine*. Stanford: Stanford University Press, 2010.

Can, Lâle. "Connecting People: A Central Asian Sufi network in turn-of-the-century Istanbul." *Modern Asian Studies* 46, no. 2 (2012): 373–401.

———. "Trans-Imperial Trajectories: Pilgrimage, Pan-Islam, and Ottoman-Central Asian Relations, 1865–1914." PhD diss., New York University, 2012.

Can, Lâle, and M. Christopher Low. "The 'Subjects' of Ottoman International Law." *JOTSA* 3, no. 2 (Nov. 2016): 223–34.

Caplan, Jane, and John Torpey, eds. *Documenting Individual Identity: The Development of State Practices in the Modern World*. Princeton, NJ: Princeton University Press, 2001.

Carlston, Erin G. *Double Agents: Espionage, Literature, and Liminal Citizens*. New York: Columbia University Press, 2013.

Cassel, Pär Kristoffer. *Grounds of Judgement: Extraterritoriality and Imperial Power in Nineteenth-Century China and Japan*. New York: Oxford University Press, 2012.

Çelik, Recep. *Milli Mücadelede Din Adamları*. İstanbul: Emre Yayınları, 2004.

Çetinsaya, Gökhan. "The Ottoman View of British Presence in Iraq and the Gulf: The Era of Abdülhamid II." *MES* 39, no. 2 (April 2003): 194–203.

Ceylan, Ayhan. *Osmanlı Taşra İdarî Tarzı Olarak Eyâlet-i Mümtâze ve Mısır Uygulaması*. İstanbul: Kitabevi, 2014.

Chalcraft, John. "Engaging the State: Peasants and Petitions in Egypt on the Eve of Colonial Rule." *IJMES* 37, no. 3 (2005): 303–25.

Choudhury, Rishad. "Hajj between Empires: Indo-Muslim Pilgrimage and Political Culture, 1707–1820." Manuscript in progress.

Clancy-Smith, Julia A. *Mediterraneans: North Africa and Europe in an Age of Migration, c. 1800–1900*. Berkeley: University of California Press, 2011.

Clifford, James. "Travelling Cultures." In *Cultural Studies*, edited by Lawrence Grossberg, 96–116. New York: Routledge, 1992.

Cohen, Julia Phillips. *Becoming Ottomans: Sephardi Jews and Imperial Citizenship in the Modern Era*. New York: Oxford University Press, 2014.

Crews, Robert. *For Prophet and Tsar: Islam and Empire in Russia and Central Asia*. Cambridge, MA: Harvard University Press, 2006.

Davison, Roderic H. " 'Russian Skill and Turkish Imbecility': The Treaty of Kuchuk Kainardji Reconsidered." *Slavic Review* 35, no. 3 (Sept. 1976): 463–83.

Deringil, Selim. *Conversion and Apostasy in the Late Ottoman Empire*. Cambridge: Cambridge University Press, 2012.

———. "The Invention of Tradition as Public Image in the Late Ottoman Empire, 1808 to 1908." *CSSH* 35, no. 1 (1993): 3–29.

———. "Legitimacy Structures in the Ottoman State: The Reign of Abdulhamid II (1876–1909)." *IJMES* 23, no. 3 (1991): 345–59.

———. "The Ottoman Empire and Russian Muslims: Brothers or Rivals?" *Central Asian Survey* 13, no. 3 (1994): 409–16.

———. " 'They Live in a State of Nomadism and Savagery': The Late Ottoman Empire and the Post-Colonial Debate." *CSSH* 45, no. 2 (April 2003): 311–42.

———. *The Well-Protected Domains: Ideology and Legitimation of Power in the Ottoman Empire, 1876–1909.* London: I. B. Tauris, 1998.

Dudden, Alexis. *Japan's Colonization of Korea: Discourse and Power.* Honolulu: University of Hawai'i Press, 2006.

Düzbakar, Ömer. "Osmanlı Devleti'nin Dilencilere Bakışı (Bursa Örneği)." *Uluslararası Sosyal Araştırmalar Dergisi* 1, no. 5 (2008): 290–312.

Dyer, Jeffery. "Pan-Islamic Propagandists or Professional Diplomats? The Ottoman Consular Establishment in the Colonial Indian Ocean." In *The "Subjects" of Ottoman International Law*, edited by Lâle Can and Michael Christopher Low. Bloomington: Indiana University Press, forthcoming.

Dym, Jordana. "Citizen of Which Republic? Foreigners and the Construction of National Citizenship in Central America, 1823–1845." *The Americas* 64, no. 4 (2008): 477–510.

Ekmekçioğlu, Lerna. *Recovering Armenia: The Limits of Belonging in Post-Genocide Turkey.* Stanford: Stanford University Press, 2016.

———. "Republic of Paradox: The League of Nations Minority Regime and the New Turkey's Step-Citizens." *IJMES* 46, no. 4 (2014): 657–79.

Ellis, Matthew. *Desert Borderland: The Making of Modern Egypt and Libya.* Stanford: Stanford University Press, 2018.

Eraslan, Cezmi. *II. Abdülhamid ve İslam Birliği: Osmanlı Devleti'nin İslam Siyaseti, 1856–1908.* İstanbul: Ötüken, 1991.

Ergin, Nina. "The Soundscape of Sixteenth-Century Istanbul Mosques: Architecture and Qur'an Recital." *Journal of the Society of Architectural Historians* 67, no. 2 (2008): 204–21.

Esmeir, Samera. "On Becoming Less of the World." *History of the Present* 8, no. 1 (2018): 88–116.

Fahmy, Ziad. "Jurisdictional Borderlands: Extraterritoriality and 'Legal Chameleons' in Precolonial Alexandria, 1840–1870." *CSSH* 55, no. 2 (April 2013): 305–29.

Faroqhi, Suraiya. *Pilgrims and Sultans: The Hajj under the Ottomans.* New York: I. B. Tauris, 2014.

Flournoy, Richard, and Manley Hudson, eds. *A Collection of Nationality Laws of Various Countries as Contained in Constitutions, Statutes and Treaties.* New York: Oxford University Press, 1929.

Fortna, Benjamin C. "The Reign of Abdülhamid II." In *The Cambridge History of*

Turkey, edited by Reşat Kasaba, 38–61. Cambridge: Cambridge University Press, 2008.

Frantantuono, Ella. "Migration Administration in the Making of the Late Ottoman Empire." PhD diss., Michigan State University, 2016.

Freely, John, and Hilary Sumner-Boyd. *Strolling through Istanbul*. London: I. B. Tauris, 2010.

Freitag, Ulrike. "Helpless Representatives of the Great Powers? Western Consuls in Jeddah, 1830s to 1914." *Journal of Imperial and Commonwealth History* 40, no. 3 (Sept. 2012): 357–81.

Fujinami, Nobuyoshi. "The First Ottoman History of International Law." *Turcica* 48 (2017): 245–70.

Gelvin, James, and Nile Green, eds. *Global Muslims in the Age of Steam and Print*. Berkeley: University of California Press, 2014.

Genell, Aimee M. "Autonomous Provinces and the Problem of Semi-Sovereignty in European International Law." *Journal of Balkan and Near Eastern Studies* 18, no. 6 (Dec. 2016): 533–49.

———. "Empire by Law: Ottoman Sovereignty and the British Occupation of Egypt, 1882–1923." PhD diss., Columbia University, 2013.

———. "The Well-Defended Domains: Eurocentric International Law and the Making of the Ottoman Office of Legal Counsel." *JOTSA* 3, no. 2 (Nov. 2016): 255–75.

Georgeon, François. *Sultan Abdülhamid*. Translated by Ali Berktay. İstanbul: Homer Kitabevi, 2008.

Gong, Gerrit. *The Standard of Civilization in International Society*. Oxford: Clarendon, 1984.

Green, Nile. "The Hajj as Its Own Undoing: Infrastructure and Integration on the Muslim Journey to Mecca." *Past & Present* 226, no. 1 (Feb. 2015): 193–226.

———. "The Rail *Hajjis*: The Trans-Siberian Railway and the Long Way to Mecca." In Porter and Saif, *The Hajj*, 100–107.

———. "Spacetime and the Muslim Journey West: Industrial Communications and the Making of the 'Muslim World.'" *AHR* 118, no. 2 (April 2013): 401–29.

———. *Sufism: A Global History*. Malden, MA: Wiley-Blackwell, 2012.

Gruber, Christiane, and Frederick Stephen Colby. *The Prophet's Ascension: Cross-Cultural Encounters with the Islamic Mi'rāj Tales*. Bloomington: Indiana University Press, 2010.

Gün, Gülay. "Flight and Refuge in 19th Century Europe: The Muhacirin Commission of the Ottoman Empire." MA thesis, European University and Bilgi University, 2013.

Gündüz, İrfan. *Osmanlılarda Devlet-Tekke Münasebetleri*. Ankara: Seha Neşriyat, 1984.

Gürler, İsa. "Eyüp'te bir Kalenderhane." *Diyanet Aylık Dergi*, May 2007, 56–57.

Gutman, David. *The Politics of Armenian Migration to North America, 1885–1915: Sojourners, Smugglers, and Dubious Citizens*. Edinburgh: Edinburgh University Press, 2019.

———. "Travel Documents, Mobility Control, and the Ottoman State in an Age of Global Migration, 1880–1915." *JOTSA* 3, no. 2 (2016): 347–68.

Hamed-Troyansky, Vladimir. "Refugees and Empires: North Caucasus Muslims between the Ottoman and Russian Worlds, 1864–1914." PhD diss, Stanford University, 2017.

Hammond, Timur. "Mediums of Belief: Muslim Place Making in 20th Century Turkey." PhD diss., UCLA, 2016.

Hanioğlu, M. Şükrü. *A Brief History of the Late Ottoman Empire*. Princeton, NJ: Princeton University Press, 2008.

Hanley, Will. *Identifying with Nationality: Europeans, Ottomans, and Egyptians in Alexandria*. New York: Columbia University Press, 2017.

———. "International Lawyers without Public International Law: The Case of Late Ottoman Egypt." *Journal of the History of International Law* 18 (2016): 98–119.

———. "What Ottoman Nationality Was and Was Not." *JOTSA* 3, no. 2 (Nov. 2016): 277–98.

Haour, Anne. *Outsiders and Strangers: An Archaeology of Liminality in West Africa*. Oxford: Oxford University Press, 2013.

Harvey, David. *The Condition of Postmodernity*. Oxford: Basil Blackwell, 1989.

Haskan, Mehmet N. *Yüzyıllar Boyunca Üsküdar*. Üsküdar: Üsküdar Araştırmaları Merkezi, Sayı 3, 2001.

Hassan, Mona. *Longing for the Lost Caliphate: A Transregional History*. Princeton, NJ: Princeton University Press, 2017.

Ho, Engseng. *The Graves of Tarim: Genealogy and Mobility Across the Indian Ocean*. Berkeley: University of California Press, 2006.

Hobsbawm, Eric, and Terence Ranger, eds. *The Invention of Tradition*. Cambridge: Cambridge University Press, 1992.

Huber, Valeska. *Channelling Mobilities: Migration and Globalisation in the Suez Canal Region and Beyond, 1869–1914*. Cambridge: Cambridge University Press, 2013.

Isin, Engin Fahri. "Citizenship after Orientalism: Ottoman Citizenship." In *Citizenship in a Global World: European Questions and Turkish Experiences*, edited by E. Fuat Keyman and Ahmet İçduygu, 31–51. London: Routledge, 2005.

Izmirlieva, Valentina. "Christian Hajjis—the Other Orthodox Pilgrims to Jerusalem." *Slavic Review* 72, no. 2 (Summer 2014): 322–46.

Kane, Eileen. "Odessa as a Hajj Hub, 1880s–1910s." In *Russia in Motion: Cultures of*

Human Mobility since 1850, edited by John Randolph and Eugene M. Avrutin, 107–25. Urbana: University of Illinois Press, 2012.

———. *Russian Hajj: Empire and the Pilgrimage to Mecca*. Ithaca, NY: Cornell University Press, 2015.

Kara, İsmail, Ş. Tufan Buzpınar, Azmi Özcan, and James W. Redhouse. *Hilafet Risâleleri: İslam Siyasî Düşüncesinde Değişme ve Süreklilik*. 6 cilt. İstanbul: Klasik Yayınları, 2003.

Kara, Mustafa. *Din Hayat Sanat Açısından Tekkeler ve Zaviyeler*. İstanbul: Dergah Yayınları, 1999.

Karakoç, Ercan. "Milli Mücadele'de Üsküdar." In *Üsküdar Sempozyumu*. Vol. 2. İstanbul: Üsküdar Araştırmaları Merkezi, 2005.

Karateke, Hakan T. "Opium for the Subjects? Religiosity as a Legitimizing Factor for the Ottoman Sultan." In *Legitimizing the Order: The Ottoman Rhetoric of State Power*, edited by Hakan Karateke and Maurus Reinkowski, 111–31. Leiden: Brill, 2005.

Karateke, Hakan T., and Maurus Reinkowski. Introduction to *Legitimizing the Order: The Ottoman Rhetoric of State Power*, edited by Hakan Karateke and Maurus Reinkowski, 1–11. Leiden: Brill, 2005.

Kargılı, Murat. *Hac, Kutsal Yolculuk: Kartpostallarla Hac Yolu*. İstanbul: Denizler Kitabevi, 2014.

Karpat, Kemal H. *The Politicization of Islam: Reconstructing Identity, State, Faith and Community in the Late Ottoman State*. Oxford: Oxford University Press, 2001.

Kayaoğlu, Turan. *Legal Imperialism: Sovereignty and Extraterritoriality in Japan, the Ottoman Empire, and China*. Cambridge: Cambridge University Press, 2010.

Kennedy, Michael D. "Globalizing Knowledge through Area Studies." *Journal of the International Institute* 9, no. 1 (Fall 2001): http://hdl.handle.net/2027/spo.4750978.0009.107.

Kern, Karen M. *Imperial Citizen: Marriage and Citizenship in the Ottoman Frontier Provinces of Iraq*. Syracuse, NY: Syracuse University Press, 2011.

Keshavarzian, Arang. *Bazaar and State in Iran: The Politics of the Tehran Marketplace*. Cambridge: Cambridge University Press, 2007.

Khalid, Adeeb. "Pan-Islamism in Practice: The Rhetoric of Muslim Unity and Its Uses." In *Late Ottoman Society: The Intellectual Legacy*, edited by Elisabeth Özdalga, 201–24. London: RoutledgeCurzon, 2005.

———. *The Politics of Muslim Cultural Reform: Jadidism in Central Asia*. Berkeley: University of California Press, 1999.

Khoury, Dina Rizk, and Sergey Glebov. "Citizenship, Subjecthood, and Difference in the Late Ottoman and Russian Empires." *Ab Imperio* 1 (2017): 45–58.

Khoury, Dina Rizk, and Dane Keith Kennedy. "Comparing Empires: The Ottoman

Domains and the British Raj in the Long Nineteenth Century." Introduction to special issue, *CSSAAME* 27, no. 7 (2007): 233–44.

Kılıç-Schubel, Nurten. "Rethinking the Ties between Central Asia and the Ottoman Empire: Travels of a Central Asian Shaykh in Ottoman Empire in the 16th Century." In *Papers of VIIIth International Congress on the Economic and Social History of Turkey*, edited by Nurcan Abacı, 259–272. Morrisville: Lulu Press, 2006.

Kim, Hodong. *Holy War in China: The Muslim Rebellion and State in Chinese Central Asia, 1864–1877*. Stanford: Stanford University Press, 2004.

Knysh, Alexander. *Sufism: A New History of Islamic Mysticism*. Princeton, NJ: Princeton University Press, 2019.

Komatsu, Hisao. "The Andijan Uprising Reconsidered." In *Symbiosis and Conflict in Muslim Societies: Historical and Comparative Perspectives*, edited by Tsugitaka Sato, 29–62. New York: RoutledgeCurzon, 2004.

Kotkin, Stephen. *Magnetic Mountain: Stalinism as a Civilization*. Berkeley: University of California Press, 1997.

Kotsonis, Yanni. "Ordinary People in Russian and Soviet History." *Kritika* 12, no. 3 (Summer 2011): 739–54.

Kuehn, Thomas. *Empire, Islam, and Politics of Difference: Ottoman Rule in Yemen, 1849–1919*. Leiden: Brill, 2011.

Kunter, Halim Baki. "Tarsustaki Türkistan Zaviyelerinin Vakfiyeleri" [Waqf endowments of the Turkestani dervish lodges in Tarsus]. *Vakıflar Dergisi* 6 (1965): 31–50.

Landau, Jacob M. *Pan-Turkism: From Irredentism to Cooperation*. London: Hurst & Co, 1995.

———. *The Politics of Pan-Islam: Ideology and Organization*. Oxford: Clarendon Press, 1994.

Lecocq, Baz. "Hajj from West Africa from a Global Historical Perspective (19th and 20th Centuries)." *African Diaspora* 5, no. 2 (2012): 187–214.

LeGall, Dina. *A Culture of Sufism: Naqshbandīs in the Ottoman World*. New York: State University of New York Press, 2005.

Lewis, Mary Dewhurst. *Divided Rule: Sovereignty and Empire in French Tunisia, 1881–1938*. Berkeley: University of California Press, 2014.

———. "Geographies of Power: The Tunisian Civic Order, Jurisdictional Politics, and Imperial Rivalry in the Mediterranean, 1881–1935." *Journal of Modern History* 80, no. 4 (Dec. 2008): 791–830.

Lieven, Dominic. *Empire: The Russian Empire and Its Rivals from the Sixteenth Century to the Present*. London: Pimlico, 2003.

Lockman, Zachary. *Contending Visions of the Middle East: The History and Politics of Orientalism*. Cambridge: Cambridge University Press, 2004.

Lohr, Eric. *Russian Citizenship: From Empire to Soviet Union.* Cambridge, MA: Harvard University Press, 2012.

Low, M. Christopher. "Empire and the Hajj: Pilgrims, Plagues, and Pan-Islam under British Surveillance, 1865–1908." *IJMES* 40, no. 2 (May 2008): 269–90.

———. *Imperial Mecca: Ottoman Arabia and the Indian Ocean Hajj.* New York: Columbia University Press, 2020.

———. "'The Infidel Piloting the True Believer': Thomas Cook and the Business of the Colonial Hajj." In *The Hajj and Europe in the Age of Empire*, edited by Umar Ryad, 47–80. Leiden: Brill, 2016.

———. "The Mechanics of Mecca: The Technopolitics of the Late Ottoman Hijaz and the Colonial Hajj." PhD diss., Columbia University, 2015.

———. "Ottoman Infrastructures of the Hydro-State: The Technopolitics of Pilgrimage and Potable Water in the Hijaz." *CSSH* 57, no. 4 (2015): 942–74.

———. "Unfurling the Flag of Extraterritoriality: Autonomy, Foreign Muslims, and the Capitulations in the Ottoman Hijaz." *JOTSA* 3, no. 2 (Nov. 2016): 299–323.

Ludden, David. "Presidential Address: Maps in the Mind and the Mobility of Asia." *Journal of Asian Studies* 62, no. 4 (Nov. 2003): 1057–78.

Maas, Willem, ed. *Multilevel Citizenship.* Philadelphia: University of Pennsylvania Press, 2013.

Makdisi, Ussama. "Ottoman Orientalism." *AHR* 107, no. 3 (June 2002): 768–96.

Maksudyan, Nazan. "Orphans, Cities, and the State: Vocational Orphanages (Islahhanes) and Religion in the Late Ottoman Urban Space." *IJMES* 43, no. 3 (August 2011): 493–511.

Malcolm X, with the assistance of Alex Haley. *The Autobiography of Malcolm X.* New York: Grove, 1965.

Marglin, Jessica M. "The Two Lives of Mas'ud Amoyal: Pseudo-Algerians in Morocco, 1830–1912." *IJMES* 44, no. 4 (2012): 651–70.

McChesney, Robert D. *Central Asia: Foundations of Change.* Princeton, NJ: Darwin, 1996.

———. "The Central Asian Hajj-Pilgrimage in the Time of the Early Modern Empires." In *Safavid Iran and Her Neighbors*, edited by Michel Mazzaoui, 129–56. Salt Lake City: University of Utah Press, 2003.

———. *Waqf in Central Asia: Four Hundred Years in the History of a Muslim Shrine, 1480–1889.* Princeton, NJ: Princeton University Press, 1991.

McKeown, Adam. *Melancholy Order: Asian Migration and the Globalization of Borders.* New York: Columbia University Press, 2011.

Merry, Sally Engle. "Colonial Law and Its Uncertainties." *Law and History Review* 28, no. 4 (2010): 1067–71.

Metcalf, Barbara D. "The Pilgrimage Remembered: South Asian Accounts of the

Hajj." In *Muslim Travellers: Pilgrimage, Migration, and the Religious Imagination*, edited by Dale F. Eickelman and James Piscatori, 85–107. New York: Routledge, 1990.

Metcalf, Thomas R. *Imperial Connections: India in the Indian Ocean Arena, 1860–1920.* Berkeley: University of California Press, 2007.

Meyer, James H. "Immigration, Return, and the Politics of Citizenship: Russian Muslims in the Ottoman Empire, 1860–1914." *IJMES* 39, no. 1 (2007): 15–32.

———. "Speaking Sharia to the State: Muslim Protesters, Tsarist Officials, and the Islamic Discourses of Late Imperial Russia." *Kritika* 14, no. 3 (2013): 485–505.

———. *Turks Across Empires: Marketing Muslim Identity in the Russian-Ottoman Borderlands, 1856–1915.* Oxford: Oxford University Press, 2014.

Mikhail, Alan. *Nature and Empire in Ottoman Egypt: An Environmental History.* Cambridge: Cambridge University Press, 2011.

Mikhail, Alan and Christine Philliou. "The Ottoman Empire and the Imperial Turn." *CSSH* 54, no. 4 (2012): 721–45.

Millward, James. *Eurasian Crossroads: A History of Xinjiang.* New York: Columbia University Press, 2009.

Minawi, Mostafa. "Beyond Rhetoric: Reassessing Bedouin-Ottoman Relations along the Route of the Hijaz Telegraph Line at the End of the Nineteenth Century." *Journal of the Economic and Social History of the Orient* 58, no. 1–2 (2015): 75–104.

———. *The Ottoman Scramble for Africa: Empire and Diplomacy in the Sahara and the Hijaz.* Stanford: Stanford University Press, 2016.

Morrison, Alexander. "Metropole, Colony, and Imperial Citizenship in the Russian Empire." *Kritika* 13, no. 2 (2012): 327–64.

———. *Russian Rule in Samarkand, 1868–1910: A Comparison with British India.* Oxford: Oxford University Press, 2008.

———. "Sufism, Pan-Islamism and Information Panic: Nil Sergeevich Lykoshin and the Aftermath of the Andijan Uprising." *Past & Present* 214, no. 1 (2012): 255–304.

Motadel, David, ed. *Islam and the European Empires.* Oxford: Oxford University Press, 2016.

Naganawa, Norihiro. "The Hajj Making Geopolitics, Empire, and Local Politics: A View from the Volga-Ural Region at the Turn of the 19th and 20th Centuries." In Papas, Welsford, and Zarcone, *Central Asian Pilgrims,* 168–99.

Necipoğlu, Gülru. *Architecture, Ceremonial and Power: The Topkapı Palace in the Fifteenth and Sixteenth Centuries.* New York: Architectural History Foundation; Cambridge, MA: MIT Press, 1991.

———. "The Life of an Imperial Monument: Hagia Sophia after Byzantium." In *Hagia Sophia from the Age of Justinian to the Present*, edited by R. Mark and A. S. Çakmak, 195–225. Cambridge: Cambridge University Press, 1992.

Ochsenwald, William. *The Hijaz Railroad*. Charlottesville: University Press of Virginia, 1980.

———. "Ottoman Arabia and the Holy Hejaz, 1516–1918." *Journal of Global Initiatives* 10, no. 1 (2015): 23–34.

Özbek, Nadir. "Imperial Gifts and Sultanic Legitimation During the Reign of Sultan Abdulhamid II, 1876–1909." In *Poverty and Charity in the Middle Eastern Contexts*, edited by Mine Ener, Amy Singer, and Michael Bonner, 203–23. New York: State University of New York Press, 2003.

———. "Osmanlı İmparatorluğu'nda Dilenciler ve Serseriler, 1750–1914." In Özbek, *Osmanlı İmparatorluğu'nda Sosyal Devlet*, 65–114.

———. *Osmanlı İmparatorluğu'nda Sosyal Devlet: Siyaset, İktidar ve Meşruiyet, 1876–1914*. İstanbul: İletişim Yayınları, 2002.

———. "Philanthropic Activity, Ottoman Patriotism and the Hamidian Regime, 1876–1909." *IJMES* 37, no. 1 (2005): 59–81.

———. "The Politics of Welfare: Philanthropy, Voluntarism and Legitimacy in the Ottoman Empire, 1876–1918." PhD diss., Binghamton University, 2001.

Özcan, Azmi. "Özbekler Tekkesi Postnişini: Buharalı Şeyh Süleyman Efendi bir 'Double Agent' mı İdi?" *Tarih ve Toplum* 100 (Nisan 1992): 204–8.

———. *Pan-Islamism: Indian Muslims, the Ottomans and Britain, 1877–1924*. Leiden: Brill, 1997.

Özsu, Umut. "Ottoman Empire." In *The Oxford Handbook of the History of International Law*, edited by Bardo Fassbender and Anne Peters, 429–48. Oxford: Oxford University Press, 2012.

———. "The Ottoman Empire, the Origins of Extraterritoriality, and International Legal Theory." In *The Oxford Handbook of the Theory of International Law*, edited by Florian Hoffman and Anne Orford, 123–37. Oxford: Oxford University Press, 2016.

Özsu, Umut, and Thomas Skouteris. "International Legal Histories of the Ottoman Empire." *Journal of the History of International Law/Revue d'histoire du droit international* 18, no. 1 (Oct. 2016): 1–145.

Özyüksel, Murat. *The Hejaz Railway and the Ottoman Empire: Modernity, Industrialisation and Ottoman Decline*. London: I. B. Tauris, 2014.

Palabıyık, Mustafa Serdar. "The Emergence of the Idea of 'International Law' in the Ottoman Empire before the Treaty of Paris (1856)." *MES* 50, no. 2 (2014): 233–51.

———. "International Law for Survival: Teaching International Law in the Late Ottoman Empire (1859–1922)." *Bulletin of the School of Oriental and African Studies* 78, no. 2 (2015): 271–92.

Papas, Alexandre, Thomas Welsford, and Thierry Zarcone, eds. *Central Asian Pilgrims: Hajj Routes and Pious Visits between Central Asia and the Hijaz*. Berlin: Klaus Schwarz, 2011.

Pearson, Michael N. *Pilgrimage to Mecca: The Indian Experience, 1500–1800.* Princeton, NJ: Markus Wiener, 1996.

Peirce, Leslie. *Morality Tales: Law and Gender in the Ottoman Court of Aintab.* Berkeley: University of California Press, 2003.

Perl-Rosenthal, Nathan. *Citizen Sailors: Becoming American in the Age of Revolution.* Cambridge, MA: Belknap Press of Harvard University Press, 2015.

Philliou, Christine. *Bibliography of an Empire: Governing Ottomans in an Age of Revolution.* Berkeley: University of California Press, 2011.

Pickett, James. "Written into Submission: Reassessing Sovereignty through a Forgotten Eurasian Dynasty." *AHR* 123, no. 3 (June 2018): 817–45.

Pierce, Richard. *Russian Central Asia, 1867–1917: A Study in Colonial Rule.* Berkeley: University of California Press, 1960.

Porter, Venetia, and Liana Saif, eds. *The Hajj: Collected Essays.* London: British Museum, 2013.

Quatert, Donald. *The Ottoman Empire, 1700–1922.* Cambridge: Cambridge University Press, 2000.

Reichmuth, Philipp. "Semantic Modeling of Islamic Legal Documents: A Study on Central Asian Endowment Deeds." Unpublished thesis, Martin-Luther-Universität Halle, 2010.

Reid, Anthony. "Nineteenth Century Pan-Islam in Indonesia and Malaysia." *Journal of Asian Studies* 26, no. 2 (Feb. 1967): 267–83.

Reynolds, Michael A. "Buffers, Not Brethren: Young Turk Military Policy in the First World War and the Myth of Panturanism." *Past & Present* 203, no. 1 (May 2009): 137–79.

———. *Shattering Empires: The Clash and Collapse of the Ottoman and Russian Empires, 1908–1918.* Cambridge: Cambridge University Press, 2011.

Rıfat Paşa, İbrahim. *Miratü'l-Haremeyn: Bir Generalin Hac Notları.* İstanbul: Yitik Hazine Yayınları, 2010.

Rodogno, Davide. *Against Massacre: Humanitarian Interventions in the Ottoman Empire, 1815–1914.* Princeton, NJ: Princeton University Press, 2012.

Roff, William. "Sanitation and Security: The Imperial Powers and the Nineteenth Century Hajj." *Arabian Studies* 4 (1982): 143–60.

Ryad, Umar, ed. *The Hajj and Europe in the Age of Empire.* Leiden: Brill, 2016.

Sahadeo, Jeff. *Russian Colonial Society in Tashkent: 1865–1923.* Bloomington: Indiana University Press, 2007.

Salzmann, Ariel. "Citizens in Search of a State: The Limits of Political Participation in the Late Ottoman Empire." In *Extending Citizenship, Reconfiguring States,* edited by Michael Hanagan and Charles Tilly, 37–66. Lanham, MD: Rowman and Littlefield, 1999.

Saray, Mehmet. *Rus İşgali Devrinde Osmanlı Devleti ile Türkistan Hanlıkları Arasındaki Siyasi Münasebetler (1775–1875).* İstanbul: İstanbul Matbaası, 1984.

———. *The Russian, British, Chinese and Ottoman Rivalry in Turkestan: Four Studies on the History of Central Asia.* Ankara: Turkish Historical Society, 2003.

Sarınay, Yusuf, ed. *Başbakanlık Osmanlı Arşivi Rehberi.* İstanbul: Devlet Arşivleri Genel Müdürlüğü, 2010.

Sarıyıldız, Gülden. "II. Abdülhamid'in Fakir Hacılar İçin Mekke'de İnşa Ettirdiği Misafirhane." *İstanbul Üniversitesi Edebiyat Fakültesi Tarih Enstitüsü Dergisi*, no. 14 (1988–94): 121–47.

———. "Hicaz'da Salgın Hastalıklar ve Osmanlı Devleti'nin Aldığı Bazı Önlemler." *Tarih ve Toplum* 104 (Ağustos 1992): 82–88.

———. *Sokak Yazıcıları: Osmanlılarda Arzuhaller ve Arzuhalciler* [Street writers: Petitions and petition writers among the Ottomans]. İstanbul: Derlem Yayınları, 2010.

Sartori, Paolo, ed. *Explorations in the Social History of Modern Central Asia (19th–early 20th Century).* Leiden: Brill, 2013.

Sartori, Paolo, and Ido Shahar. "Legal Pluralism in Muslim-Majority Colonies: Mapping the Terrain." *Journal of the Economic and Social History of the Orient* 55, no. 4–5 (2012): 637–63.

"Saudi Arabia Citizenship System." Kingdom of Saudi Arabia Ministry of Interior Ministerial Agency of Civil Affairs. Decision no. 4 of 25/1/1374 [23 Sept. 1954]. www.moi.gov.sa/wps/wcm/connect/121c03004d4bb7c98e2cdfbed7ca8368 /EN_saudi_nationality_system.pdf?MOD=AJPERES.

Scully, Eileen P. *Bargaining with the State from Afar: American Citizenship in Treaty Port China, 1844–1942.* New York, Columbia University Press, 2012.

———. "Taking the Low Road to Sino-American Relations: 'Open Door' Expansionists and the Two China Markets." *Journal of American History* 82, no. 1 (1995): 62–83.

Shefer, Miri. "Charity and Hospitality: Hospitals in the Ottoman Empire in the Early Modern Period." In *Poverty and Charity in Middle Eastern Contexts*, edited by Michael Bonner, Mine Ener, and Amy Singer, 121–45. Albany: State University of New York Press, 2003.

Shissler, Holly. *Between Two Empires: Ahmet Ağaoğlu and the New Turkey.* London: I. B. Tauris, 2003.

Silverstein, Brian. "Sufism and Governmentality in the Late Ottoman Empire." *CSSAAME* 29, no. 2 (2009): 171–85.

Singha, Radhika. "Passport, Ticket, and India-Rubber Stamp: 'The Problem of the Pauper Pilgrim' in Colonial India, ca. 1882–1925." In *The Limits of British Colonial Control in South Asia: Spaces of Disorder in the Indian Ocean Region*, edited by Ashwini Tambe and Harald Fischer-Tiné, 49–84. London: Routledge, 2008.

———. "Punished by Surveillance: Policing 'Dangerousness' in Colonial India, 1872–1918." *Modern Asian Studies* 49, no. 2 (2015): 241–69.
Slight, John. *The British Empire and the Hajj, 1865–1956.* Cambridge, MA: Harvard University Press, 2015.
Smiley, Will. "The Burdens of Subjecthood: The Ottoman State, Russian Fugitives, and Interimperial Law, 1774–1869." *IJMES* 46, no. 1 (2014): 73–93.
———. *From Slaves to Prisoners of War: The Ottoman Empire, Russia, and International Law.* Oxford: Oxford University Press, 2018.
Smith, Grace Martin. "The Kaşgari Dergâh in Istanbul." *Archivum Ottomanicum* 14 (1995–96): 213–21.
———. "The Özbek Tekkes of Istanbul." *Der Islam* 57, no. 1 (1980): 130–39.
Sonyel, Salahi R. "The Protégé System in the Ottoman Empire." *JIS* 2, no. 1 (1991): 56–66.
Spagnolo, John T. "Portents of Empire in Britain's Ottoman Extraterritorial Jurisdiction." *MES* 27, no. 2 (April 1991): 256–82.
Stein, Sarah Abrevaya. *Extraterritorial Dreams: European Citizenship, Sephardi Jews, and the Ottoman Twentieth Century.* Chicago: University of Chicago Press, 2016.
Stephens, Julia. *Governing Islam: Law, Empire, and Secularism in Modern South Asia.* Cambridge: Cambridge University Press, 2018.
———. "An Uncertain Inheritance: The Imperial Travels of Legal Migrants, from British India to Ottoman Iraq." *Law and History Review* 32, no. 4 (2014): 749–72.
Stern, John P. *The Japanese Interpretation of the "Law of Nations," 1854–1874.* Princeton, NJ: Princeton University Press, 1979.
Tagliacozzo, Eric. *The Longest Journey: Southeast Asians and the Pilgrimage to Mecca.* Oxford: Oxford University Press, 2013.
———. "Snouck Hurgronje and the Politics of Pilgrimage." In *Southeast Asia and the Middle East: Islam, Movement, and the Longue Durée,* edited by Eric Tagliacozzo, 135–55. Stanford: Stanford University Press, 2009.
Tanman, M. Baha. "Buhara Tekkesi." In *Dünden Bugüne İstanbul Ansiklopedisi.* İstanbul: Kültür Bakanlığı ve Tarih Vakfı, 1994.
———. "Hırka-i Şerif Camii." In *İslam Ansiklopedisi.* Vol. 17. İstanbul: Türkiye Diyanet Vakfı, 1998.
———. "Özbekler Tekkesi." In *Dünden Bugüne İstanbul Ansiklopedisi.* Vol. 6. İstanbul: Kültür Bakanlığı ve Tarih Vakfı, 1994.
Tanpınar, Ahmed Hamdi. *Beş Şehir.* İstanbul: Dergi Yayınları, 1995.
Thum, Rian. *The Sacred Routes of Uyghur History.* Cambridge, MA: Harvard University Press, 2014.
Torpey, John. *The Invention of the Passport: Surveillance, Citizenship, and the State.* Cambridge: Cambridge University Press, 2000.
Tsing, Anna. "The Global Situation." *Cultural Anthropology* 15, no. 3 (2000): 327–60.

Turan, Namık Sinan. *Hilafetin Tarihsel Gelişimi ve Kaldırılması.* İstanbul: Altın Kitaplar, 2004.

Turna, Nalan. *19. Yüzyıldan 20. Yüzyıla Osmanlı Topraklarında Seyahat, Göç ve Asayış Belgeleri: Mürûr Tezkereleri.* İstanbul: Kaknüs Yayınevi, 2013.

Turner, Victor. "Betwixt and Between: The Liminal Period in Rites de Passage." In *The Forest of Symbols*, edited by Victor Turner, 93–112. Ithaca, NY: Cornell University Press, 1967.

———. "The Center Out There: Pilgrim's Goal." *History of Religions* 12, no. 3 (1973): 191–230.

Türkiye Diyanet Vakfı İslâm Ansiklopedisi. İstanbul: Türkiye Diyanet Vakfı, 1988–2013. https://islamansiklopedisi.org.tr.

Van den Boogert, Maurits. *The Capitulations and the Ottoman Legal System: Qadis, Consuls, and Beratlıs in the 18th Century.* Leiden: Brill, 2005.

van Schendel, Willem. "Spatial Moments: Chittagong in Four Scenes." In *Asia Inside Out: Connected Places*, edited by Eric Tagliacozzo, Helen F. Siu, and Peter C. Perdue, 98–128. Cambridge, MA: Harvard University Press, 2015.

Vora, Neha. *Impossible Citizens: Dubai's Indian Diaspora.* Durham, NC: Duke University Press, 2013.

Werth, Paul. *The Tsar's Foreign Faiths: Toleration and the Fate of Religious Freedom in Imperial Russia.* Oxford: Oxford University Press, 2016.

White, Joshua M. *Piracy and Law in the Ottoman Mediterranean.* Stanford: Stanford University Press, 2018.

Wolfe, Michael. *One Thousand Roads to Mecca: Ten Centuries of Travelers Writing About the Muslim Pilgrimage.* New York: Grove, 1999.

Wortman, Richard. *Scenarios of Power: Myth and Ceremony in Russian Monarchy from Peter the Great to the Abdication of Nicholas II.* Princeton, NJ: Princeton University Press, 2006.

Yaşayanlar, İsmail. "Hicaz Yolunda Kolera: Rusya Müslümanlarının Kullandığı Hac Yolu ve Koleranın Yayılımına Etkisi." *Avrasya İncelemeleri Dergisi* 4, no. 2 (2015): 178–203.

Yeşilot, Okan, Yüksel Çelik, and Muharrem Varol, eds. *İstanbul'daki Türkistan Tekkeleri: Ata Yurt ile Ana Yurt Arasındaki Manevi Köprüler* [The Turkestan Tekkes: Spiritual Bridges between the Fatherland and Motherland]. İstanbul: Türkçek, 2015.

Yıldırım, Nuran. "Osmanlı Coğrafyasında Karantina Uygulamalarına İsyanlar, 'Karantina İstemezük!'" *Toplumsal Tarih Degisi* 150 (2006): 18–27.

Yılmaz, Hüseyin. *Caliphate Redefined: The Mystical Turn in Ottoman Political Thought.* Princeton, NJ: Princeton University Press, 2018.

Yılmaz, İlkay. *Serseri, Anarşist ve Fesadın Peşinde: II. Abdülhamid Dönemi Güvenlik*

Politikaları Ekseninde Mürur Tezkereleri, Pasaportlar ve Otel Kayıtları. İstanbul: Tarih Vakfı Yayınları, 2014.

Zarcone, Thierry. "Histoire et croyances des derviches Turkestanais et Indiens a Istanbul." In *Anatolia Moderna: Yeni Anadolu*. Vol. 2, edited by Thierry Zarcone and Jean-Louis Bacqué-Grammont, 137–200. Paris: Librairie d'Amérique et d'Orient Adrien Maisonneuve, 1991.

———. "Kalenderhane Tekkesi." In *Dünden Bugüne İstanbul Ansiklopedisi*. Vol. 4. İstanbul: Kültür Bakanlığı ve Tarih Vakfı, 1994.

———. "Kaşgari Tekkesi." In *Dünden Bugüne İstanbul Ansiklopedisi*. Vol. 4. İstanbul: Kültür Bakanlığı ve Tarih Vakfı, 1994.

———. *Sufi Pilgrims from Central Asia and India in Jerusalem*. Kyoto: Center for Islamic Area Studies at Kyoto University, 2009.

Ziyodov, Shovosil. "The Hajjnâmas from the Manuscript Collection of the Oriental Institute at the Academy of Sciences, Uzbekistan." In Papas, Welsford, and Zarcone, *Central Asian Pilgrims*, 227–28.

Zürcher, Erik J. *The Young Turk Legacy and Nation Building: From the Ottoman Empire to Atatürk's Turkey*. London: I. B. Tauris, 2010.

INDEX

Page numbers in italics refer to illustrative material.

Abd al-Ahad (emir of Bukhara), 117
Abdullah Nidai Efendi (Sufi shaykh), 71
Abdülhamid II (Ottoman sultan): claims of spiritual leadership, 8, 123, 166; imperial processions and pan-Islam, 43–47, *46*; invocation in Andijan Uprising, 2; philanthropy, 74–75, 91, 114; promotion of Hagia Sophia as seat of caliphate, 41; ties to Buharalı Şeyh Süleyman Efendi, 73, 114, 205n13
Abdülmecid (Ottoman sultan), 74, 130–31, 167, 176
Adıvar, Halide Edip, 75, 205–6n20
Administration of Public Assistance (Müessesat-ı Hayriye-i Sıhhıye İdaresi), 138
affiliation switching. *See* legal pluralism
Afghanistan: British protectorate, 8–9, 108; hajj routes and shrines, 38, 50; Ottoman view as semi-sovereign state, 11, 103–7, 158; Second Anglo-Afghan War, 8
Afghans, in Ottoman Empire: British protection, 99, 101–6, 107–8, 211n32; lodges, 71, 72, 77–78; and Ottoman protection, 11–12, 96, 102–5, 224n3; rights to foreign nationality, 96, 98, 103–6, 108; at Sultantepe Özbekler Tekkesi, 7, 78, 80. *See also mahmi;* "protection question"
ahdname (Ottoman grants of extraterritorial privileges). *See* Capitulations
Alexandria: in *Hajjnoma-i Turkiy*, 34, 36, 51; in petitions for hajj travel, 130–31; protégés in, 14, 15, 111
Altishahr, 41, 50, 110. *See also* Chinese Turkestan
Anadolukavağı, 135–36, *137. See also* quarantine
Andijanis: in Chinese Turkestan, 15, 110–11, 124; as de facto Ottomans, 151–53, 179; petitions from, to Ottoman state, 140–42, 169; resident in Sultantepe Özbekler Tekkesi, 71, 87, 90
Andijan Uprising (1898), 2, 54, 219n4
Arafat (plain in Mecca), 57, 149–50, 161
arzuhal (petition). *See* petitioning

INDEX

Assembly of Shaykhs (Meclis-i Meşayih), 73, 88–89

Atâ Efendi, Şeyh (postnişin of Sultantepe Özbekler Tekkesi), 9, 74–76, 205–6n20

Atatürk, Mustafa Kemal, 2–3, 9, 76, 181, 205–6n20

Basri Pasha (governor of Medina), 175–76

Batumi, 48

Bedouin tribes: attacks on pilgrims, 34, 58, 59–60, 141, 142, 147, 161; Ottoman payments for pilgrims' safe passage, 164, 204n6

Bekir bin Azım (Kashgari child pilgrim at Sultantepe Özbekler Tekkesi), 65–68, 204n6

Benton, Lauren, 107

berat (certificates of protection), 14, 98–100. *See also* Capitulations

Beytülmal. *See* treasury

Black Sea, 7, 125, 156; pilgrims' experience crossing, 39, 135–36; Russian investment in routes through, 7, 38, 138. *See also* quarantine

Bombay, 1, 38, 48, 105

Bosphorus (straits), 5, 39, 40, 48, 51, 64; and quarantine stations, 135–37

Britain: Anglo-Russian rivalry in Asia and extraterritoriality, 14, 26, 95–96; attempts to expand jurisdiction via Afghans, 3, 10, 98, 99, 101–3, 107; attempts to expand power via protégés in the Hijaz, 26–27, 112, 212n48; creation of protectorate in Kabul, 8, 98; efforts to undermine Ottoman sovereignty in Hijaz, 112, 158–59, 212n48; hajj patronage, 23–24; Ottoman challenges to British protection, 11–12, 103–6, 108

Brophy, David, 110, 115, 194–95n10, 196n23

Buhara Dergâhı (Bukhara Lodge), 73–74, 77, 84, 86, 89, 131, 182, 195n13

Bukhara: associations with Islamic piety, 132, 165–67; Ottoman conflation with Russian Turkestan, 165, 178, 209n11; Ottoman use of term, 9

Bukhara, emirate, 8, 15, 18, 55, 73, 74; Ottoman classification as semi-sovereign state, 11; Russian conquest, 8

Bukharans, in Ottoman Empire: ambivalence on status as *ecnebi*, 113, 154, 156–57, 160, 173–74; communities in Istanbul, 71, 149–51; communities in the Hijaz, 20, 150, 162–63, 170; cultural capital, 165–67; diplomats and elites, 73, 114, 116; as *mücavirin*, 165–66, 167–69; naturalization of, 153, 154–55; Ottoman protection, 11–12, 20, 15–16, 94, 96, 139, 179; petitioners, 125–27, 130–32, 139, 168–69; pilgrimage leader, 116, 214n60; pious endowments, 161, 213n59; and property rights, 113, 114, 121, 154, 158, 211n31; and question of protection, 94–95, 97–102, 103–6, 107–10; seeking capitulatory privileges, 11, 14, 15–16, 176–77. *See also mahmi;* "protection question"

caliph. *See* sultan-caliph

caliphate, Ottoman: abolition in republican Turkey, 181; burdens and limits of, 13, 123–24, 139–46; integration into power structure, 13, 19, 166, 180; Istanbul as seat of, 38; role in combating extraterritoriality, 16, 30; promotion of, 11, 16–17. *See also* sultan-caliph

Capitulations: abrogation, 151–53, 173; definition, 10; in early modern period (*ahdname*), 13–14, 98; exemptions in the Hijaz, 26, 111–13, 158, 178; formalization and expansion of with Paris Peace Treaty, 10; increases in naturalization applications after

INDEX

abrogation, 151, 153, 154–55, 177–78; privileges provided by, 10, 13–14, 97–98, 105, 152, 211n33; threats to Ottoman jurisdiction, 123–24. *See also* extraterritoriality; legal pluralism; nationality reform, Ottoman

Capitulatory regimes, and foreign Muslims, 10, 13–16, 98–100; European attempts to expand reach of and project power, 10–11, 14–16, 99, 101, 106–9, 107, 158–59; Ottoman anxieties, 27, 173; Ottoman efforts to restrict abuses of, 29–30, 93, 102–11, 123–24, 175–76, 213n51. *See also* extraterritoriality; legal pluralism; *mahmi*; protégés; sovereignty

Catherine II ("the Great"), 8

Celal bin Hekim (Bukharan native in landmark protection case), 97–102, 105, 119

Central Asia: nineteenth-century conquests of, 8–9; Ottoman designations for, 9. *See also specific polities and regions*

Central Asians, in Ottoman Empire: as European protégés, 14–15, 24, 96, 99, 172–73; and extraterritoriality in global context, 15, 111, 124; and Porte's paradoxical position on status of, 19–20, 123–24; as subjects of history, 12–13, 26–27. *See also* Afghans, in Ottoman Empire; Andijanis; Bukharans, in Ottoman Empire; Chinese Muslims, in Ottoman Empire; Kashgaris; *mahmi*

Chaghatay (Turki), 35, 67, 131

China, 7, 8, 9, 18, 36, 67, 142, 194n10; extraterritoriality in Xinjiang and treaty ports, 15, 16, 102, 110–11, 124, 194–95n10, 196n26; lack of diplomatic relations with Ottoman Empire, 14, 158. *See also* Chinese Turkestan; Qing Empire

Chinese Muslims, in Ottoman Empire: and Austro-Hungarian protection, 176–77; capitulatory rights, 14, 96, 105–6, 108, 124; classification as foreigners, 3, 20, 115, 119; hajj routes, 38; Kashgaris in the Hijaz, 115, 117, 121, 122; as *mahmi*, 20, 96, 105, 108, 139, 179; references to, in *Hajjnoma-i Turkiy*, 28, 60–61; Ottoman use of term, 9; petitions from, 17–18, 126, 130, 131–32, 139, 140–45, 147; and repatriation, 125–26, 142–47; and Russian protection, 109–10. *See also mahmi*

Chinese Turkestan, 65, 80, 110–11; Andijanis in, 110–11, 124, 223n67; Ottoman efforts to discourage hajj from, 147–48; pilgrims originating from, 5, 65, 74, 78, 80, 85, 204n6; Russian projection of influence in, 110, 111; use of term, 9. *See also* Xinjiang

cholera, 23–24, 55–56, 89, 125, 135–37, 141, 164. *See also* quarantine

citizenship: definition, 15; distinctions from nationality, 15–16, 157, 196n24, 209n5; "dual citizenship" among transimperial migrants, 155–56; genealogies in late Ottoman and early Republic Turkish era, 3, 179, 181; imperial citizenship, 22, 173, 179, 195n18, 197n39, 198–99n50; secular dhimmitude and "step citizens" in Turkish Republic, 3, 181; religion and, 173, 223n70; Russian "attract and hold" policies, 214n64; in Saudi Arabia, 172; "spiritual citizenship," 195n17. *See also* nationality

Citizenship Affairs Bureau, 102, 116, 169, 223n72

Cohen, Julia Phillips, 22

Committee of Union and Progress (CUP), 18, 90–91, 152

communitas, 32, 37; ideals in *Hajjnoma-i Turkiy*, 36–37, 60–61
Concert of Europe, 10, 16, 47
Constantinople, Muslim conquest of, 147. *See also* Istanbul
contested subjects, 29, 81–82, 95. *See also* death, and contested estates; de facto subjecthood
Crimean War (1853–56), 10, 46–47, 112

death: focus on in *TVG*, 56–58; and burial at Sultantepe, 29, 90, 184; in *Hajjnoma-i Turkiy*, 36, 59–60
death, and contested estates, 14, 94–95, 109–10, 120, 122, 158–59, 201n17
de facto subjecthood (Ottoman), 29, 104, 151, 152–61, 173–74, 179
dergah. *See* Sufi lodges
Deringil, Selim, 46, 143, 196n27, 198n49, 213n51, 224n74
dhikr (Sufi remembrance of God), 6, 67, 76, 204n5
differentiated rule. *See* foreign Muslims, and differentiated rights
Directorate of Imperial Foundations (Evkaf-ı Hümayun Nezareti), 88

Eastern Question, 10
East Turkestan, 5, 9, 65. *See also* Chinese Turkestan
ecanib-i Müslimin. *See* foreign Muslims
ecnebi (foreigner): application to pilgrims and Central Asians, 20, 30, 123; historical associations with term, 100, 209n15; multiplicity of meanings, 181; problems in application to Central Asians, 151, 154, 159, 170; as Tanzimat-era legal classification, 7, 11, 20. *See also* foreign Muslims
Edhem Efendi, Şeyh (postnişin of Sultantepe Özbekler Tekkesi), 66, 84, 204nn2,6

Egypt: British occupation of, 159; hajj routes and, 38, 67, 130; Mehmed Ali Pasha and suppression of Wahhabi revolt, 112; Ottoman conquest of, 7; and support of *mücavirin*, 164, 167. *See also* Alexandria
Ekmekçioğlu, Lerna, 181, 193n1, 224n14
extraterritoriality, 3, 10, 97–98; benefits, 97, 98, 105; connections to petitioning and patronage, 126, 146–47; convergences with hajj, 13, 111; expansion to foreign Muslims, 27, 29–30, 99–100, 111; global dimensions, 98, 110, 111; limits of, 30; Ottoman attempts to counter, 30, 97, 108–9, 179. *See also* Capitulations; protection; protégés
Eyüp (neighborhood), 71, 78, 92, 93, 144, 150, 152; tekkes in, 86, 95, 153, 168, 177, 194n3. *See also* Kalenderhane Tekkesi; Kaşgari Tekkesi
Eyüp el-Ensari (Halid bin Zeyd Ebu Eyüp el-Ansari), Istanbul shrine, 48–49, 50; in *Hajjnoma-i Turkiy*, 49; in Ottoman history, 48–49

fana' (annihilation of the ego), 36, 62
Farid ud-Din Attar, *The Conference of the Birds*, 36
Faroqhi, Suraiya, 24–25
Fatma Tevhide Hanım (Ottoman woman married to foreign subject), 152, 160
Ferghana Valley, 2, 5, 7, 10, 54, 80, 110, 130, 142, 150, 152, 171, 206n34
foreign Muslims (*ecanib-i Müslimin*): ambivalent status of, 106, 119, 123, 173–74; classification of non-Muslims as, 7, 10–11, 20, 100; control and regulation (in Sufi lodges), 28–29, 87, 89, 91–92; and marriage, 154, 158–61; Ottoman anxieties about, 23, 26–27, 112–13, 159–61, 173, 198n49; and

INDEX

Ottoman nationality boundary, 12–13, 176; and property rights, 100–101, 112–22, 154, 157–59. See also *mahmi; mücavirin;* naturalization; petitioning; repatriation; *and regional descriptors for non-Ottoman Muslims*
foreign Muslims, and differentiated rights, 20, 26, 30–31, 96, 118–19, 178, 198–99n50

Galata Bridge (Istanbul), 43, 44, 45, 72, 134
Galib Pasha (Hijaz governor), 176
globalization: "charisma" of, 25–26; connections to extraterritoriality, 111; and hajj, 25–26, 85; tensions and paradoxes, 19, 20, 35
Gureba-yı Müslimin (hospital), 66, 89–90, 94, 204n3

Hacı Habib (Afghan native in landmark protection case), 102–5, 106, 119
Hacı Mirza bin Rehim (Istanbul resident in contested estate case), 94–95, 122
Hacı Sahib (de facto Ottoman naturalized after abrogation of Capitulations), 152–53, 177
Hacı Said (pilgrim stuck in quarantine), 136–37
Hadrami diaspora, 110, 159, 170–71
Hagia Sophia, 39, 41, 42, 43, 49, 144; corruption of name by Central Asians, 41, 201n21; in *Hajjnoma-i Turkiy,* 39–41
hajj, and migration, 13, 26, 95, 151–52, 155; blurred lines between, 131, 132–33; challenges of limiting, 123, 139; connections to labor and education, 7, 84–85; and long-term pious residence, 152. *See also* de facto subjecthood; *mücavirin; muhacirin*
hajjnoma (hajj account) 35, 37, 165. See also *Hajjnoma-i Turkiy; Turkiston Viloyatining Gazeti*

Hajjnoma-i Turkiy (early-twentieth-century Central Asian hajj account): authorship of, 35, 200n3; and contextualization of hardship and admonition to go on hajj, 34–36, 39, 52, 58–62; and emphasis on spiritual dimensions of hajj, 36, 42–43, 59–62; on Islamization of Istanbul, 38–47, 51–52, 63–64; on Istanbul, 36–38; on "madhhab of love" and the heart, 34, 36, 41–43, 52; subjectivity of author, 51–52, 62–64; on Russian colonial hajj, 52–53; and travel in industrialized hajj, 35–37
hajj patronage, European, 23–24, 25, 106–7, 211n33; and Anglo-Russian rivalries, 14, 110; and expansion of European jurisdiction in Ottoman Empire, 10, 24, 29, 95–96, 106–7; role of consuls in provision of support and protection, 14–15, 24, 94–95, 122. *See also* Britain; Russia, and extraterritoriality; Russia, and hajj
hajj patronage, Ottoman, 7, 17, 22, 24–26; and petitioning dynamics, 126–27; relationship to legitimacy and loyalty, 15–16, 24, 25, 105, 111; relationship to domestic reforms and order, 133–34; and tensions of empire, 13, 20, 30, 95–96, 123; and understudied dilemmas, 24–25, 139–46. See also *mücavirin;* petitioning; repatriation
hajj routes, from Central Asia, 38, 53, 71, 201nn11,14; changes in steamship era, 38, 47–48, 50; in *Hajjnoma-i Turkiy,* 35, 38, 63; historiographical mappings of, 25, 62–64; and networks as paths to migration, 3, 152, 182
hadimü'l-Haremeyn (custodian of the Holy Cities), 7, 24, 40
Hamidian era: catalysts for protection question, 96; emergence of Office of Legal Counsel, 96, 103, 123; and

legitimation of power, 16–17, 45–47, 196n27, 202n31. *See also* public health and order

han (inn): Davud Han, 39, 145; Fincancı Han, 131; inns listed in Sultantepe Özbekler Tekkesi records, 84

Hanley, Will, 15, 104, 196n24

hemşeri (countryman), 1, 9, 87, 183

Hijaz (Ottoman province), 7; competing jurisdiction, 111–19; exceptional status, 15, 26, 100–101, 152; fears of European intervention, 15, 26, 29, 111–12, 198n49; foreign Muslims and property rights in, 100–101, 112–19, 120–21, 154, 157–59, 174; population, 163; shared sovereignty with sharif, 112, 164; sultanic provisioning and philanthropy, 91, 163–64. *See also* Holy Cities; Jeddah; Mecca; Medina; *mücavirin*

Ho, Engseng, 62, 170–71

Holy Cities (*Haremeyn*): Central Asian migration to and communities in, 99, 117, 161, 164–65, 169; and experience of *communitas*, 31–32; Ottoman custodianship and provisioning, 7, 8, 24–25, 111–12, 163–64. *See also* Mecca; Medina; *mücavirin*

Huber, Valeska, 19–20

Hukuk Müşavirliği İstişare Odası. *See* Office of Legal Counsel

İbrahim Rıfat Paşa (author, *Miratü'l-Haremeyn*), 162, 164

identity: in Altishahr, 49–50; and legal nationality, 15–16; limits as category of analysis, 178–79; Turkic, 21, 76. *See also* nationality, Ottoman

imtiyazat (extraterritorial rights and privileges), definition of, 10, 98. *See also* Capitulations

imperial citizenship. *See* citizenship

Indians, in Ottoman Empire: and British protection, 107, 112, 158–59; in Jerusalem, 162, 219–20n12; migrants in Iraq provinces, 102, 111, 210n25; as potential British protégés in the Hijaz, 26–27, 112, 212n4; as "real" colonial subjects, 26, 107, 117, 178

İnönü, İsmet, 75, 205–6n20

international law, 195n14; and Capitulations, 98, 107; civilizational hierarchies, 25, 102; convergences with hajj, 13, 95; and legal nationality, 15, 95, 112, 178; limits of, in Ottoman context, 122, 199n51; Ottoman engagement with, 11, 29, 102–6, 177, 178, 212n48

Iraq: as arena of growing European interest, 10, 24; and British protection, 102–5, 158, 196n21, 214n63; shrines in, 50

Istanbul: and Allied occupation, 9, 75; boroughs of Greater Istanbul, 71, 72; Central Asian lodges of, 68, 69–71, 71–75; as crossroads of transimperial hajj routes, 6, 7, 9–10, 27, 30, 48, 52, 63, 68; and de facto Ottomans, 152–53, 154–55; as destination for Central Asians, 5, 7, 12, 34, 38, 88, 125–26, 149; hajj and concerns about order, 132–39; pilgrims stranded in, 17–19, 78, 125–26, 131–32, 140–46, 146–48; as seat of caliphate, 41, 74; Sufi and hajj networks, 12, 28–29, 85, 91; year-round management of hajj traffic, 125, 132–33, 136

Istanbul municipal administration (Şehremaneti), 18–19, 90, 125, 132, 136, 142–47

Jawis, in Hijaz province, 112, 159, 163, 211n38, 221n37

Jeddah, 14, 28, 52, 66, 97, 99, 163; Bukharan seeking Russian protection in, 97–102; European consulates,

14, 101–2, 120–21, 137, 196n21; passage to, and hajj routes, 34, 38, 59, 66, 131, 132, 135, 136, 144; population of, 163; in *TVG*, 56–57. *See also* Hijaz

Jerusalem, 29, 40, 93; Central Asian connections to, 16, 150, 152, 218n1; in extended hajj networks, 48, 51

jurisdictional disputes, 82; and estates of dead, 94–95, 122; and landmark cases on protection, 97–102, 102–5, 106, 119. *See also* Capitulations; Capitulatory regimes, and foreign Muslims

Kaaba (House of God), 6, 32, 40, 48, 164; in *Hajjnoma-i Turkiy*, 36, 61–62; invocation in petitions, 130, 140

Kalenderhane Tekkesi, 71, 73, 205n10

Kaşgari Tekkesi, 71, 72, 89, 204–5n9, 205n10, 206n22

Kashgar, 3, 15, 114, 130; emirate of, 8, 13, 115; and "tazkirah-shrine system," 49–50. *See also* Chinese Turkestan; Xinjiang

Kashgaris. *See* Bekir bin Azım; Chinese Muslims, in Ottoman Empire

Kaufman, K. P., 54

Keshavarzian, Arang, 77

Khiva Khanate, 8, 55, 74, 80, 94, 114, 202n51

Khoqand: khanate, 8, 54, 73, 94, 110, 114; natives of city and/or khanate at Sultantepe Özbekler Tekkesi, 87, 207n42, 219n12, 221n42; petitioners from, 130

kul (subject), 17–18; as caliphal subjects, 126; in petitioning, 127–29, 130, 140

Kyrgyz pilgrims, Mirim Khan on, 60–61

La'lizade Abdülbaki Efendi, 71–73, 114

land tenure, and restrictions on foreign Muslims, 158, 159–60; circumvention by Central Asians in Mecca and Medina, 112–19; enforcement, 112, 154–55; and marriage, 137–38; resistance from Hijaz authorities, 120–22. *See also* Law on the Rights of Foreign Citizens to Own Land

Law on Ottoman Nationality (1869), 7, 19, 95, 99–100, 101, 104, 153, 154, 223n70. *See also* nationality reform, Ottoman

Law on the Rights of Foreign Citizens to Own Land (1867), 112–13, 157–58; impact of provision requiring individual protocols with Porte, 118–19, 154, 211n31, 212n50

Lazarev (Russian steamship), 136, 138

legal imperialism, 7, 107. *See also* Capitulations; Capitulatory regimes, and foreign Muslims; Russia, and extraterritoriality

legal pluralism, 16, 33, 155–56; affiliation switching, 97–98, 102–3; "borrowed nationality," 96, 102, 209n4; and competing jurisdictional sovereignty, 30, 111–19; "forum shopping," 30, 97; legal posturing, 127; limits of, 96, 102, 105–6, 119–24, 175. *See also* Celal bin Hekim; Hacı Habib

legitimacy: and European protection, 106–7; and legal maneuvering, 16, 25, 33, 111

legitimacy, Ottoman, 7–8, 24–25, 26, 111–12; in Concert of Europe, 10, 16; dual nature of, 18–19, 123; "factual legitimacy," 166, 221–22n50; Hamidian legitimation attempts, 46–47

liminality, 19, 31–32, 37, 69, 119, 124, 171–72, 177–78, 181, 199n56

Lohr, Eric, 120, 195n18, 214n65

Low, Michael Christopher, 26, 55, 159, 211n38, 213n51, 221n38

Ludden, David, 62

mahmi (protected subject): ambiguity surrounding status of, 118–19, 124, 139–40,

175; emergence of term, 11, 26–27, 29–30, 101–3, 104, 139; as distinct from colonial subjects, 101; as distinct from European protégés, 104; limited rights and dead ends faced by, 106, 119–23; Moroccans as, 176–77; as ongoing issue in World War I, 175, 176–77; and Ottoman material responsibilites, 17–18, 126–27, 132, 139–41, 146–47. *See also* "protection question"

Malcolm X, 32

marriage, 93, 157–58, 159–61, 171. *See also* Fatma Tevhide Hanım; Murad Efendi

mass pilgrimage: intersection with European protection, 10, 14, 16, 20. See also *Hajjnoma-i Turkiy;* pauper pilgrims; steamship-era hajj

Mecca, 115–17, 161, 162, 165; in *Hajjnoma-i Turkiy,* 34–35, 59–61; population of, 163; in *TVG,* 57; Zamzam well, 40. *See also* Hijaz; Holy Cities; *mücavirin*

Meclis-i Meşayih. *See* Assembly of Shaykhs

Medina, 30, 50, 150, 163; Bukharan pious endowments in, 117, 161–62; Central Asian presence, 114–15, 121–22, 161, 165–70; population of, 163; religious significance of, 161; in *TVG,* 57. See also Hijaz; Holy Cities; *mücavirin*

Maksudyan, Nazan, 133

Marjani, Shihabbadin, 165

Mehmed Ali Pasha (governor of Egypt), 112

Mehmed Kazım Pasha (governor of Hijaz), 109

Mehmed Salih Efendi, Şeyh (*postnişin* at Sultantepe Özbekler Tekkesi), 66, 67, 204n6

Mehmed II (Ottoman sultan), 39–40, 48–49

Mir Bedreddin bin Sadreddin (Bukharan notable in the Hijaz), 115–17, 213n59

Mirim Khan (Muhammad Oxund Toshkandi), 28, 35–38, 71, 166. See also *Hajjnoma-i Turkiy*

military service: for *muhacirin,* 103; Ottoman mobilization, 156; volunteers among Central Asians, 156–57, 220nn19,20,24

Ministry of Pious Endowments, 74, 142, 148, 167, 204n2

mobility, transimperial: afterlife of, 172; challenges of restricting, 112, 138, 145–46; facilitation by Sufi lodges, 75, 76–87, 90–91, 92–93; unevenness, 19–20. *See also* networks; steamship-era hajj

mobility documents, passports, 20, 53, 65, 219n5; limits of, as proof of legal nationality, 94, 122; obtaining from European powers, 101, 105, 111, 152

Moroccans, 15, 139, 177, 180; categorization as *mahmi,* 176–77

Mudros Armistice, 9

muhacirin (Muslim migrant and refuge; sing., *muhacir*), 103, 105, 151, 156, 183, 222–23n63; distinction from *mücavirin,* 161, 169–70

Muhacirin Komisyonu (Muslim Refugee Commission), 135–36

Murad Efendi (de facto Ottoman naturalized abrogation of Capitulations), 154–55

Muslim world, as an idea, 17, 23; in industrialized hajj, 51–52

mücavirin (long-term pious resident of Holy Cities; sing., *mücavir*), 100, 112, 122, 161–65, 171, 175–76, 221n35, 222n53; attempts to limit, 169–70, 174; in estate cases, 158–59; legitimation of Ottoman power, 166–67; Ottoman patronage of, 161, 164, 166, 167–69;

INDEX

role in financing local lodges, 114, 117; in Saudi Arabia, 1, 172. *See also* de facto subjecthood
mürur tezkeresi, 66, 204n4

Naqshbandi (-yya), 6, 67, 71, 76, 87
nationality: definition, 15–16, 209n5; distinction from subjecthood/citizenship, 15–16, 157, 194n24, 209n5; Ottoman conception of "real" nationality/subjecthood, 11, 26, 98, 103–4, 108; "nationality games," 95
nationality, Ottoman (*Osmanlı*), 11, 99, 176; de facto, 29, 104, 151, 152–61, 173; and identity papers (*tezkire-i osmaniye*), 88, 116, 175, 179, 219–20n12, 220n19; and role of religion, 173–74, 179–81. *See also* naturalization
nationality reform, Ottoman, 12, 29; and difficulty enforcing, 10–11, 20, 30; and Law on Ottoman Nationality (1869), 7, 19, 95, 99–100, 101, 104, 153, 154, 223n70
naturalization, 171, 173; impetus for after abrogation of Capitulations, 151, 153, 154–55, 173–78; and marriage, 154, 158–61; procedures, 153, 154; reversion (*terk-i tabiiyet*), 121, 222n62; role of Sufi lodges and shaykhs in, 12, 93, 154; Russian impediments to, 120–21, 123–24, 175–76; and *tebdil-i tabiiyet* (nationality conversion), 120, 153, 177; *telsik* (World War I–era term), 151, 153–55, 173, 219–20n12
Neciboğlu, Gülru, 40
networks, 23, 25–27, 76–77; and hajj routes as paths to migration, 3, 152, 179–80, 182; Sufi and hajj networks in Istanbul, 12, 28–29, 85, 91–92; at Sultantepe Özbekler Tekkesi, 5, 68, 71, 76–87, 92–93, 95, 182. *See also* mobility, transimperial

Nur Muhammed, Hacı (pilgrim/migrant at Sultantepe Özbekler Tekkesi), 82–85, 86, 151

oaths, 116, 121, 156, 176
Ochsenwald, William, 163
Odessa, 18, 27, 38, 48, 58, 67, 135–36, 142, 144, 146, 147, 148
Office of Legal Counsel (Hukuk Müşavirliği): emergence of, 103; opinions on protection and foreign Muslims' rights, 29–30, 96, 98, 101–2, 103–5, 109–110, 182; position on foreign Muslims' property rights, 159; on protection question and *mahmi* in First World War, 176–78, 182. *See also* "protection question"
"ordinary people," 59, 69, 180; use of term, 31, 37, 199n55
Osmanlı (Ottoman). *See* nationality, Ottoman
Ostroumov, Nikolai Petrovich, 54
Ottoman Public Debt Administration, 47, 210n26
Özbek, Nadir, 138, 215n19, 216n23
Özbekkangay, Ethem, 69, 75–76
Özbekkangay, Necmeddin (Şeyh), 69, 183–84, 224n16

pan-Islam(-ism): and caliph's power, 29, 73, 140; European fears of, 23–24, 53–54; in *Hajjnoma-i Turkiy*, 43–47, 51–52; as factor in petitioning and patronage, 132, 145; limits of as category of analysis, 2, 17, 20–21, 22–23, 31, 96, 144, 178–80; use of term, 13, 17, 20, 180–81
pan-Turkism, 2, 21–22, 23, 75, 151, 178, 197n33
Paris Peace Treaty (1856), 10
pauper pilgrims, 37, 134–35, 201n9; attempts to restrict and discourage travel to Istanbul, 135–37, 144, 147–48

petitioning: mediation by petition-writer (*arzuhalci*), 127, 128; in Ottoman history, 17, 127–29

petitioning, by Central Asians: burdens on Ottoman state, 18–19, 30, 110, 139–48; changes in Hamidian era, 131; connections to extraterritoriality and caliphal protection, 17–18, 30, 126, 132, 140–41, 146–48; effective tropes and strategies, 126, 132, 143–44, 146; granting of, as means of speeding departures, 139–40, 146–48; from *mücavirin*, 167–68; for passage to Jeddah, 130–32; and reification of sultan-caliph's spiritual authority, 126–27; for repatriation, 78, 125, 126, 140–44, 146; supplications from ulema and dervishes, 129–31

property rights. *See* land tenure, and restrictions on foreign Muslims; Law on the Rights of Foreign Citizens to Own Land

Prophet Muhammad, 5, 28, 35, 39, 40, 51, 161; relics in Istanbul, 51–52

protection: competing regimes of, 26–27; importance of, for migrants, 11; in other imperial settings, 15; Russian and British, 98–99, 101; Russian attempts to protect Chinese Muslims, 109–11. *See also* Britain; Capitulations; legal imperialism; legal pluralism; Russia, and hajj; Russia, and extraterritoriality

protection, caliphal, 8, 27, 30, 94, 96, 102–5, 123, 124, 182, 199n51; and patronage, 126–27, 139–41, 146–47

"protection question," 31, 96, 119–20, 182; intractability of, 122–23, 175–76; landmark legal decisions, 103–6; 107–11. *See also mahmi*

protégés: definition, 14; difference from *mahmi*, 118–19; foreign Muslims as new type, 10, 13–16, 96, 99, 101, 104; and impetus for nationality reform, 100, 104. *See also* Capitulations; extraterritoriality

public health and order: domestic reforms and policing of urban space, 133–34, 138–39; as factor driving Ottoman patronage, 18, 30, 89–90, 126, 138–39, 142–43, 146; as tropes in petitioning, 126, 132, 143–44, 146; in *TVG*, 55

Qing Empire, 7, 14, 18, 67, 110, 111, 115, 194–95n10; conquest of Emirate of Kashgar, 8, 15

quarantine, 20, 35, 125, 135–37, 137, 214–15n2. *See also* cholera; Hacı Said

railroads: Hijaz Railroad, 166, 222n51; Russian investment in, 7, 53, 58; Tashkent-Orenburg line, 38; Trans-Caspian Railway, 38, 65, 142

repatriation, 17, 30, 110; petitioning and, 78, 125, 126, 140–44, 146

Russia, and extraterritoriality: attempts to formalize jurisdiction over colonial subjects and Bukharans, 101, 107–8, 109–11; attempts to protect Chinese Muslims, 109–11; connection to Anglo-Russian rivalries in Asia, 14, 95–96; consulate in Istanbul, 89, 94–95, 101, 107; consulate in Jeddah, 101, 109–10, 115, 120, 137, 210n17; impediments to naturalization of Central Asians, 120–21, 123–24, 175–76. *See also* contested subjects; death, and contested estates

Russia, and hajj: attempts to dissuade in *TVG*, 55–58, 63; and imperial ambivalence, 53–54, 55; investment in infrastructure, 7, 38, 53, 65, 142; Mirim Khan's views on in *Hajjnoma-i Turkiy*, 52–53; patronage of pilgrims, 53, 58, 92, 197–98n41

Russian Turkestan (governor-generalship), 9, 15, 34–35, 202n51, 210n19; conquest of, 8; Office of Legal Counsel's distinction between subjects of and protected states, 102–3, 106, 118–19; Ottoman conflation with Bukhara, 178, 209n1

Russo-Ottoman War (1877–78), 47, 74, 103, 134

Sayyid Muhammad Amin Khudayor Marhumoghli, 55

Şehremaneti. *See* Istanbul municipal administration

Selim "the Grim" (Ottoman sultan), 7, 24, 40, 41, 164

Sephardi Jews, 22, 174

Sevastopol, 34, 38, 39, 48, 59, 63, 143

shari'a: (Islamic law): as law governing people from/in protected states, 15, 102; and Ottoman jurisdiction vis-à-vis foreign Muslims, 98, 112, 211–12n40; "speaking shari'a" 109, 211n39

shrine visitation: changes to in steamship era, 47–49, 50–51; culture of, 47–51; and Mirim Khan, 48–49; Wahhabi opposition to, 50

Smiley, Will, 120, 209n5, 214n65

Smith, Grace Martin, 68–69, 71, 206n22, 207n36

social welfare: connections to modernization, 89, 133–34, 138–39, 215n19; provision by Sufi lodges, 28, 29, 66, 89–90; sultanic and state patronage, 90–92, 138–39. *See also* petitioning; public health and order

sovereignty: concession of to foreign consuls, 176–77; European guarantees of territorial sovereignty in 1856, 10, 112; new modes of marking, 166; shared sovereignty in the Hijaz, 112, 164; view of protected states as semisovereign, 98, 104–5, 154, 158, 178, 209n9. *See also* extraterritoriality; legal pluralism

Soviet Union, 1, 21, 195n13

spiritual subjecthood, 11–12, 13, 126–27, 140, 177–81. See also *mahmi*

steamship-era hajj, 19, 43, 201n14; in *Hajjnoma-i Turkiy*, 36, 51, 59; impact on Ottoman Empire and relations with foreign Muslims, 24, 93; and Sufi lodges, 68, 74

Stein, Sarah Abrevaya, 98, 195–96n19, 210n18

subjecthood, *vs.* legal nationality, 157, 173

Suez Canal, 7, 19–20, 38

Sufi lodges (*tekke, dergah*), 24–25, 28–29, 72; bureaucratization and regulatory functions, 28–29, 88–92, 133–34; Central Asian lodges in the Hijaz, 114–15, 117; closure in Turkish Republic, 9, 76, 181; connections among Central Asian lodges, 67, 84, 86; death and burial, 29, 90, 184; legacy in Turkey, 9, 182–84, 195n13; role in transimperial hajj, 25, 27–28, 66, 68, 74–75, 177; shaykhs as guarantors and mediators, 77, 154; social welfare functions, 66, 89–90; as spaces of integrating and absorbing foreign Muslims, 25, 27–28, 68, 177. *See also* Buhara Dergahı; Kaşgari Tekkesi; Sultantepe Özbekler Tekkesi

Sufism (*tasavvuf*): and culture of shrine visitation (*ziyara*), 49–50; mystical ideals in *Hajjnoma-i Turkiy*, 28, 34–35, 42–43, 58–62; significance in Central Asian Islam, 35; significance in Ottoman society, 28–29; tazkirah-shrine system, 50. *See also* Sufi lodges

sultan-caliph, 7, 8, 13, 96, 123, 127, 181; connections between spiritual and material authority (*maddi manevi*), 18–19, 180–81; responsibilities, 22–23, 147; as

spiritual sovereign of *mahmi*, 26–27, 199n51. *See also* protection, caliphal
Sultantepe Özbekler Tekkesi, *ii*, 5–6, 12, 29, 31, 70, 71–76, 95, 183; archive, 6, 67–71, 74; as central node of Central Asian networks, 5, 68, 71, 76–87, 92–93, 95, 182; and intersections of patronage and regulation, 74–75, 88–92; legacy in Turkey, 9, 182–84; lodgers' military service, 165–67; norms at lodge, 86–87; profile of guests, 78–82; and provision of healthcare, 66, 89–90; and residents' circulations between, 82–84, 86, 207n42; shaykhs' role in assisting hajjis, 9–10, 66, 154, 155; in Turkish history and historiography, 6, 9, 69, 75–76, 77
Sunnism, and salience for naturalization, 3, 173–74, 223n72
Süleyman Efendi, Buharalı Şeyh (*postnişin* of Buhara Dergahı and Ottoman statesman), 73, 77, 114, 117, 118

tabiiyet. *See* nationality
Tabiiyet-i Osmaniye Kanunnamesi (Law on Ottoman Nationality). *See* nationality reform, Ottoman
Tanpınar, Ahmed Hamdi (author), 149–50, 151
Tanzimat Reforms (1839–76), 16, 26, 46–47, 99; impact on foreign Muslims, 100–101, 123, 133
tariqa, 59, 77. *See also* Sufism
Tarsus Türkistan Zaviyeleri (lodges), 150, 205n18, 218n1
tasavvuf. *See* Sufism
Tashkent, 27, 34, 52, 54, 96; natives of at Sultantepe, 86; and new rail lines, 38, 56, 58
tebdil-i tabiiyet. *See* naturalization
tekke. *See* Sufi lodges
telsik. *See* naturalization

time-space compression, 27, 199n52
Topkapı (Palace), Mirim Khan's visit to, 51
Trans-Caspian Railway. *See* railroads
treasury: and contested estates, 94, 109–10; idea of a "Muslim" treasury in petitions, 17–18, 130–31; and subsidies for *mücavirin*, 164, 168
Treaty of Küçük Kaynarca (1774), 8
Treaty of Lausanne (1923), 181
Treaty of St. Petersburg (1881), 111
Tsing, Anna, 25–26
Tunisians, and connections to extraterritoriality, 102, 104–5, 106, 121, 175–76, 177, 196n23
Turkey, Republic of: and non-Muslim citizens, 3, 181, 193n1; pan-Turkist influence on history of Central Asians in empire, 21–23, 75–76, 151, 181; secularism and rejection of Ottoman legacy, 2–3, 181
Turkestan. *See* East Turkestan; Chinese Turkestan; Russian Turkestan
Turkestani ("Türkistanlı"), 9, 143, 149–50, 183
Turkestanskie Vedomosti, 54
Turkiston Viloyatining Gazeti (*TVG*; newspaper), 54–55; *hajjnoma* series, 55–58, 63
Turner, Victor, 32

umma: Central Asian hajjis as case study within, 17, 26; and sultan-caliph's spiritual authority, 11–12, 19, 26, 166. *See also* foreign Muslims, and differentiated rights
Uwais al-Qarani, 51, 168
Üsküdar, 5, 71, 74, 92, 193n1; and Central Asian communities, 85, 155

Vora, Neha, 171, 223n68

Wolfe, Michael, 32

World War I, and Ottoman Empire, 2, 9; abrogation of Capitulations, 151, 173; anti-foreign sentiment during, 152–53; de facto subjects and naturalization, 152–61; impact on Central Asian hajjis, 148, 173; loss of Medina and Mecca, 9; military mobilization, 153, 156, 220n20; and protection question, 123

Xinjiang, 8; extraterritoriality in region and Chinese treaty ports, 15, 16, 102, 110, 124, 194–95n10, 196n26; religious practice and identity formation in, 49–50; Russian projection of influence in, 110–11, 124. *See also* Chinese Turkestan; Kashgar

Yıldız Hamidiye Camii (Mosque), 43–47, 46, 166

Young Turk era, 16, 95, 103, 123, 126, 138–39, 174, 176, 178. *See also* Committee of Union and Progress

ziyara. *See* Sufism